Samuel Johnson
and Three Infidels

Samuel Johnson and Three Infidels

Rousseau, Voltaire, Diderot

Mark J. Temmer

The University of Georgia Press

ATHENS AND LONDON

© 1988 by the University of Georgia Press
Athens, Georgia 30602
All rights reserved
Set in Linotron 202 Garamond Number 3
The paper in this book meets the guidelines for
permanence and durability of the Committee on
Production Guidelines for Book Longevity of the
Council on Library Resources.

Printed in the United States of America
92 91 90 89 88   5 4 3 2 1

Library of Congress Cataloging in Publication Data

Temmer, Mark J.
    Samuel Johnson and three infidels.

    Bibliography: p.
    Includes index.
    1. Johnson, Samuel, 1709–1784—Philosophy.
2. Johnson, Samuel—Criticism and interpretation.
3. Rousseau, Jean-Jacques, 1712–1778. 4. Voltaire,
1694–1778. Candide. 5. Diderot, Denis, 1713–1784.
Neveu de Rameau. 6. Philosophy in literature.
7. Literature, Comparative—English and French.
8. Literature, Comparative—French and English.
9. French literature—18th century—History and
criticism. I. Title.
PR3537.P5T4   1988   828'.609   87-5930
ISBN 0-8203-0962-1 (alk. paper)

British Library Cataloging in Publication Data available.

Per la Fata
e gli amici di Yale,
Alex, Charlie, e Maurice

Mrs. Kennicot, in confirmation of Dr. Johnson's opinion, that the present was not worse than former ages, mentioned that her brother assured her, there was now less infidelity on the Continent than there had been; Voltaire and Rousseau were less read. I asserted, from good authority, that Hume's infidelity was certainly less read. JOHNSON. "All infidel writers drop into oblivion, when personal connections and the floridness of novelty are gone; though now and then a foolish fellow, who thinks he can be witty upon them, may bring them again into notice."

—Boswell, *Life of Johnson*

Contents

Acknowledgments

First must figure the name of Donald Greene, a loyal and learned Johnsonian, who has encouraged me, kept me from committing many blunders, and shared his knowledge of the eighteenth century, as imaginative as it is precise. Many thanks are also due to my friends Georges May, Jacques Voisine, Basil Guy, and Maurice Lecuyer. Moreover, I am beholden to my colleagues Jean Gandesbury, William Frost, Howard Clarke, Tom Steiner, Ernest Sturm, and Paul Fonteyn, as well as to reference librarians Liselotte Fajardo and Donald Fitch of the University of California at Santa Barbara library. Bouquets of gratitude to Mrs. Lucille Aubrey for administrative compassion, to Mmes Uthe, Aldrich, and Smitheram of the Interlibrary Loan Department, and to Phyllis Gibson, Pat Wilson, and Ann Matlovsky who typed and retyped the manuscript without ever losing their patience. I should also like to thank the Committee on Research of the University of California at Santa Barbara for its financial support of my project; Karen Orchard, associate director and editor, and Nancy Holmes, assistant editor, at the University of Georgia Press, who have guided me with precious suggestions always respectful of this author's intentions; Kathleen Bonds, John Harris, Frank and Celeste McConnell, Martin Hernandez, George Carr, and John Peck, the poet, for their friendship; and last, but not least, Faye Nennig. Her literary and stylistic insights have made her editorial assistance invaluable to me.

An abbreviated version of chapter 2 appeared under the title "*Candide* and *Rasselas* Revisited" in *La Revue de littérature comparée* 56, no. 2 (April–June 1982): 176–93. Parts of chapter 3 were presented in a talk at the *Colloque de* Cerisy-la-Salle, July 1983.

Abbreviations for Johnson Sources

A   Piozzi, Hester Lynch. *Anecdotes of the Late Samuel Johnson, LL.D.* Edited by Arthur Sherbo. New York, 1974.

H   Hawkins, Sir John. *The Life of Samuel Johnson, LL.D.* London, 1787. Reprint. New York: Garland Publishing Co., 1974

L   Boswell, James. *Life of Samuel Johnson, LL.D.* 6 vols. Edited by George B. Hill. Revised by L. F. Powell. Oxford, 1934–50.

R   Johnson, Samuel. *The Rambler.* Edited by Walter Jackson Bate and Albrecht B. Strauss. *Yale Edition of the Works of Samuel Johnson.* Vol. 5. New Haven, 1965.

I   Johnson, Samuel. *The Idler.* In *The Idler and the Adventurer.* Edited by W. J. Bate, John M. Bullit, and L. F. Powell. *Yale Edition.* Vol. 2. 1959.

Ad   Johnson, Samuel. *The Adventurer.* In *The Idler and the Adventurer.* Edited by Bate, Bullit, and Powell.

P   Johnson, Samuel. *Poems.* Edited by E. L. McAdam, Jr., with George Milne. *Yale Edition.* Vol. 4. 1964.

T   Balderston, Katharine C., ed. *Thraliana: The Diary of Mrs. Hester Lynch Thrale (Later Mrs. Piozzi).* 2 vols., 1776–1809. Oxford, 1942.

Ras   Johnson, Samuel. *The History of Rasselas, Prince of Abissinia.* Edited by R. W. Chapman. Oxford, 1927.

B   Bate, W. J. *Samuel Johnson.* New York, 1977.

BA   Bate, W. J. *The Achievement of Samuel Johnson.* New York, 1955.

G   Greene, Donald. *The Politics of Samuel Johnson.* New York, 1960.

GS   Greene, Donald. *Samuel Johnson.* New York, 1970.

Introduction

"La dernière chose," claims Pascal, "qu'on trouve en faisant un ouvrage, est de savoir celle qu'il faut mettre la première."[1] Indeed, often only after a book has been completed does the author become aware of its true nature and of his own intent. Here then are my afterthoughts by way of a preface.

In the first chapter, I have juxtaposed Johnson and Rousseau, a comparison which has been shunned by Johnsonians, with the exception of Boswell and Mrs. Piozzi and, in our time, Jean Hagstrum, who stresses that both thinkers display a lively interest in pragmatism. The risks involved in drawing parallels between these extraordinary men are manifest. Is there a critical structure flexible enough to accommodate Rousseau's and Johnson's ideas, subtle enough not to maim their artistic achievements—a structure deep enough to account for semiological discrepancies between French and English? Answers to these questions are far from easy. Moreover, we should keep in mind that our vision of Rousseau results mainly from his autobiographical works whose significance must be determined in part by his readers (for such is the psychoanalytic task he assigns to us), whereas the seemingly more stable ideas we hold about Johnson issue from biographies as well as from his writings. Is it fair then to compare the image of a man created, to a large extent, by himself with a likeness of another man created, for the most part, by others? Georges May's study *L'autobiographie* offers a lucid commentary on the genre, showing that its complications are as numerous as they are maddening. However, his answer to the question, What is an autobiography? is applicable to biography as well: namely, one ought to assume the matter of definition settled and speak of autobiography "comme si nous savions de quoi il s'agit."[2] A license not to be stymied by definitions would allow us to interpret Boswell's *Life* as an autobiography, if we agree with Chauncey Tinker that Johnson used Boswell to write it. Then, reversing our approach, we could read the *Confessions* as if they were a biography of Jean-Jacques by Rousseau. Indeed, he speaks of himself at times as if he were the severe biographer of a boy quite distinct from the one he was or might have been, although at the end of the fourth book he declares: "quoique né homme à certains égards, j'ai été longtems enfant et je le suis encore à beaucoup d'autres" (1:174).[3] Exiled in England, sick and old, he threads his way through raptures and woes of bygone days, conjuring up an image of a runaway not only from Geneva but also from himself: a projection whose vraisemblance increases as a function of artistic effort and skill. The new self, he prophesies in the preamble to his *Confessions,* will be a man radiant with truth: "et cet homme, ce sera moi"(1:5). This detachment towards himself reaches an almost eerie intensity in *Rousseau juge de Jean-Jacques.*

Thus, assuming that the two genres furnish enough evidence to permit a comparison between Johnson and Rousseau, my reader will be justified in asking whether I have followed a strict method. My answer must be a prudent no. In a comparison of two men of whom the first has defined his life by himself according to his genial insights, while the second may be said to have defined his life principally with the collaboration of a superb biographer, it seems presumptuous to superimpose on these lives—viewed as *ontological masterpieces*—value systems less sophisticated than those by which they have become immortal. These lives, and not the critic that I would be, are *la matière* of the first chapter. When faced with existential enigmas, I have chosen to resort to a straightforward account of what appears inexplicable rather than to cut-and-dried systematizations which run roughshod over the delicate and often cryptic singularities of my heroes' mortal ways. Why not respect matters which defy subsumption under Viennese or Parisian categories, and why not occasionally make a choice verified by intuition? Why not ponder, now and then, Jean-Jacques's anarchical fancies as well as Johnson's unacknowledged whimsies which, in turn, elicit mine? I am unable to read either man without wishing to converse with him—a temptation I have not always resisted.

There is no need to emphasize that the title of my first chapter refers to Plutarch, who writes at the beginning of his *Life of Alexander* ('the parallel' being, of course, Julius Caesar): "Our intent is not to write histories, but only lives (οὔτε γὰρ ἱστορίας γράφομεν, ἀλλὰ βίους").[4] The phrase, ironic or not, gives pause to reflect and reveals what will be evident to anyone familiar with the *Parallel Lives:* namely, that my "method" reflects ever so faintly Plutarch's procedure and that, on a much higher level, Boswell's *Life* is also visited by the spirit of Plutarch, whom the Scot called the "Prince of Biographers." Because the Greek historian was also Rousseau's darling author,[5] it seems reasonable to discern a kinship between the *Life* and the *Confessions,* a rapport which may be defined as an enchanting way of telling a marvelous life. This kinship, I believe, is intensified by Rousseau's influence on Boswell's descriptive technique, expressed by the latter's "Flemish" realism. I should add that my manner of proceeding does not mean to slight, by implication or otherwise, contemporary systematization of narrative theory regarding autobiography. I have not relied on it because I do not think it appropriate, either to the parallel lives or to my temper.

The sequence of the three chapters of this book is not haphazard. By sketching first the outlines of Johnson's and Rousseau's lives and by providing a summary of their respective achievements, I should like to reacquaint Johnsonians with Rousseau the man and author, because an unfortunate, though understandable, prejudice against Jean-Jacques has kept many Johnsonians and Boswellians from recognizing his true worth. In addition, I should like to remind some *dix-huitiémistes* of the powerful heart, mind, and personality of the Englishman. I hope that this presentation of Rousseau and Johnson not only will facilitate appreciation of similarities and oppositions between the two men but also will clarify the relationship between Johnson and Voltaire and between Johnson and Diderot. Thus, far from being in Johnson's words "an infidel," Rousseau proclaims and practices a pietism which often matches in intensity Johnson's otherworldly yearnings—a major point in the beginning and end of the second chapter, in which I relate Voltaire's *Candide* to *Rasselas,* one of Johnson's masterpieces. To a man, Voltaireans have disregarded the story of the Ethiopian prince, whereas Johnson scholars have never failed to mention *Candide* in their treatment of *Rasselas* without, however, doing full justice to the aesthetic and stylistic values of Voltaire's chef-d'oeuvre. I propose, therefore, to fit these beguiling tales within the context of the history of ideas and of European literature. It may surprise Johnsonians and Boswellians to learn that Rousseau's *Lettre sur la providence* (1756), addressed to Voltaire, often dovetails in mood with *Rasselas*—a concordance which, in turn, clarifies the spiritual opposition between the two *contes philosophiques*, both written in 1759.

Fortunately, this integration of *Rasselas* and *Candide* into the history of eighteenth-century literature is, relatively speaking, a simple matter. The two tales are masterpieces whose authors are without forerunners or epigones, and, although published during the same year, they betray no signs of a reciprocal influence.[6] Thus, before immersing myself in the inner space of the two novels, my only task was to outline the philosophical background from which *Candide* and *Rasselas* detach themselves. In his *Introduction to the Comparative Study of Literature,* Jan Brandt Corstius characterizes the prerequisites for such an immersion: "We shall always have to begin by becoming fully absorbed in the work, observing it as well as submitting to it, through rallying all the sensitivity that we have been given originally by nature and which we keep alive through our contact with literature."[7] As regards my literary approach, I am indebted to my teacher Henri Peyre and to Leo Spitzer, who have shown how one may achieve a satisfactory equilibrium between historical contemplation and stylistic exploration. In view of the abundance of commentaries on *Rasselas* and *Candide,* at times I have sought to intensify the subjective aspect of the inquiry and, this exploration completed, to determine whether the insights which crystallized as a result of such a journey correspond to "objective" literary realities. Exemplary of this procedure is the discovery of a covert declaration of love in *Candide,* surely an almost heretical revelation, and its correlation to Voltaire's love letters to his niece Mme Denis. What I heard from Cunégonde's lips I imagined hearing from Pekuah's, a lady-in-waiting neglected by

Johnsonians, even by Sheldon Sacks who remarks that "one can hardly imagine bells being rung for the safe return of Pekuah!"[8] Thus, by virtue of a literary daydream, I have amplified the episode of Pekuah and her Arab ravisher into a potential novel about Pascal, love, and gold, in order to direct attention to the consuming repression which pulsates beneath the pensive surface of this curious story. Proceeding along different lines, I have compared the Astronomer's dilemma to Hume's analysis of causation, suspecting that Johnson would have derived much satisfaction from a perusal of the *Critique of Pure Reason* which appeared in 1781, three years before his death. As for the analysis of *Candide* and *Rasselas* in the light of the *Bildungsroman,* it develops in an orthodox manner. Similarly, discussions about differences and resemblances in characters, attitudes, style, diction, and humor unfold according to traditional patterns.

The third chapter consists of a comparison between *The Life of Richard Savage* and *Le Neveu de Rameau* which, I hope, may bring about a reevaluation of current views concerning these remarkable works. There is a strong possibility that Diderot's masterpiece may have been influenced by Johnson's *Life of Savage,* as well as by Savage's *An Author to be Lett.* I emphasize again that the relationship between Rousseau and Johnson must be understood if one is to recognize some of the spectres which hover behind the *neveu.*

To sustain these hypotheses, I have devised a method different from those which characterize the first and second chapters of this triptych, precisely because the comparison between Johnson, pious biographer of an English hanger-on, and Diderot, moralizing foil to a French parasite, is the first of its kind—a clear handicap as well as a thrilling advantage. Thus, I have had to prepare my case by first acquainting my readers with the two anti-heroes. This familiarization involves excursions into history, autobiography, biography, fiction, and satire, as well as some psychic sleuthing, before arriving at tentative results. What may appear digressive is, in fact, essential to the case. Regardless of whether my conclusions find favor or are rejected, I hope that the contrasts brought out between Diderot and Johnson reveal hitherto neglected aspects of their persons and works, and that the integration of the *Life of Savage* into the general framework of continental literature will elicit approval from those who know and love Samuel Johnson.

Thus, the chapters of this volume are separate studies, articulated according to different methods, and should not be viewed as modules smoothly integrated into a book governed by a rigorous thesis. Yet Johnson (like Rousseau and, to a lesser degree, Voltaire and Diderot) is omnipresent in each chapter. Because the Englishman is successively confronted by personalities, minds, and achievements as mighty as his own, a reader interested in Plutarch's comparative ideal as well as in comparative literature will discern among these chapters filiations, explicit and implied. Furthermore, it is hoped that an increased awareness of these filiations may enhance understanding of Johnson's relationships to the three masters of French eighteenth-century prose.

By the same token, some of the concepts and hypotheses which issue from this study should be linked to specific moments in the literary history of Anglo-French relationships during the eighteenth century, an epoch characterized by a dismal sequence of French geopolitical failures. Despite the victory at Fontenoy on May 11, 1745, which, in the words of Napoléon, "fit vivre la monarchie quarante ans de plus qu'elle n'aurait dû,"[9] France continued to lose its empire to the English. It is against this slow, but inevitable, slide towards the abyss of '89 that Anglo-French literary relations should be viewed—a history in which Rousseau, Voltaire, and Diderot played their roles. But whether their interaction with English writers and thinkers affected the fundamental cultural characteristics of the two nations remains an open question. Frederick C. Green asserts in his splendid book *Minuet* that the cultural climates of France and England in the eighteenth century were too different for one to influence the other, that the English manner of thinking was formed in the tradition of Bacon and Shakespeare, and that French thought patterns reflected the method and values of Descartes and Racine. Furthermore, he observes:

> Nations like individuals, can be intensely curious about each other, and, having satisfied their curiosity, continue to behave

as before. Besides, literary genius is essentially racial and the
books which exercise an international appeal are very rare. To
the foreign palate the art of a great writer will always seem
strange and disconcerting because of its native tang. . . .
Voltaire became a European figure not because he was a great
artist but because he was a superb polemist. Literature, if it
will conform to alien taste, must almost of necessity sacrifice
its essential beauties, which lie, not in ideas, but in their form
of expression. [10]

Nowadays, such views may seem old-fashioned, but a glance at
French literary publications during the last four decades proves
almost painfully the degree to which Cartesian methodology still
dominates French thinking. Many have taken exception to Green's
assertions, among them Alice Green Fredman who views Diderot
as an anti-Cartesian in method and ideal and claims that he "does
not seem to fit into the pattern contrived for his contemporaries."[11]
In addition, she, as well as a host of Diderotphiles from every
borough of New York City—including the late, and so likeable,
Robert Loy—have shown how well Diderot understood Bacon,
Newton, Locke, Hume, Shakespeare and Garrick, Fielding, Richardson, Sterne, Lillo (not to mention Hobbes, Bolingbroke,
Shaftesbury, and Hutcheson) and how famously Sterne, unlike the
irascible Smollett, got along in France, where he met Crébillon-fils
and became a fixture in the effervescent crowd at Granval. Fredman
relates that Sterne even preached a sermon in Paris in May 1764,
attended by Hume, Diderot, and the Baron d'Holbach "among a
concourse of all nations and religions too."[12] That Fredman over-
looked the Diderot-Johnson connection seems forgivable. After all,
Diderot was wont to apprise the world of his idols but hid his *neveu*
ever so carefully from everyone, so that his book review of the *Life
of Savage* could not be compared to the *Neveu de Rameau*—thus
diverting the attention of modern scholars from a telling parallelism between his *compte-rendu* and Johnson's gloomy biography.
One should also note that the index of Green's *Minuet* does not list
Candide, Rasselas, or *Le Neveu de Rameau.* Furthermore, while at-
tacking Joseph Texte for overstressing Rousseau's influence on later
generations, Green loads the dice by stating that "Rousseau,
though a born Swiss, was in every other respect absolutely a

Frenchman."[13] With such a *parti-pris* Texte's argument crumbles, whereas if one maintains that Rousseau wrote in French, thought in German, and sang in Italian—for such is my conviction—Texte's position is once more strengthened.

What holds true for Diderot also applies in varying degrees to Prévost, Voltaire, Montesquieu, Marivaux, Rousseau, and later Chenier and Mme de Staël: namely, that English thought and literature became a source of fascination and inspiration. Equally affected were the French libertine intellectuals who devoured the Huguenots' translations and adaptations of the English freethinkers which reached France via Dutch printing presses. The ensuing Anglomania has been evoked by F. C. Green,[14] whose masterful style does justice to *la douceur de vivre* of yore. It is important to remember that the graceful life of the rich unfolded against a background of poverty and repression—grim realities that found abstract expression in Hegel's *Phenomenology of Mind* and, eventually, in mirthless Marxist disquisitions. That this Anglomania was followed by a wave of Anglophobia, preceding and following the Revolution, is a matter of history, just like Burke's attack against *la Terreur*. Eventually, these hostile feelings gave way to friendlier sentiments—to wit, Edward Bulwer-Lytton's aside to Talleyrand, to whom he dedicated his *England and the English:* "We no longer hate the French."[15]

Viewing France from across the Channel, one should distinguish, on the one hand, English curiosity about France and, on the other hand, French influences on English behavior, art, and thought. The former was intense. This curiosity focused not only on French duchesses and sultry chambermaids during more or less "sentimental" journeys, as well as on "the visibilities of Paris" (L, 2:401), but above all on the Sage of Ferney, who complained in March 1768: "J'ai été pendant quatorze ans l'aubergiste de l'Europe, et je me suis lassé de cette profession."[16] André Michel Rousseau's exhaustive *Voltaire en Angleterre* provides a lively account of visitors at Ferney, including Boswell as well as William Beckford and Lord Bristol, of hotel fame, while David Garrick never quite got there.

Before summarily evaluating French literary and cultural influences in England during the Age of Johnson, two political events should be called to mind: first, the arrival of perhaps eighty thousand Huguenots as the result of the repeal of the Edict of Nantes in 1685, and earlier, in 1660, the Restoration of Charles II. When Charles and his court returned from their continental exile, they brought with them a predilection for Gallic wit and gallantry as well as an awareness of French classical writers and sometimes an acquaintance with thinkers on the order of Descartes and Pascal, who were soon to be matched by Hobbes, Newton, and Locke. It is noteworthy that neither of the eminent English critics of the time—Dryden and Rymer—ever wholeheartedly submitted to what Pope came to call the "foreign laws." But, regardless of this quasi-chthonic resistance, translations appeared of Boileau, Bossu, le Père Rapin, Corneille, Molière, Racine, Calprenède (*Cassandre*), Voiture, La Rochefoucauld, La Bruyère, Mme de la Fayette, Mme de Sévigné, and other French authors. Montaigne's *Essais* found gifted imitators in Abraham Cowley and Sir William Temple; Tom Brown translated Mme d'Aulnoy, Saint-Evremond (who lived in London), LeClerc, Fontenelle, and Scarron.

When l'abbé Prévost first visited England, only a few Frenchmen were aware of the existence of Shakespeare, whereas across the Channel any cultured gentleman had at his disposal, or could avail himself of, the best French authors. Given these favorable circumstances, Voltaire soon reigned supreme in the realms of polemics, criticism, and history. Goldsmith experienced his sway, as did Chesterfield, Hume, Gibbon, and Horace Walpole who, in the company of many others, frequented the salons of Mme de Geoffrin and Mme de Tencin (dubbed by Diderot "la belle et scélérate chanoinesse"[17]), the drawingrooms of the Marquise du Deffand, Julie de Lespinasse, the Duchesse de Choiseul, and Mme Hélvetius—salons spurned by the *Citoyen de Genève*. There, visitors could rub shoulders with Buffon, Diderot, Grimm, d'Holbach, l'abbé Galiani, and d'Alembert. Samuel Johnson kept his distance, being more interested in three representatives of the *grand siècle*— Bayle, Pascal, and Boileau—than in his French coevals. Surprisingly, however, he sought out Fréron, Voltaire's archenemy who, to be sure, was not an infidel. Curiosity concerning Rousseau was intense, as was his influence over English sentiments and intellects; its extent in eighteenth- and early nineteenth-century England has been studied in depth by Henri Roddier and Jacques Voisine.[18]

Keeping F. C. Green's thesis in mind, one should not, however, forget that France and England have shared and still share values which neither country proclaims officially and which are not easy to define. In fact, it is one of the purposes of this book to investigate such affinities, hitherto undiscovered or disregarded— for example, similarities between Johnson and Rousseau or between *The Life of Savage* and *Le Neveu de Rameau*. Likewise, the comparison between *Candide* and *Rasselas* will not only show aesthetic agreements regarding neoclassicism but will also point to their authors' ability to invest their prose with a high degree of intellectual energy.

This kind of *entente culturelle,* more easily achieved in conversation than in print or politics, must have been experienced often in Twickenham and Paris during chats between Pope (whose *Essay on Man* enjoyed great popularity on the Continent) and Voltaire, as well as between the master of Strawberry Hill and his elderly, blind, infatuated interlocutress, Mme du Deffand. On second thought, however, one wonders whether Horace Walpole was a genuine representative of Old England. More indicative of the nature of this elusive cultural commonwealth seems to be an episode related by Boswell which must be quoted in its entirety:

> Here let me not forget a curious anecdote, as related to me by Mr. Beauclerk, which I shall endeavour to exhibit as well as I can in that gentleman's lively manner; and in justice to him it is proper to add, that Dr. Johnson told me I might rely both on the correctness of his memory, and the fidelity of his narrative. "When Madame de Boufflers was first in England (said Beauclerk,) she was desirous to see Johnson. I accordingly went with her to his chambers in the Temple, where she was entertained with his conversation for some time. When our visit was over, she and I left him, and were got into Inner Temple-lane, when all at once I heard a noise like thunder. This was occasioned by Johnson, who it seems, upon a little recollection, had taken it into his head that he ought to have done the honours of his literary residence to a foreign lady of quality, and eager to show himself a man of gallantry, was hurrying down the stair-case in violent agitation. He overtook

us before we reached the Temple-gate, and brushing in between me and Mme de Boufflers, seized her hand, and conducted her to her coach. His dress was a rusty brown morning suit, a pair of old shoes by way of slippers, a little shrivelled wig sticking on the top of his head, and the sleeves of his shirt and the knees of his breeches hanging loose. A considerable crowd of people gathered round, and were not a little struck by this singular appearance." (L, 2:405–6)

Almost like a myth, this anecdote—some will deem it trivial—harbors its own truth which, if analyzed, would lose its delightful sense and import. That the Comtesse de Boufflers, mistress of the Prince de Conti (both affectionate friends to Jean-Jacques), should have climbed a dark staircase to honor the person and conversation of Samuel Johnson is in itself quite noteworthy. That Samuel Johnson, suddenly overcome by an impulse to be gallant, should have rushed to the street to escort this ambassadress, *sans portefeuille,* seems even more remarkable and suggests an exhilarating possibility: at one time or another, Rousseau and Johnson may have been charmed by the same woman (surely an intersection of their parallel lives), just as l'abbé Prévost and Richard Savage were dazzled, unbeknownst to each other, by Mrs. Oldfield, a lovely actress who was mistress to a Churchill. To complete this magic circle, I should add that l'abbé Prévost later became chaplain to the Prince de Conti—an improbable closure which even Richardson could not have imagined.

It will not startle all readers if, in concluding this preface, I claim that the best way to gauge the intensity of English involvement with the French is to compare it to the English love of Italy and, in recent times, the interest in Germany and Russia. No Englishman ever, Chaucer excepted, got as much from France as did Milton from Rome. English men and women went to Paris to clear their heads, to Florence to lose them and, with a little luck, to die there.[19]

Yet, after all is said and written about literary relationships, one ought to bear in mind that literary history, more often than not, appears as flat and two-dimensional as the pages on which it is printed, this study being no exception to the rule. For every artist lives and creates within his private timeframe which vanishes with death, as well as within a cultural timeframe which transcends it. To share an artist's sense of time seems impossible, unless, by some grace, one succeeds in synchronizing one's heart with his or hers and thus becomes one with the rhythm of what he or she dances, sings, composes, paints, sculpts, builds, or writes. Because of this difficulty in achieving critical synchronization, which is impossible if the artist is no longer a coeval, most historians of artistic endeavors "detemporalize" those who undertook them and restrict themselves to fitting artistic achievements within a historical frame of reference, according to categories of style, genre, theme, and technique. But, when the very lives of artists become works of art, when life and literature intermingle and even fuse, when the coalescence of the private and cultural experience of time (*das Zeiterlebnis*) is crucial, as is the case with Johnson, Rousseau, Voltaire, and Diderot, critics trying to come to terms with such complexities face a task which defies their analytical and evocative powers. Indeed, it would take a critical demiurge, endowed with Proust's quasi-divine understanding of temporal prisons and paradoxes, to accomplish what I seek to do: first, to compare the parallel lives of Jean-Jacques Rousseau and Samuel Johnson; second, to show how *Rasselas* and *Candide* address the question of the "choice of a life"; third, to trace the kinship between the *Life of Savage* and *Le Neveu de Rameau;* and, finally, to try to deduce what the three infidels may have known about Samuel Johnson and what he may have thought about them, without ever revealing all of his feelings to his companions and listeners.

1 Johnson and Rousseau: Parallel Lives That Never Intersected

Si je n'étois ce que je suis . . .
—Rousseau

This is my history; like all other histories, a narrative of misery.
—Johnson

Dare one compare incomparable men—a defender of the status quo, who fought against slavery, with a melancholic champion of human happiness, tempted by a totalitarian utopia? Is it possible to contrast the English oracle from Lichfield, deaf to music and blind to color, with the Genevan prophet of Romanticism, an artist to his fingertips? Each man seems to oppose the other in thought and manner of living; each man contradicts himself so much that Diderot's remark about his *neveu* suits either temperament: "Rien ne dissemble plus de lui que lui-meme."[1] Notwithstanding these complications, the subject matter appears tempting. After all, the desire to compare is natural and, I should add, quite harmless, whether it be books or spouses. Thus absolved, I should like to please myself by contrasting the two authors who please me most.

Perhaps I should have written *vergleichen* rather than "compare," because the German verb immediately evokes the concept of *Gleichung* or equation. To date, however, no one has succeeded in developing an algebra that permits the formulation of a human equation respectful of what is humane—in other words, capable of taking into account the elusive factors that determine the symbiosis between existence and art. Freud's failure in his analysis of Leonardo da Vinci is a case in point, and so is Sartre's hyper-intelligent study of Baudelaire. Let it be understood that I do not wish to discourage anyone from trying to relate Rousseau to Johnson within a rigorously defined frame of reference. Aside from the unavoidable ambiguities inherent in comparative literature, the project would also involve pointing out semiological contrasts between French and English, not to speak of the task of first assaying, and then comparing, the aesthetic values of two idioms, one in semblance as robust as the other is supposedly transparent. Will anyone ever succeed in such an undertaking? I strongly doubt it, for the issues are too convoluted, the unconscious prejudices too subtle, the bibliographies too voluminous. Faced by such intricacies, the best I can hope for is to achieve an affectionate juxtaposition of the complex lives and equally complex works of the two men. While such a program seems, at first sight, relatively modest, its execution looms forbidding, for even a simple juxtaposition implies worrisome questions. Who is Johnson's Johnson, asks Donald Greene, as distinct from " 'dear old Doctor Johnson' and, in the end, ridiculous old Doctor Johnson'?"[2] And what relation do all these fanciful Johnsons bear to Boswell's Johnson—Boswell, the creator of a major mythic figure of European literature? His unequalled portrait (some refuse to consider it a biography)[3] brings to mind a canvas by Picasso on which a lady's eyes, nose, and cheeks are positioned according to laws promulgated by the painter's intellect and sensibility. Boswell's attitudinal modulations bear some analogy to such a perceptual reorganization. The late Frank Brady has clearly summarized Boswell's procedure, which in turn engenders new questions about the portrait of his majestic friend: "Boswell, in the *Life of Johnson,* achieves complex variations in perspective by mingling the first-person form of the diarist (the subject seen by himself in the present) and the autobiographer (the subject seen by himself in retrospect) with the third-person forms: the limited (the subject seen by contemporaries) and the quasi-omniscient (the subject seen by the biographer)."[4]

Fortunately, it is Johnson himself who gives me leave to rise above this perplexing situation, for he claims in his "Dissertation on the Art of Flying" that "nothing . . . will ever be attempted, if all possible objections must be first overcome" (Ras., p. 31). Such airy encouragement is even more needed in the treatment of the second life under discussion—the mortal days of Jean-Jacques, who is his own Boswell. And by the same token, what are we to make of Rousseau who changes Jean-Jacques's aspirations into fiction and into social myths of incalculable importance, thereby creating a confusion so bewildering that his admirers often envy students of *La Chanson de Roland*, whose daydreams are rarely troubled by questions regarding the identity of Turoldus? And, as if to compound all these questions into a Spanish question mark, Professor Greene reminds French scholars that English "insularity or independence persists, and that it is dangerous at any time for the student to lump together English literary and intellectual phenomena with those of a Continental movement such as 'Enlightenment' or 'Romanticism' without making due allowance for the stubborn idiosyncrasy of the English."[5]

Need I emphasize that Johnson's dislike of Rousseau augments one's difficulties? Furthermore, his dismissal of Rousseau as a man who deserves to be sent to the American colonies, as a man who knows he is talking nonsense, and as a lover of paradoxes (an addiction shared by Johnson) has indubitably increased the almost instinctual scorn of the mild-mannered autodidact by loyal Johnsonians (with the notable exception of Jean Hagstrum) and may have kept them from understanding the significance of fragments left by Boswell and Mrs. Piozzi. However, there is little to be gained by relying on too many anecdotes, although to disregard them entirely is to miss a few smiles and chuckles, especially if one happens to be French, unacquainted with what is old hat to the English. Furthermore, some of these stories and quips—occasionally apocryphal—indicate heartfelt attitudes, for instance: "The French are an indelicate people; they will spit upon any place" (L, 2:403), or Johnson's reputed reply to a bystander who complimented him on the success of his *Dictionary* at a time when the lexicographers of the *Académie Française* were making little, if any, headway: "Why, what would you expect, dear Sir, from fellows that eat frogs" (A, 78)? Although Rousseau is not French, he readily shares Gallic prejudices and delights much like Johnson, in sending arrows across the Channel. Ascertaining that the victuals of primitive men must have been like food consumed by present-day savages, he declares *ex cathedra:* "Pour concevoir les repas des anciens on n'a qu'à voir aujourd'hui ceux des sauvages: j'ai failli dire ceux des Anglais" (*Essai,* 519). Little did he dream in 1761 that five years later he would be eating pudding.

Regardless of these entanglements, prejudices, and complications, it is surprising that none of the scholars who have written on Rousseau and Johnson has relied on Boswell's and Mrs. Piozzi's testimonies.[6] Few among Johnson's many friends knew him better, biographically speaking, than these two persons, one a genius in biography and the other a highly intelligent and experienced woman who cared for Johnson with affection and patience.[7] On January 4, 1766, Boswell in Lyons writes to Rousseau:

> I am told that you are going to England. What a wonderful prospect for me! I am sure that there is no man on earth more keenly disposed to contribute to your happiness than I, and you will be sure of it too; and in time you will rely on the young friend of my Lord Marischal. I propose a perfect satisfaction for myself in introducing Mr. Johnson to you, about whom I told you so much at Môtiers, and of whom you said, "I should love that man, I should respect him"—and that after having heard that he would scarcely respect you. But I know you both, and although the one employs his powers to uphold the wisdom of the centuries, and the other to feed the fires of his own sublime and original spirit, I am sure that your great souls will acknowledge each other with warmth. And you shall go to Scotland, and you shall visit our romantic country-seat; and Rousseau shall meditate in the venerable woods of my ancestors, and he shall share my beliefs that nymphs, genii, angels, and all kinds of benevolent and happy spirits hold their choirs there. Farewell, my dear Sir. How impatient I am to see you, and to tell you a thousand enchanting anecdotes of Corsica. The moment I arrive in Paris I shall send to Mme. Duchesne's, where I hope to find a line from you. I am ever yours, as I was at Môtiers.[8]

Alas, the English bear and *l'ours suisse* were never to gaze on one another—an encounter that would have been comparable to that of Aeschylus and Euripides in the Underworld, and surely more dramatic than the meeting between Johnson and John Wilkes.

Unaware of the existence of this letter, Mrs. Piozzi relates the following conversation with her guest at Streatham:

> When he had told me this odd anecdote of his childhood concerning his youthful doubts regarding the truth of Revelation; "I cannot imagine (said he) what makes me talk of myself to you so, for I really never mentioned this foolish story to anybody except Dr. Taylor, not even to my *dear dear* Bathurst, whom I loved better than I ever loved any human creature; but poor Bathurst is dead!!!" —Here a long pause and a few tears ensued. Why Sir, said I, how like is all this to Jean-Jacques Rousseau! as like, I mean, as the sensations of frost and fire, when my child complained yesterday that the ice she was eating *burned* her mouth. Mr. Johnson laughed at the incongruous ideas; but the first thing which presented itself to the mind of an ingenious and learned friend whom I had the pleasure to pass some time with here at Florence, was the same resemblance, though I think the two characters had little in common, further than an early attention to things beyond the capacity of other babies, a keen sensibility of right and wrong, and a warmth of imagination little consistent with sound and perfect health. (A, 66)

Whereas Boswell realizes a potential accord between the two "great souls," one entrusted with the values of the past and the other with the hopes for the future, Mrs. Piozzi recognizes with extraordinary perspicacity and with the advantage of having most certainly read Rousseau's *Confessions* (which had appeared during the years 1782 and 1789) that their respective youths exhibit a common sensibility and "warmth of imagination." The theme of the likeness of the two unlike men recurs in Mrs. Piozzi's memoirs:

> Johnson has been often in the Course of these wretched Gleanings compared to Rousseau; he resembled him however in two Things more important than any I have mentioned yet—his Fear of Death, & his high Notions of the hard Task of Christianity—He never thinks that he has done or can do enough,—and dreads the Time when he shall be beaten with

> many Stripes—Le vrai Chretien says Jean Jacques—in the same
> Spirit—trouve tous les Jours sa Tâche audessus de soi; the
> whole passage is beautiful but I have not it by me, & quite on
> Johnson's Principle.—I shewed it him once and he said so
> too—. (T, 1:203–4)

Elsewhere, after discussing the dangers that beset women too fond
of secrets, Mrs. Piozzi notes, with tongue in cheek, that our specialists on love agree that solitude is far more dangerous to girls
than life in town:

> But I have not yet done with the resemblance between
> Johnson's Sentiments and those of Rousseau—in the Affair of
> Love too! but so it is, that they are both of opinion that
> Solitude is the Nurse of *this* as well as of every Passion, that in
> the Tumult of Company, & Hurry of Preparation, a Girl has
> neither Time nor Inclination to listen to tender Speeches, nor
> can She retain the Remembrance of them in her Mind—the
> Ball, the Show are not the dangerous Things—no! tis the Tête
> à Tête, the private Friend, the kind Consoler, the constant
> Companion that is dangerous; the publick Lover is not to be
> feared. (T 1:204)

Without annoying her celebrated friend, she tells him of his resemblance to his supposed archenemy: "I used to tell Dr. Johnson
without displeasing him at all, how like he was to Jean-Jacques
Rousseau; a Thing at 1st View paradoxical enough" (T, 2:765). And
she concludes how it used to amaze her "how very similar the two
Minds must originally have been made; and how much both were
altered from the first Resemblance by Education, Prejudices, Habits and Aims" (T, 1:172).

It is these affinities and contrasts with regard to their psyches,
thoughts, and destinies that I wish to ponder. In order to arrange
such juxtapositions, it will be necessary first to outline Rousseau's
and Johnson's respective works; then to sketch the contours of their
lives (background, childhood, education, departure from home,
marriage, and so forth), compare the structures of their psyches,
relate their characters and evaluate their thoughts, contrast their
sensibilities as well as their caprices, and finally cast a retrospective
glance on the two men by focusing each life on the other—making
Rousseau the mirror of Johnson, and the latter the looking glass of

the former. What Mrs. Piozzi writes in her *Anecdotes of the late Dr. Samuel Johnson* (1786) holds doubly true for my evocation of the man from Lichfield and the exile from Geneva: "Mine," she admits, "is a mere *candle-light* picture of his latter days, where every thing falls in a dark shadow except the face, the index of the mind; but even that is seen unfavorably, and with a paleness beyond what nature gave it" (A, 141).[9]

In 1750 and 1755, Rousseau shocked Europe with his *Discours sur les sciences et les arts* and his *Discours sur l'origine de l'inégalité*. In these tracts he inaugurated that vehement critique of contemporary values which he continued for the rest of his life—a critique that lay the foundations for modern sociology and ethnography from Durkheim to Lévi-Strauss. The latter celebrates Rousseau's contribution to these social sciences with an electric fervor which sparks across the two centuries yawning between *Le Discours sur l'origine de l'inégalité* (1755) and *Tristes Tropiques* (1955):

> Rousseau, tant décrié, plus mal connu qu'il ne fut jamais, en butte à l'accusation ridicule qui lui attribue une glorification de l'état de nature—où l'on peut voir l'erreur de Diderot, mais non pas la sienne—car il dit exactement le contraire et reste seul à montrer comment sortir des contradictions où nous errons à la traîne de ses adversaires; Rousseau, le plus ethnographe des philosophes . . . Rousseau, notre maître, Rousseau, notre frère, envers qui nous avons montré tant d'ingratitude, mais à qui chaque page de ce livre aurait pu être dédiée, si l'hommage n'eût pas été indigne de sa grande mémoire. . . . Jamais Rousseau n'a commis l'erreur de Diderot qui consiste à idéaliser l'homme naturel [Lévi-Strauss refers indubitably to Diderot's *Supplément au voyage de Bougainville* (1772), published in 1796]. Il ne risque pas de mêler l'état de nature et l'état de société; il sait que ce dernier est inhérent à l'homme; mais il entraîne des maux; la seule question est de savoir si ces maux sont eux-mêmes inhérents à l'état. Derrière les abus et les crimes, on recherchera donc la base inébranlable de la société humaine.[10]

Lévi-Strauss does not exaggerate when he asserts that Rousseau has never been more disparaged and misunderstood than he is now. The late Paul de Man concurs:

> Rousseau is one of the group of writers who are always being
> systematically misread. . . . When, especially as in the case of
> Rousseau, the ambivalence of the original utterance is itself a
> part of the philosophical statement, this is very likely to
> happen. . . . It is as if the conspiracy that Rousseau's paranoia
> imagined during his lifetime came into being after his death,
> uniting friend and foe alike in a concerted effort to
> misrepresent his thought. . . . In Rousseau's case, this
> misreading is almost always accompanied by an overtone of
> intellectual and moral superiority, as if the
> commentators . . . had to apologize or to offer a cure for
> something that went astray in their author. [11]

One frequent misreading by Johnsonians is exemplified by the venerable commonplace claiming that Rousseau preaches a "return to nature," when in truth such a return represents for him a hypothetical construct. Such is the sense of the preface of the second *Discours,* which delineates the dilemma of all ethnographic efforts and also stresses the theoretical nature of any attempt to understand the true nature of man:

> J'ai commencé quelques raisonnements; j'ai hazardé quelques
> conjectures, moins dans l'espoir de resoudre la question que
> dans l'intention de l'éclaircir et de la reduire à son véritable
> état. D'autres pourront aisément aller plus loin dans la même
> route, sans qu'il soit facile à personne d'arriver au terme. Car
> ce n'est pas une légére entreprise de démêler ce qu'il y a
> d'originaire et d'artificiel dans la Nature actuelle de l'homme,
> et de bien connoître un Etat qui n'existe plus, qui n'a peut-être
> point existé, qui probablement n'existera jamais, et dont il est
> pourtant nécessaire d'avoir des Notions justes pour bien juger
> de nôtre état présent. (3:123)

In the same essay, Rousseau also posits the pleasure principle in a manner that announces Freud: "Nous ne cherchons à connoître, que parce que nous désirons de jouïr" (3:143). With his passionate definition of freedom and his attack against the repressive aspects of the social structures of his time, he creates effects quite similar to those by modern revolutionary pamphlets. Whereas Locke defines freedom as the right to possess property, Rousseau defines it as the right to fulfill the potential of soul and heart, disregarding and even condemning at times the concept of property as a basis for a definition of freedom. In this respect, Thoreau may be viewed as one of Jean-Jacques's most important disciples.[12] *Le Contrat social* (1761) defines freedom as the right to do one's duty. This severe equation between *Freiheit und Pflicht* leads to Kant, Hegel, and all Marxist thinkers, including those of the New China. The historical importance of *Le Contrat social* is incalculable, for it became the bible of revolutionaries like Saint-Just, who held it in his hand when asking that the king and his queen be put to death. Its innovative ideas are the concept of the general will and the idea of pure right, which influenced Kant as well as the German Idealists. In the first part of this paradoxical treatise, Rousseau maintains that it is possible for the state to force a citizen to be free once he has agreed to be free and that, in extreme cases, violations of this ill-defined consent might be punishable by death—an absolutist theory which has known cruel interpreters. It should be added that the second part of the *Contrat social* is far more relativistic than the first part, since it bears the imprint of Montesquieu's *Esprit des lois*.

La Nouvelle Héloïse appeared in 1761. According to Ernst Cassirer, it contains the source of Kant's categorical imperative and, according to Havelock Ellis, has generated a new conception of time in literature which leads to *A la recherche du temps perdu*. Schopenhauer ranks *La Nouvelle Héloïse* with Goethe's *Wilhelm Meisters Lehrjahre, Tristram Shandy,* and *Don Quixote* as among the finest novels ever written, because these works concern themselves with life itself (*das Leben an sich*) and thus spurn what he chooses to call *die werklosen Gaukeleien der Phantasie* (the useless dreams of fantasy). *La Nouvelle Héloïse* is also a *Bildungsroman,* the first of its kind in European literature, and in the next chapter I shall outline some of the characteristics of this genre. Like *Wilhelm Meisters Lehrjahre,* Rousseau's epistolary novel traces the measured progression of individuals, haunted by questions and stimulated by errors, forever moving towards a higher degree of active self-realization. Saint-Preux, like Wilhelm, is led by mentors and gradually succeeds in shaping his own ethos. Because of the impact of Rousseau's novel on Goethe's, its influence can be detected in German novels from Gottfried Keller's *Der grüne Heinrich* through Stifter's *Der Nachsommer* to Thomas Mann's *Magic Mountain*.[13]

The *Emile,* the basis of modern educational theories, appears in 1762. Aside from its powerful sway on pedagogues, this book also affected Tolstoy's educational theories as well as John Dewey's pragmatic views on education. Its religious core, *La Profession de foi du vicaire savoyard,* consists of a critique of Revelation and proposes an emotional proof of the existence of God; it exerted a decisive influence on Schleiermacher and, through him, on the American Transcendentalists.

After Rousseau's death in 1778 appeared *Les Confessions* (1782–89), *Les Rêveries du promeneur solitaire* (1782), and *Les Dialogues: Rousseau juge de Jean Jacques* (1778). The first two of these autobiographical works rank high among his artistic masterpieces. *Les Confessions* is unique in that it justifies the life he has lived in purely human terms; despite the initial invocation to God, Rousseau attempts to be his own savior. *Les Rêveries,* specifically *La Cinquième Promenade,* transcends mortal anguish by overcoming dispersion in time in order to find peace in *le présent vécu:* "où l'âme trouve une assiete assez solide pour s'y reposer toute entiére . . . où le temps ne soit rien pour elle . . . où le présent dure toujours" (1:1046). Other works by Rousseau include an opera *Le Devin du village* (1752) and a play *Narcisse ou l'amant de lui-même* (1752); in addition, he wrote *La Lettre sur la Providence* (1756), *Lettre à d'Alembert sur les spectacles* (1758), *L'Essai sur l'origine des langues* (1761), *Lettres à Malesherbes* (1762), *Lettre à Christophe de Beaumont* (1763), *Lettres écrites de la montagne* (1764), *Dictionnaire de musique* (1767), *Projet de constitution pour la Corse* (incomplete, published posthumously), and *Considérations sur le gouvernement de Pologne* (1772).

Even a glance at Johnson's bibliography reveals that he is somewhat more conservative than Rousseau. The latter creates his own myths—the myth of a "new man" in the *Emile* and *Les Confessions,* of a "new family"in *La Nouvelle Héloïse,* and of a "new state" in *Le Contrat social.* By contrast, Johnson—like Rousseau, already a quasi-mythical figure in his lifetime—defends the status quo as often as he attacks it and, therefore, should not be viewed as a champion of superannuated causes. I have alluded to the endemic prejudice held by Johnsonians (with the exception of Donald Greene and Jean Hagstrum) against Rousseau. For example, discussing the ethical wholeness of Johnson the man and of his works, Bate quotes approvingly the opinion of another distinguished Johnsonian, Sir Walter Raleigh, whose viewpoint I cannot endorse: "Johnson . . . 'is great by his reserves . . . his books are mere outworks' whereas so many other writers—and Raleigh cites Rousseau as an example—tenderly husband their gifts, economically tamp their insights into one or a few books, and leave a drained specimen and 'mere husk of a man for the reader who later tries to approach him' " (BA, 229). Raleigh's other remark about Rousseau matches the first: "Rousseau is not more individual in his cultivation of sentiment than Johnson in his dislike of it."[14] Hester Thrale, whom I have quoted, knew better.

Ceci dit, a review of Samuel Johnson's principal works is in order. These include his genial contribution as a hack to the *Gentleman's Magazine,* writings that feature his Parliamentary Debates from 1740 to 1743 (consisting partly of speeches written by Johnson, supposedly made by Pitt). We are told that the classical scholar Philip Francis, who had spent eight years in the study of Demosthenes, praised one of the putative speeches by Pitt as being unsurpassed by any one of Demosthenes' orations and that, according to Arthur Murphy the playwright, Johnson admitted to having "written the speech rapidly with little care, in a garret in Exeter Street" (L, 1:504). Donald Greene stresses that Johnson was composing speeches rather than reporting them and that his method was "to take one important controversial topic and make of it a set piece, a formal and exhaustive dissertation in dialogue form" (G, 114). He also offers samples of Johnson's ghostly eloquence: [Pitt] "The Minister who neglects any just opportunity of promoting the power or increasing the wealth of his country is to be considered as an enemy to his fellow subjects; but what censure is to be passed upon him who betrays that army to defeat, by which victory might be obtained; impoverishes the nation whose affairs he is intrusted to transact by those expeditions which might enrich it, who levies armies only to be exposed to pestilence, and compels them to perish in sight of their enemies without molesting them?" (G, 126). "This," comments Donald Greene, "is demagogery of the highest, or lowest, order—one hears in it the authentic note of the French

Revolution" (G, 126). Indeed, the intensity of Johnson's rhetoric calls to mind Rousseau's angry protest which ends his *Discours sur l'origine de l'inégalité:* "il est manifestement contre la Loi de la Nature, de quelque manière qu'on la définisse, qu'un enfant commande à un vieillard, qu'un imbécille conduise un homme sage, et qu'une poignée de gens regorge de superfluités, tandis que la multitude affamée manque du nécessaire" (3:194). In contrast to all those who fancy political theory, Greene sees Johnson as a kind of spokesman of the average Anglo-Saxon from Staffordshire who suspects that "most schemes of political improvement are . . . laughable" (G, 257). Greene concludes: "It is an attitude that is, almost by definition, unformulated and inarticulate—it is the Bolingbrokes and Burkes, the Rousseaus and Marxes, the people with ingenious theories to propound, who write the books and make the speeches and get the publicity. But insofar as it has a spokesman, it is hard to say who would fill that role better than Johnson" (G, 257).

That Karl Marx made an *Address to the Communist League* in London in 1850 is indeed a matter of history; but I am on the point of protesting that Rousseau never spoke in public, when I recall his "archimandrite . . . homme à grande barbe avec un habit violet à la grecque, un bonnet fouré, l'équipage et l'air assez noble . . . ne parlant qu'un jargon presque indéchiffrable, mais plus ressemblant à l'italien qu'à nulle autre langue" (1:154). The meeting with this delightful imposter occurs in the fourth book of the *Confessions;* young Jean-Jacques becomes his interpreter and is even called upon to address Their Excellencies, the Senators at Berne: "Voila la seule fois de ma vie que j'aye parlé en public et devant un souverain, et la seule fois aussi, peutêtre, que j'ai parlé hardiment et bien" (1:156). One should note, however, that Rousseau, like Johnson, could be quite pragmatic and even prophetic—to wit, his conclusion to his *Considérations sur le gouvernement de Pologne et sur sa réformation projet-tée* (1772), addressed to Count Wielhorski and his fellow citizens: "Vous ne serez jamais libres tant qu'il restera un seul soldat Russe en Pologne, et vous serez toujours menacés de cesser de l'être tant que la Russie se mêlera de vos affaires" (3:1037).

Generally speaking, Johnson is far less interested in political theory than Rousseau: "[Johnson] will have nothing to do with lofty abstractions, 'the will of the people,' 'the spirit of the nation,' 'the social contract,' as the source of political power: government is simply certain human beings, who are fallible and greedy like the rest, invested in power over others" (GS, 148). Greene proceeds to quote a passage from Johnson's review of Soame Jenyns's *Free Inquiry into the Nature and Origin of Evil:* "Of political evil, if we suppose the origin of moral evil discovered, the account is by no means difficult, polity being only the conduct of immoral men in public affairs" (GS, 148). However, Greene makes it clear that, according to Johnson, "power is . . . intended to minimize its actual use" (GS, 150). Furthermore, he insists that Johnson's conversational "violence" against the Whigs is ironic and jocular.

Unlike Rousseau, Johnson is a major poet whose works include verse in Latin and Greek as well as translations. How is one to compare *London* (1738) and *The Vanity of Human Wishes* (1749), poems ranked by T. S. Eliot among "the greatest verse satire of the English or any other language,"[15] to Rousseau's tame alexandrines? What virtues, what characteristics allow the comparatist to cast a bridge from the poetic bulwark of these satires to the pretty and at times fluid chansons, romances, and pastourelles that constitute a less-than-solid foundation for a bridgehead? Without common denominators a connection cannot be made, and it is therefore expedient to offer *rousseauistes* a sampling of clearly phrased heroic couplets on Paris rather than a smattering of verses from *The Vanity of Human Wishes,* difficult even for specialists to read (in the making of syntactical mazes, Johnson almost rivals Mallarmé):

> London! the needy villain's gen'ral home,
> The common shore of Paris and of Rome;
> With eager thirst, by folly or by fate,
> Sucks in the dregs of each corrupted state.
> Forgive my transports on a theme like this,
> I cannot bear a French metropolis
>   (P, 53)[16]

This outburst took place long before Johnson journeyed to Paris in the good company of Mr. and Mrs. Thrale. To repeat, the differences between Johnson's and Rousseau's poetry are insurmountable and do not permit serious critical comparison. On the one hand, we have the results of the tradition initiated by Dryden and

Pope, not to mention Horace and Juvenal—satirical, didactic, reflective as well as circumstantial; on the other hand, we gaze into
Le Verger de Madame la Baronne de Warens with its "Plaisirs toûjours
doux, toûjours purs" (2:1124), weakly echoing the serene melody
of La Fontaine's *Adonis:* "Jours devenus moments, moments filés de
soie."[17] Still more *mièvre,* or finical, are Jean-Jacques's homages *Pour
{la Zulietta},* a lyrical tidbit (pun ineluctable) which proclaims the
charms of the Venetian courtesan whose immortal advice to Jean-
Jacques to forego women in favor of mathematics might have been
sanctioned by the author of the *Rambler,* had he taken the trouble
to read *Les Confessions.* But, to return to the *Vanity of Human Wishes,*
one should bear in mind that neither English nor French literature
offers verse which matches Johnson's Christian-Stoic poem, with
respect to compression of abstract concepts and feelings within a
highly structured formal pattern; in fact, the only author whose
voice reminds me of Johnson's is Gryphius (1616–64), the German
baroque poet whose message rings equally terse and serious. Even
the title of one of his poems, "Es ist alles eitel" (All is vain), is akin
to that of Johnson's satire. For the purpose of an additional contrast
between Rousseau, *poète,* and the English poet, who felt that he
deserved a tomb in Westminster Abbey, I should direct my French
reader to such poems as "On the Death of Dr. Robert Levet," "To
Mrs. Thrale," and "A Short Song of Congratulation," which deploy
a rhythmic strength and embody a texture never found in Rousseau
(and, for that matter, rarely in any French poet after Villon). Exemplary of such *rugosité anglaise* is the second stanza of "An Extempore
Elegy," about which Fanny Burney writes: "While we were thus
alone one evening we made an extempore elegy, Dr. Johnson, Mrs.
Thrale and myself *spouting* it alternately:

> She was once as cherry plump,
>   Red her cheek as Cath'rine pear,
> Tossed her nose, and shook her rump,
>   Till she made her neighbors stare.
>
> There she soon became a jilt,
>   Rambling often to and fro'
> All her life was naught but guilt,
>   Til purse and carcase both were low.
>   (P, 300)

One suspects that Johnson is the sole author of these stanzas and regrets that he did not warble more often in this mode.

Light years removed from such verse is his neoclassical tragedy *Irene,* almost completed in 1737 and eventually performed by David Garrick. It was not even a *succès d'estime.* What E. L. McAdam and George Milne say about it holds true, roughly speaking, for Rousseau's dramatic poetry: "[Johnson] could write *about* people, for he could comment on their actions, but he could not let them talk without making them awkwardly comment on themselves. . . . Johnson's characters cannot talk like human beings" (P, xxiii).[18] Similarly, Rousseau's dramatis personae lack any kind of vraisemblance—for example, Pygmalion, who sighs upon seeing Galathée step down from the pedestal: "Dieux immortels! Vénus! Galathée! ô prestige d'un amour forcené!" (2:1230) A few years after having completed his tragedy, Johnson wrote the *Life of Richard Savage.* Its relationship to Diderot's *Neveu de Rameau* is the subject matter of the last chapter of this book. But the *Life of Savage* also bears comparison to Rousseau's story of Mme de Warens. Just as Johnson's biography may be considered the first modern biography of a parasitic poet, so Rousseau's admirable portrait of his *Maman* represents the first objective in-depth biography of a woman.[19]

Other works by Johnson include his *Dictionary of the English Language* (1755), a work of seminal importance which attempts to resolve questions of good usage as well as of propriety. *Mutatis mutandis,* one might juxtapose it with Rousseau's *Dictionnaire de musique* (1763). Regarding Johnson's essays in the *Rambler* (1750–52), the *Adventurer* (1752), and the *Idler* (1758–60), Rousseau's bibliography offers no matching counterparts, although some passages in l'*Emile, La Nouvelle Héloïse,* and *Les Confessions* intersect thematically with Johnson's views.

Mention must also be made of *Rasselas* (1759), a philosophical tale, characteristically Johnsonian in mood. Because of its spiritual concerns, *Rasselas* is comparable in some ways to *La Nouvelle Héloïse,* which also elaborates a theme typical of the *Bildungsroman*—namely, "the choice of life." Chapter 2 relates *Rasselas* to *Candide* and to Rousseau's *Lettre sur la Providence.* In 1769 appeared the edition of Shakespeare's works with a preface that, according to Adam Smith, is "the most manly piece of criticism ever published in any country" (BA, 41). *The Journey to the Western Islands* (1755) and *The Lives of the Poets* (1779 and 1781) are literary efforts of a kind never attempted by Rousseau, unless one reduces the *Confessions* to *une vie romancée et poétique*.

With their respective achievements in mind, we may proceed to sketch the contours of Rousseau's and Johnson's lives. Both began with tragedy. Jean-Jacques's mother died in childbirth: "je coûtai la vie à ma mère, et ma naissance fut le premier de mes malheures" (1:7). Throughout his life, he bore the self-imposed guilt of her death, and he may have abandoned his five children not only to have them relive his traumatic sense of loss but also to commit a real crime in order to justify unconscious guilt feelings that weighed heavily upon his psyche. Heidegger's concept of *Geworfenheit* illustrates Rousseau's ontological drama (*werfen* means "to cast" but also "to whelp")—a drama that was reenacted when Rousseau found himself locked out from his hometown: "Je frémis en voyant en l'air ces cornes terribles, sinistre et fatal augure du sort inévitable que ce moment commençoit pour moi" (1:42). Although he protected the memory of his father, the latter clearly cared little for his son who was left to his own devices. Johnson's entry into the world was also ill-starred: a traumatic birth, followed by the scrofula, cast a long shadow on his young life. Almost blind, he later confided to Hawkins that he had never known a day without pain. His mother was a difficult woman, and he harbored little love for his father Michael, a bookseller by trade. It is generally believed that the depressing description of family life by Nekayah, Rasselas's sister, reflects the habitual mood of Johnson's home: "Parents and children seldom act in concert: each child endeavours to appropriate the esteem or fondness of the parents, and the parents, with yet less temptation, betray each other to their children; thus some place their confidence in the father, and some in the mother, and, by degrees, the house is filled with artifices and feuds" (Ras, p. 116).

Never does Johnson idealize the bitter years of his youth. Jean-Jacques, however, more fortunate than the boy from Lichfield, knows or imagines an affectionate home life which he adorns with a poetic halo—a humble world of tenderness, transfigured by the artist into a myth of universal significance: "Comment serois-je devenu méchant, quand je n'avois sous les yeux que des exemples de douceur, et autour de moi que les meilleures gens du monde? Mon pere, ma tante, ma mie, mes parens, nos amis, nos voisins, tout ce qui m'environnoit ne m'obéissait pas à la vérité, mais m'aimoit; et moi je les aimois de même" (1:10). Jean-Jacques never attends school, and his creative genius, unfettered by tradition, fulfills his potential to the point that Kant will hail him as the Newton of the moral world. Young Sam, on the other hand, is the schoolboy *par excellence,* although Hawkins relates that "the course of his studies was far from regular: he read by fits and starts, and in the intervals, digested his reading by meditation, to which he was ever prone" (H, 12). His poverty at Pembroke College has become legendary, almost Dickensian, and his intellectual exploits, specifically his capacity to remember, brings to mind similar feats performed by Julien Sorel who astounds Monsieur de Rênal's family, *femme de chambre comprise.* True, Henri Beyle's hero is imagined, whereas Johnson lived; eventually, however, through the art of Boswell, the memory of Johnson's life assumes the vibrant and imaginary quality of a character in a well-known story.[20]

Both youths leave *home;* in that sense Lichfield equals Geneva. Jean-Jacques runs away only to find a protectress, a *Maman,* in the person of Mme de Warens who cares for the boy during many years; Johnson meets his pathetic Tetty, twenty years his senior, whom he loves without perhaps ever loving her the way he will love Molly Aston (who is to judge?) and eventually Mrs. Thrale. Likewise Rousseau, at the age of forty-five, "redevenu tout à coup le berger extravagant" (1:427), finds himself bewitched by the pockmarked charms of Sophie, *la comtesse d'Houdetot,* and suddenly mindless of Thérèse Levasseur, his mistress and the mother of his children. A strange creature she was—his *gouvernante*—who may be viewed as the prototype of all the *Dienstmädchen* who ever scurried up and down the staircases in real and fictional nineteenth-century homes. Ranking high among these humble heroines are Hazlitt's Sara Walker, that "lodging-house hussy," who humiliated her admirer so much, as well as Lene Demuth who was to bear a son to Karl Marx. It has to be significant in a world conspicuously lacking in demonstrable meaning that the name Levasseur is derived from the late Latin *vassus* (servant) and that *Demuth* signifies humility. Need one stress that neither man, Johnson nor Rousseau, ever possessed his ideal woman?[21]

The Englishman leaves for London; the Genevan, for Paris. The former journeys in the company of David Garrick, sharing with him one horse and carrying in his satchel his unfinished tragedy *Irene,* which tells the story of the Sultan Mahomet who slays a Greek Christian he loves.[22] Jean-Jacques strolls to the French capital on foot, possessed by the high hope of becoming *Maréchal* Rousseau "avec un beau plumet blanc" (4:158). What Hawkins writes about his man holds true for Jean-Jacques:

> Bred to no profession, without relations, friends, or interests, Johnson was an adventurer in the world, and had his fortunes to make: the arts of insinuation and address were, in his opinion, too slow in their operation to answer his purpose; and, he rather chose to display his parts to all the world, at the risk of being thought arrogant, than to wait for the assistance of such friends as he could make, or the patronage of some individual that had power or influence, and who might have the kindness to take him by the hand, and lift him into notice. (H, 50–51)

Indeed, both lives exhibit picaresque elements: Johnson, destitute, tramping through the streets of London in the company of his friend Savage; rubbing shoulders with the rabble, with whores and their pimps, with men from underground and hack writers living in garrets (so wittily evoked in *The Rambler*), with impostors like Psalmanazar, metaphysical tailors—in short, all the quasi-Dostoyevskian and Balzacian types who emerge at sunset in large cities. Jean-Jacques, too, knows intermittently the life of the *pícaro.* The list of his trades and professions includes lackey in Turin, as well as professional convert, exhibitor of his *fontaine de Héron,* assistant to the affable pseudoarchimandrite, land surveyor without enthusiasm, untrained conductor of a symphony orchestra in Lausanne, assistant to Claude Anet (Mme de Warens's *intendant* and lover), secretary to the aristocratic and desirable Mme Dupin (who, *en déshabillé,* turns his head), as well as secretary to the French ambassador in Venice with whom he quarrels. Furthermore, in conformity with his future authorship of the *Emile,* he teaches M. de Mably's son in Lyon and nips on the sly, whenever possible, from a bottle of wine. Much of his life takes place outdoors, and he has bequeathed a lovely description of a night spent *à la belle étoile;* space and time figure as the coordinates of his *Sehnsucht.* Johnson, on the other hand, prefers to sleep in the streets of London rather than behind a garden wall and, unlike Rousseau, finds fulfillment in enclosures—taverns, drawingrooms, churches, judicial courts, or libraries. To be sure, Johnson inspects Paris and marches and rides through the gray-and-russet valleys of the Hebrides. *Pícaros* they are indeed, but of a special kind. Both are adventurers, as hungry for salvation as they are thirsty for happiness. "La soif du bonheur ne s'éteint point dans le coeur de l'homme" (1:413), confesses Rousseau, and the echo of this lament resounds throughout his life. It is worth noting that he exhales this sigh in Wootton (where he composes *L'idylle des cerises*), only twenty-six miles from Lichfield—a town proud of its sons Johnson and Garrick and of its daughter Anna Seward, "the swan of Lichfield."[23]

What they lived they teach. Both are instructors of mankind, both will continue to be heard, and both will be better known to posterity than any other men of the eighteenth century. Rousseau shapes his existential experience into an intricate, yet luminous metaphor which, in turn, casts a light on his existence as he knew it. His life is his textbook. Johnson, on the other hand, does not entrust us with the intimate metaphor of his life; if he ever wrought it, he consigned it to the fire in his hearth before his death. Rather, he teaches his story by way of allegories whose sense will forever fascinate and reassure his students.

Do we learn more about the two men if we read descriptions of their appearance? Here is Bernardin de Saint-Pierre's portrait of his moody friend:

> Il était maigre et d'une taille moyenne . . . il avait le teint
> brun, quelques couleurs aux pommettes des joues, la bouche
> belle, le nez très-bien fait, le front rond et élevé, les yeux
> pleins de feu. . . . On remarquait dans son visage trois ou
> quatre caractères de la mélancolie, par l'enfoncement des yeux

et par l'affaissement des sourcils; de la tristesse profonde par les rides du front; une gaieté très-vive et même un peu caustique, par mille petits plis aux angles extérieures des yeux, dont les orbites disparaissaient quand il riait . . . sa figure . . . offrait à la fois, je ne sais quoi d'aimable, de fin, de touchant, de digne de pitié et de respect.[24]

All is grace and finesse in Rousseau: "J'aime à manger sans être avide; je suis sensuel et non pas gourmand" (1:35). According to Mrs. Piozzi, however, "Mr. Johnson's own Pleasures—except those of Conversation—were all coarse ones: he loves a good dinner early—eats it voraciously, and his notions of a good Dinner are nothing less than delicate—a Leg of Pork boyl'd till it drops from the bone almost, a Veal Pye with Plumbs and Sugar, and the outside Cut of a Buttock of Beef are his favourite Dainties, though he loves made Dishes Soups etc: sowces his Plumb Pudding with melted Butter, and pours Sauce enough into every Plate to drown all Taste of the Victuals" (T, 185–86). Jean-Jacques is as fastidious as a cat; Johnson, as rough as the proverbial English bulldog—at least in appearance:

> He had a loud voice, and a slow deliberate utterance, which no doubt gave some additional weight to the sterling metal of his conversation. His person was large, robust, I may say approaching to the gigantick, and grown unwieldy from corpulency. His countenance was naturally of the cast of an ancient statue. . . . He was now in his sixty-fourth year, and was become a little dull of hearing. His sight had always been somewhat weak. . . . His head, and sometimes also his body shook with a kind of motion like the effect of palsy. . . . He wore a full suit of plain brown clothes, with twisted hair-buttons of the same colour, a large bushy greyish wig, a plain shirt, black worsted stockings, and silver buckles. (L, 5:18– 19)[25]

The last likeness of Johnson, painted by his friend Sir Joshua Reynolds, brings to mind the Rembrandt of the late self-portraits, whose kindly eyes are steeped in pain and resignation. But Johnson looks *at* you and envelops you in his gaze, whereas Rousseau's glance flows past idle spectators in the museum.[26] He does not see you, for is he not the greatest Narcissus that ever lived? Similarly, his death mask suggests intense introspection, while Johnson's mask intimates a dearly bought release from the heartache of life.

Turning our attention to a comparison of the psyches of the two authors, we note a crucial divergence. According to Bate,

> Johnson is probably the most extraordinary example in modern times of a man who in his own character concretely and dramatically exemplifies the Augustinian tradition of individualism and "interiority"—that "it is within the soul itself that man must search for truth and certitude" (*in interiore homine habitat veritas*)—and yet, far from welcoming it or turning to it with conscious choice, distrusted and in many ways tried to resist it. In this respect, he is of enormous interest in illustrating the transition to the modern inwardness of the religious life and the problem of elusiveness and self-doubt that attended it. (B, 455)

Indeed, Johnson's interests are polarized: on the one hand, his critical mind fastens on the truths of tradition as well as on *le pour et contre* of cant and wealth; on the other hand, the same mind yearns for dissolution in the hereafter. Johnson clings to facts though they wound him. Rousseau, by contrast, often sidesteps them: "Ma mauvaise tête ne peut s'assujettir aux choses. . . elle veut créer" (1:71–72). Unlike Jean-Jacques, who creates a moral system of his own which absolves him of many failings (at least on the conscious level), Johnson is always severe with himself and appears obsessed by an ever-present sense of moral and religious responsibility that transmutes his weaknesses (for instance, torpor) into painful and destructive guilt. Bate subjects these feelings to a psychoanalytical interpretation:

> A pervasive incorrigible sense of "guilt"—as distinct from specific "remorse"—is the inevitable result of the structural character of the human psyche, in which aggressiveness is taken over by a portion of the ego, and then internalized and directed back against the rest of the ego by a "super-ego"; and the punishment of the vulnerable ego from this rigid internalization of oppression into self-demand is essentially through a chronic sense of "guilt." The more highly developed the super-ego, the more severely exacting and the more sleepless the punishment of the ego through irrational and chronic "guilt" (unless, of course, it is projected on others,

which Johnson was in general incapable of doing). Hence, as
Freud emphasized, those who have carried "virtue" farthest, to
the point even of saintliness (*Heiligkeit*), will inevitably—not
because of what they have done (for the ego can never win in
such a struggle) but because of the structure of their
character—feel chronic guilt the most strongly. In fact, as
Freud mused near the end of his life, they serve as a kind of
spearhead illustrating that "the price we pay for our advance in
civilization is a loss of happiness through the heightening sense
of guilt." (B, 386)

Bate's commentary is especially appropriate to our discussion, because Freud's analysis of the relationship between guilt and civilization has some of its roots in Rousseau's critique of societal attitudes
and values so strongly championed by *les philosophes*. One should
add that Boswell's insistence on the contradictory aspects of his
hero's character is justified, by and large, by contemporary interpretations[27] of Samuel Johnson's psychological make-up:

So morbid was his temperament, that he never knew the
natural joy of a free and vigorous use of his limbs: when he
walked, it was like the struggling gait of one in fetters. . . .
At different times, he seemed a different man, in some
respects; not, however, in any great or essential article. . . .
Nor can it be denied that he had many prejudices [cf.
Rousseau: "je préfère être homme à paradoxes qu'homme à
préjugés" (4:323)] . . . He was steady and inflexible in
maintaining the obligations of religion and
mortality . . . impetuous and irritable in his temper, but of a
most humane and benevolent heart. . . . He loved praise,
when it was brought to him; but was too proud to seek
it. . . . In him were united a most logical head with a most
fertile imagination, which gave him an extraordinary
advantage in arguing. (L, 4:425–29)

However intense Johnson's contradictory nature may have
been, his religious orthodoxy allowed him to adjust quite satisfac-
torily to the spiritual climate in which he lived. Johnson felt at ease
with his fellow men and their world. Rousseau was a stranger to it.
Perpetually maladjusted, he was forever tempted by two opposing
ideals of unity—a contradiction expressed nowhere more movingly
than in the first book of the *Emile:* "Entraînés par la nature et par

les hommes dans des routes contraires, forcés de nous partager entre ces diverses impulsions, nous en suivons une composée qui ne
nous mène ni à l'un ni à l'autre but. Ainsi combatus et flotans
durant tout le cours de nôtre vie, nous la terminons sans avoir pu
nous accorder avec nous, et sans avoir été bons ni pour nous ni pour
les autres" (4:251). Jean-Jacques's dilemma is clear: he is the prey of
two ideals that neutralize each other.[28] The first may be defined as
an effort to include himself in the heart of the present, an attempt
to be and *to be aware* of being. Rousseau strives to concentrate all of
his being in the here and now: "De quoi jouit-on dans une pareille
situation? De rien d'extérieur à soi, de rien sinon de soi-même et de
sa propre existence, tant que cet état dure on se suffit à soi-même
comme Dieu" (1:1047). God is conscious of all that is, and it is
Rousseau's deep desire to know this nonmediated awareness of life's
plenitude. These attempts at self-possession alternate with cravings
to become one with nature by achieving the transparency of space
and the fluidity of water. This twofold quest for divine self-sufficiency and pantheistic passivity takes place in the pure present,
and there is no need of past and future. Rousseau's second ideal
strives towards the past and future while the present, formerly the
dimension of fulfillment, is now a dimension of sorrow and de-
struction. Every day that he lives divides a spiritual and moral
unity, which Rousseau never experiences directly but whose reality
he divines with ardor and faith in order to end the disintegration of
his daily life: "J'aspire au moment où, délivré des entraves du corps
je serai *moi* sans contradiction, sans partage, et n'aurai besoin que
de moi pour être heureux: en attendant je le suis dès cette vie parce
que j'en compte pour peu tous les maux, que je la regarde comme
presque étrangère à mon être" (4:604–5). Now, Rousseau's past
experiences and his hopes for the future contain the essential parts
of his self, and he aspires to experience this oneness outside the
earthly boundaries of life. This second ideal is but superficially
related to *Paradise Lost* and *The City of God,* which are connected, so
to speak, by the Vale of Tears. The contradiction of Rousseau's
strivings is complete, and his visions do not imply saintly beati-
tudes as they do for Johnson; on the contrary, they suggest the
growing secularization of Christian ideals and point to the dilem-

mas created by such a transformation. I say "dilemmas," because it is clear how Rousseau's efforts to achieve oneness oppose and defeat each other. One is not possible without the other: Rousseau's first search for unity presupposes a present independent of past and future, while his second depends solely on past and future, which are, without the present, only lifeless categories of the mind.

Although the impact of Rousseau's works is of incalculable importance in the evolution of European intellectual, literary, and political history, I venture to affirm that his mission as a catalyst of the contradictory experience which Chateaubriand calls *le mal du siècle* is perhaps even more momentous than the influence he exerted willfully through his writings—a mission of which he could not be aware but which he accomplished, in the words of Coleridge, "with a fullness of heart . . . employing the whole of his being to do aught effectually."[29] Almost every Romantic has spoken or written about the fire Rousseau poured into his or her soul. George Eliot's testimony exemplifies Jean-Jacques's impact on her feelings:

> I might admit all this; and it would be not the less true that Rousseau's genius had sent electric thrill through my intellectual and moral frame which has awakened me to new perceptions, which has made man and nature a fresh world of thought and feeling to me; and this not by teaching me any new belief. It is simply that the rushing mighty wind of his inspiration has so quickened my faculties that I have been able to shape more definitively for myself ideas which had previously dwelt as dim "Ahnungen" in my soul; the fire of his genius has so fused together old thoughts and prejudices that I have been ready to make new combinations.[30]

Even a philosopher such as Fichte uses similar language to evoke the excitement that emanated from this strange man ("Er hat Feuer in manche Seele gegossen," [He poured fire into many souls]), whose life had become a symbol of the possibility of salvation for the modern world.

Unlike Rousseau, Johnson yearns only for one victory and one kind of unity.[31] His character stands out not only because it is allied to a herculean mind but also because it reflects his unceasing struggle, which causes everything he says and does to be delineated by sharp edges. Hence his compulsive habits, often resulting from neurological dysfunctions, express also a "powerful unconscious need to release nervous tension through order, pattern, or rhythm" (B, 382) which affects his style. If ever Buffon's adage, *le style c'est tout l'homme* holds true, it has to be in the case of Samuel Johnson who, had he not been so immensely intelligent and kind, would have been a somewhat comic character, almost a Pangloss, as I suggest at the beginning of my discussion of *Candide* and *Rasselas*. But his nimble genius, "l'habitant de [ses] pensées," to paraphrase Valéry, allows him to manipulate abstract structures with an agility that masks their Aristotelian origin as well as their implicit and explicit rigidity. And where there are edges, there are contrasts— shadows on snow. Without obstacles, Johnson is unthinkable.[32] Rousseau, on the other hand, yearns for transparency, for dissolution, for being one with water, land, and sky, not to speak of his fellow men. To be transparent is Jean-Jacques's fond desire, and his most beautiful pages are characteristically luminous, while Johnson's finest prose is bedecked with dazzling patterns in black and white. Thoughts read on paper make a music that is not only heard but also understood. When juxtaposing the writings and reported conversations of Rousseau and Johnson, one should therefore devote as much attention to their melodic designs as to the arabesques of their thoughts and fancies.

A comparison of souls invites a comparison of characters, ideas, and caprices: a labyrinthine task, if one calls to mind the unending convolutions engendered by Rousseau's subjective quest for truth as well as the wealth of anecdotes, sketches, and biographies devoted to Johnson. Rousseau's splendid *Lettres à Malesherbes* (1762) offers a convenient point of departure:

> Mais Monsieur quoique je haïsse souverainement l'injustice et
> la mechanceté, cette passion n'est pas assés dominante pour me
> determiner seule à fuir la societé des hommes. . . . Je suis né
> avec un amour naturel pour la solitude qui n'a fait
> qu'augmenter à mesure que j'ai mieux connu les hommes. Je
> trouve mieux mon compte avec les etres chimeriques que je
> rassemble autour de moi qu'avec ceux que je vois dans le

monde, et la société dont mon imagination fait les frais dans
ma retraite achève de me degouter de toutes celles que j'ai
quittées. (1:1131)

Is there a self-portrait more unlike Rousseau's than Johnson's evocation of his gregarious self?

> There are others to whom idleness dictates another expedient,
> by which life may be passed unprofitably away without the
> tediousness of many vacant hours. The art is, to fill the day
> with petty business . . . to keep the mind in the state of
> action, but not of labour. This art has for many years been
> practiced by my friend Sober with wonderful success. Sober is
> a man of strong desires and quick imagination. . . . [H]is
> chief pleasure is conversation; there is no end of his talk or his
> attention; to speak or to hear is equally pleasing; for he still
> fancies that he is teaching or learning something. . . . But
> there is one time at night when he must go home, that his
> friends may sleep; and another time in the morning, when all
> the world agrees to shut out interruption. These are the
> moments of which poor Sober trembles at the thought. (I, 97)

No one has better delineated Johnson's daily dilemma than his
friend Sir Joshua Reynolds: "The great business of his life . . . was
to escape from himself; this disposition he considered as the disease
of his mind, which nothing cured but company" (L, 1:144). The
comment rings with Pascalian overtones, for Johnson's obsessive
need to be with someone dovetails with Pascal's concept of *le diver-
tissement;* however, Johnson, unlike Pascal, is unable to remain
twenty-four hours by himself. Rousseau, on the contrary, focuses
his energy on being alone and proceeds not only to prove the theoretical feasibility of attaining happiness but also swears to have
known it: "Ici commence le court bonheur de ma vie; ici viennent
les paisibles mais rapides momens qui m'ont donné le droit de dire
que j'ai vécu" (1:225). And if one recalls how strongly Rousseau
reacted to Diderot's remark "Il n'y a que le méchant qui soit seul,"
one understands not only to what degree Rousseau felt alone in his
need to be alone in the most gregarious of ages but also how deeply
Johnson's need of company may have had its roots in an ontological
awareness of his own corruption (possibly related to onanism and
other sexual concerns) which he could forget or avoid during social

intercourse. Mrs. Piozzi, at the time Mrs. Thrale, relates a conversation which occurred while she was sending her son to school: " 'Make your boy tell you his dreams: the first corruption that entered into my heart was communicated in a dream.' 'What was it, Sir?' said I. '*Do* not ask me,' replied he with much violence, and walked away in apparent agitation. I never durst make any further enquiries" (A, 67).

This morbid melancholy, this "English malady," accompanied by a compulsive fear of loneliness, always torments Johnson. Never free from physical and mental discomfort, his life is but a struggle against pain whose intensity matches the miseries of Rousseau's later years, which are darkened by acute urinary retention and by a persecution complex. But, unlike Johnson who seeks solace with friends, drinking numberless cups of tea until late into the night, Jean-Jacques finds his cure in nature and, in his younger days when still relatively healthy, by meeting the dawn: "L'aurore un matin me parut si belle que m'étant habillé précipitamment, je me hâtai de gagner la campagne pour voir lever le soleil" (1:135). Johnson never tires of deprecating what he cannot bear himself: "These specious representations of solitary happiness, however opprobrious to human nature, have so far spread their influence over the world, that almost every man delights his imagination with the hopes of obtaining some time an opportunity of retreat" (Ad, no. 126, p. 427). And his attack against those who delight in "the society of solitude" seems to be aimed at the very life and ideal of Rousseau: "There is indeed scarcely any writer who has not celebrated the happiness of rural privacy, and delighted himself and his reader with the melody of birds, the whisper of groves, and the murmur of rivulets; nor any man eminent for extent of capacity, or greatness of exploits, that has not left behind him some memorials of lonely wisdom, and silent dignity" (R, no. 135, p. 351).

In his first letter to Malesherbes (1762), Rousseau seeks to lay bare the reasons which make him hate social life. Could it be that he is wanting in conversational wit? No, declares Jean-Jacques: the real cause is "cet indomptable esprit de liberté que rien n'a pû vaincre, et devant lequel les honneurs, la fortune et la reputation meme ne me sont rien. Il est certain que cet esprit de liberté me vient moins d'orgueil que de paresse; mais cette paresse est incroyable. . . . Un mot à dire, une lettre à ecrire, une visitte à faire, des qu'il le faut, sont pour moi des suplices. Voila pourquoi, quoique le commerce ordinaire des hommes me soit odieux, l'intime amitié m'est si chere parce qu'il n'y a plus de devoirs pour elle. On suit son coeur et tout est fait. Voila encore pourquoy j'ai toujours tant redouté les bienfaits" (1:1132). In truth, Jean-Jacques only wants to see friends and no one else. Johnson, also pining for friendship, remains objective in his dealings with the world at large. His *esprit de liberté* waxes and wanes. "The pride of independence," comments Hawkins, "was most strong in Johnson at those periods of his life when his wants were greatest, and though at other times he would subject himself to great obligations, he was uniform, except in one instance, in an opinion that an offer of pecuniary assistance was an insult" (H, 192). Yet, his almost antiquated respect for "high people" and the ecclesiastical hierarchy clashes with Rousseau's furious need for independence. Mrs. Piozzi concludes her anecdotal account by stressing this one singularity: "That though a man of obscure birth himself, his partiality to people of family was visible on every occasion; his zeal for subordination warm even to bigotry; his hatred to innovation, and reverence for the old feudal times, apparent, whenever any possible manner of shewing themselves occurred" (A, 160).

Perhaps no issue clarifies better the difference in viewpoints concerning independence held by Rousseau and Johnson than the delicate question of a pension from King George III. Boswell's reflections on their respective attitudes are quite illuminating:

> To such a degree of unrestrained frankness had he now accustomed me, that in the course of this evening I talked of the numerous reflections which had been thrown out against him on account of his having accepted a pension from his present Majesty. "Why, Sir," (said he, with a hearty laugh) "it is a mighty foolish noise that they make. I have accepted of a pension as a reward which has been thought due to my literary merit; and now that I have this pension, I am the same man in every respect that I have ever been; I retain the same principles. It is true, that I cannot now curse (smiling) the House of Hanover; nor would it be decent for me to drink

> King James's health in the wine that King George gives me
> money to pay for." (L, 1:429)

Boswell's letter to Deleyre, dated October 15, 1766, conveys with
remarkable acuity Rousseau's situation; his analysis precipitates in
the reader's mind a sense of being *there*, with the great man almost
before his eyes:

> I have an idea that M. Rousseau would have been willing
> enough to accept a pension. But he wished to have it on a
> footing that no man can ever have a pension on. He has ideas
> of independence that are completely visionary and which are
> unsuitable for a man in his position. Tell me, I ask you how
> Jean-Jacques Rousseau *can* live independently, except as regards
> his mind, the activity of which never depends on anything but
> the extraordinary vigor granted by Nature? But as regards his
> external situation, he must necessarily be dependent. If Jean-
> Jacques were young and robust and hardy, like one of those
> savages he wishes to make us admire so much, then he could
> ignore the human race, and running through the woods cry,
> "Vivo et regno." But Jean-Jacques is actually a man advancing
> in years, and a man whose life has not been easy. He is infirm,
> ill, and delicate to a degree that I would never have believed
> had I not seen it. He is a man who is fond of his little
> delicacies even, and who would be very discontented if he were
> deprived of good food and a soft bed. He can think the
> thoughts of a Hercules. But behold the man as he is, and tell
> me if such a man does not need a great deal of attention and a
> great deal of affection from his fellows—and consequently if he
> does not depend on them as we all depend on one another?[33]

However perspicacious we may deem Boswell's perception of
Rousseau's quandary, we need to consider three facts. One seems
incidental: an engraving of George III adorned the wall of Rousseau's modest apartment in Paris, in the rue Platrière (now, rue
Jean-Jacques Rousseau). The Citizen of Geneva was grateful to the
English monarch for the offer, and Bernardin de Saint-Pierre relates
that Rousseau's refusal of the pension may have been the result of a
misunderstanding.[34] The second consideration relates to the pe-
rennial question of money. Rousseau scorns it. Never does he sell
out. I have already emphasized that Rousseau objects to reducing
the essence of freedom to the concept of property. For him, freedom

is identical with dignity as well as with the right to do one's duty toward the state and toward oneself (the fulfillment of one's potential of happiness . . . "ce qu'on se doit à soi-même" [1:1028]). Yet Rousseau confesses to being a little avaricious, whereas Johnson is almost saintly in his generosity and, according to Hawkins, "never greedy for money" (H, 84). Upon being asked by a clergyman to compose a homily, Johnson is said to have replied tongue in cheek: "I will write a sermon for thee . . . but thou must pay me for it" (H, 84–85). Rousseau, however, typically extreme in his view, insists on the incompatibility of lucre and genius:

> Je sentois qu'écrire pour avoir du pain eut bientot étouffé mon génie et tué mon talent qui étoit moins dans ma plume que dans mon coeur, et né uniquement d'une façon de penser elevée et fiére qui seule pouvoit le nourrir. Rien de vigoureux, rien de grand ne peut partir d'une plume toute vénale. La nécessité, l'avidité peut-être, m'eut fait faire plus vite que bien. . . . Non, non, j'ai toujours senti que l'état d'Auteur n'étoit, ne pouvoit être illustre et respectable qu'autant qu'il n'étoit pas un métier. Il est trop difficile de penser noblement quand on ne pense que pour vivre. (1:402–3)

The third fact to be pondered is that Rousseau's sundry activities include domestic employment, to which Johnson never had to stoop. "Quoi toujours laquais?" (1:92). Who does not recall Jean-Jacques's exclamation, and who has forgotten his account of "ce moment . . . court, mais délicieux à tous égards" (1:95) when Mlle de Breil raises her eyes to the young lackey, who has surprised the guests with a philological explanation, and then turns her glance towards "son grand papa," asking him to praise the young scholar? For Rousseau, money always has distasteful connotations ("Il ne me faut que des plaisirs purs, et l'argent les empoisonne tous" [1:36]), whereas for Johnson money remains a necessary commodity devoid of metaphysical implications.[35] Why does Rousseau fear a helping hand and how does this fear intensify his *esprit de liberté?* His answer is unequivocal: "tout bienfait exige reconnoissance" (1:1132). If one remembers that divine self-sufficiency represents one of Rousseau's most cherished fantasies, it becomes clear that any kind of assistance from an aristocrat implies a diminution of his own powers. Johnson, an intensely religious man to whom any form of self-divinization is abhorrent, has the capacity to be grateful. The incident with Henry Hervey, who had been good to him, illustrates Johnson's attitude: "He was a vicious man, but very kind to me. If you call a dog HERVEY, I shall love him" (L, 1:106).

One may, however, like Mrs. Piozzi, discern other likenesses in the temper of the two authors. Rousseau begins his second letter to Malesherbes by isolating within himself two opposing tendencies: "Une âme paresseuse qui s'effraye de tout soin, un tempérament ardent, bilieux, facile à s'affecter et sensible à l'excès à tout ce qui l'affecte semblent ne pouvoir s'allier dans le même caractère, et ces deux contraires composent pourtant le fond du mien" (1:1134). Does this self-portrait not bear a surprising resemblance to the severe, almost Calvinistic, sketch drawn by Hawkins? "And here we cannot but reflect on that inertness and laxity of mind which the neglect of order and regularity in living, and the observance of stated hours, in short, the waste of time, is apt to lead men to: this was the source of Johnson's misery throughout his life; all he did was by fits and starts, and he had no genuine impulse to action, either corporeal or mental" (H, 205). Rousseau, unlike Johnson, metamorphoses his "weakness" into an enriching virtue which fulfills itself in what I have called "the first search for unity," experienced exclusively in the "pure present." He calls this experience *rêverie*; the celebrated *Cinquième promenade* describes how, drifting in a boat, he frees himself from the pleasure and pain of abstract thought in order to just *be:* "Le flux et le reflux de cette eau, son bruit continu, mais renflé par intervalles frappant sans relache mon oreille et mes yeux suppléoient aux mouvements internes que la rêverie étoignoit en moi et suffisoient pour me faire sentir avec plaisir mon existence, sans prendre la peine de penser" (1:1045). Marcel Raymond has written admirable pages on the sense of Rousseau's dream-states where "le dépouillement est poussé à la limite" and where "Rousseau, l'homme du désir, en arrive à ne plus rien désirer, à ne plus rien imaginer. Il faut que ce coeur soit assez déshumanisé pour ne plus souffrir et ne plus espérer" (1:xciii). And, he adds, "*Vivre,* c'est peut-être cela: se sentir délié de la volonté de vivre. Alors, le coeur du monde s'ouvre; l'intimité des choses se révèle (*interiora rerum*), et pourtant ces choses demeurent intouchables" (1:xci).

It goes without saying that such an abdication of reason would have been odious to Johnson "whose supreme enjoyment was the exercise of his reason" (L, 1:66) and to whom, writes Boswell, "the disturbance or obscuration of that faculty was the evil most to be dreaded" (L, 1:66). Given his dread of solitude, it is understandable that he fights "the morbid melancholy . . . lurking in his constitution" (L, 1:63) by exercising his magnificent intellect among friends whose approval can only be comforting—in other words, by talking and being exceedingly entertaining: "Conversation was all he required to make him happy," declares Mrs. Piozzi, and adds that "his notions rose up like dragon's teeth sowed by Cadmus, all ready clothed, and in bright armour too, fit for immediate battle. He was therefore (as someone is said to have expressed it) a tremendous converser, and few people ventured to try their skill against an antagonist with whom contention was so hopeless" (A, 128). Rousseau, to be sure, is too much of a loner to be, or wish to be, the king of wits, and he often bewails his *esprit de l'escalier*. The only Frenchman capable of matching, in French, Johnson's dazzling verbal magic was Diderot, whose conversation had an ineffable grace and lightness; his written words scintillate with a sparkle not often found in Voltaire's finest lines. Diderot excels in dialogues; Johnson, in monologues. "How he does talk," confides Miss Beresford to Boswell: "Every sentence is an essay" (L, 4:284). Must we not agree with Miss Beresford that Johnson's speech seems identical to his writing (admittedly, it is speech, doctored by Boswell *et al*); furthermore, is the twentieth-century reader not also struck by the resemblance between Johnson's poetry and his criticism? This likeness manifests itself at times so strongly that his verse appears as critical as his critical manifestos are poetic. "Whatever his verbal medium," declares Geoffrey Tillotson, "he was always a poet."[36] If we consult *A Dictionary of the English Language,* we see that our lexicographer defines the word *speech* as: "1. The power of articulate utterance; the power of expressing thoughts by vocal words; 2. Language; words considered as expressing thoughts; 3. Particular language, as distinct from others; 4. Anything spoken; 5. Talk, mention; 6. Oration, harangue; 7. Declaration of thoughts."[37] None of these definitions makes mention, or even alludes, to the role of feeling, passions, gesticulations, mimicry. Yet the origin of language, we are told, "must have come by inspiration. A thousand, nay, a million children could not invent a language. . . . When I maintain that language must have come by inspiration, I do not mean that inspiration is required for rhetorick, and all the beauties of language. . . . I mean only that inspiration seems to me to be necessary to give man the faculty of speech . . . which I think he could no more find out without inspiration, than cows or hogs would think of such a faculty" (L, 4:207). What he means by "inspiration" is not explained. Rousseau, on the contrary, devotes his *Essai sur l'origine des langues* (1761), to the development of speech and begins his discourse by considering the language of voice and gesture as natural, compared to the written language which becomes the questionable privilege of *l'homme de l'homme*: "D'abord on ne parla qu'en poésie; on s'avisa de raisonner que long-tems après" (p. 506). And, as if to beguile himself with an ideal message which does not betray its sender (one thinks of Mme Basile, meeting young Jean-Jacques's glance in the mirror), Rousseau appeals to the mute eloquence of love: "Que celle qui traçait avec tant de plaisir l'ombre de son amant lui disait de choses! Quels sons eût-elle employés pour rendre ce mouvement de baguette?" (*Essai*, 502).

I have already referred to Rousseau's fond hope to *be* crystal clear. In the context of the issue under discussion, Jean Starobinski's well-known commentary casts more light on the contrasts between our two men:

> Comment surmontera-t-il ce malentendu qui l'empêche de s'exprimer selon sa vraie valeur? Comment échapper aux risques de la parole improvisée? A quel autre mode de communication recourir? Par quel autre moyen se manifester? Jean-Jacques choisit d'être *absent* et *d'écrire*. Paradoxalement, il se cachera pour mieux se montrer, et il se confiera à la parole écrite: "J'aimerais la société comme un autre, si je n'étais sûr de me montrer non seulement à mon désavantage, mais tout autre que je ne suis. *Le parti que j'ai pris d'écrire et de me cacher*

est précisément celui qui me convenait. Moi présent, on
n'aurait jamais su ce que je valais."[38]

Such admissions are unthinkable from Johnson's lips or quill.
However, one must remember that Rousseau wants to tell all: "Je
me suis montré tel que je fus, méprisable et vil quand je l'ai été"
(1:5). Johnson, on the contrary, burns or hides what Boswell calls
the *tacenda,* and the price of achieving a successful fusion between
his written and spoken word may have been nothing less than the
truth.

As if to mock the semiotic perplexities of the most "uncluba-
ble" of his contemporaries, Johnson forms a club in the winter of
1749 at the King's Head, a beefsteak house in Ivy Lane near St.
Paul's. "Thither," relates Hawkins, "he constantly resorted, and,
with a disposition to please and be pleased" (H, 219): " 'As soon,'
said he, 'as I enter the door of a tavern, I experience an oblivion of
care, and a freedom from solicitude: when I am seated, I find the
master courteous, and the servants obsequious to my call; anxious
to know and ready to supply my wants: wine there exhilarates my
spirits, and prompts me to free conversation and an interchange of
discourse with those whom I most love: I dogmatize and am con-
tradicted, and in this conflict of opinions and sentiments I find
delight' " (H, 87). For a *rousseauiste,* however, it is almost painful to
imagine his hero in the boisterous setting of an eighteenth-century
London inn, just as it is preposterous to visualize John Bull in
Clarens with Julie, M. de Wolmar, and Saint-Preux, savoring "une
matinée à l'angloise, réunis et dans le silence, goûtant à la fois le
plaisir d'être ensemble et la douceur du recueillement" (2:557–
58). To be sure, Rousseau also recalls delightful hours *chez Maman*
who, "playing" alternately the chemist and the harpsichord, covers
his face with extracts made of absinthe and *genièvre* (1:181). But,
with the passing of the years, Rousseau's life is burdened with ever-
increasing sadness:

Il mondo invecchia ed invecchiando s'intristisce.[39]

It is a paradox that Rousseau, who swears to have known happiness, should end his days as an outcast, a stranger in exile, whereas
Johnson, whose youth exemplifies pain and poverty, not to mention

his breakdown, should be known for his concern with good humor (a willingness to be pleased). However, Mrs. Thrale, who knew him as well as anyone, gave Boswell 19 points on a scale of 20 for good humour, Sir Joshua Reynolds 10, and Johnson 0, the latter receiving the same mark as her husband.[40] Also pertinent is Boswell's evocation of Johnson, "stretching himself at his ease in the coach, and smiling with much complacency," turning to him, saying: "I look upon *myself* as a good humoured fellow." "I answered, also smiling," continues Boswell: "No, no Sir; that will *not* do. You are good natured, but not good humoured: you are irascible" (L, 2:362–63). In any case, Johnson dislikes those who claim to be happy. "It is all *cant* (he would cry), the dog knows he is miserable all the time" (A, 284). What might have been his comment, had he read these lines: "Je me levois avec le soleil et j'étois heureux; je me promenois et j'étois heureux, je voyois Maman et j'étois heureux, je la quittois et j'étois heureux . . . le bonheur me suivoit par tout; il n'étoit dans aucune chose assignable, il étoit tout en moi-même, il ne pouvoit me quitter un seul instant" (1:225–26)? When Johnson exclaims: "Are we to think Pope was happy, because he says so in his writings?" (L, 3:251), one is tempted to replace the Augustan's name with that of the apostle from Geneva. As for public manifestations of joy, Johnson and Rousseau share Pascal's views: "Nothing is more hopeless than a scheme of merriment," declares the *Idler* (1:190), and on seeing the Pantheon in London, Johnson confides to Boswell: "Yes, Sir, there are many happy people here. There are many people here who are watching hundreds, and who think hundreds are watching them" (L, 2:169). And in the same vein: "The world in its best state is nothing more than a large assembly of beings, combining to counterfeit happiness which they do not feel" (Ad, 468). It is needless to emphasize that, for Rousseau, the discrepancy between *être* and *paraître* looms large in his critique of his age, and he condemns with Calvinistic fervor all forms of societal hypocrisy and deception, especially if practiced by actors: "Qu'est-ce que la profession du comédien? Un Métier par lequel il se donne en représentation pour de l'argent . . . et met publiquement sa personne en vente."[41] Johnson too demeans actors but, in his later years, relents (to wit, his friendship with Kitty Clive and Mrs. Siddons) and even assumes a

Tartuffian pose when telling Garrick: "I'll come no more behind your scenes, David; for the silk stockings and white bosoms of your actresses excite my amorous propensities" (L, 1:201).

Despite his religious and constitutional objections to happiness, Johnson succeeds in being not only moderately cheerful but also kind and compassionate. "He gave away all he had," relates Mrs. Piozzi, "and all he had ever gotten, except the two thousand pounds he left behind" (A, 95). In her *Thraliana,* there is a long passage testifying to Johnson's seemingly rational attitude regarding good deeds—a point of view that contradicts Rousseau's concept of pity, which is generated by feeling:

> Mr. Johnson has more Tenderness for Poverty than any other Man I ever knew; and less for other Calamities: the person who loses Parent, Child or Friend he pities but little—these says he are the Distresses of Sentiment—which a Man who is *indeed* to be pitied—has no leisure to feel: the Want of Food and Raiment is so common in London adds Johnson, that one who lives there has no Compassion to spare for the Wounds given only to Vanity or Softness.
>
> In consequence of these Principles he has *now* in his house whole Nests of People who would if he did not support them be starving I suppose:—
>
> A Blind woman & her Maid, a Blackamoor and his Wife, a Scotch Wench who has her Case as a Pauper depending in some of the Law Courts; a Woman whose Father once lived at Lichfield & whose Son is a strolling Player,—and a superannuated Surgeon to have Care of the whole *Ship's Company.* Such is the present State of Johnson's Family resident in Bolt Court—an Alley in Fleet Street, which he gravely asserts to be the best Situation in London; and thither when he is at home he keeps a sort of odd Levee for distress'd Authors, breaking Booksellers, & in short every body that has even the lowest Pretensions to Literature in Distress. Mean while he has a Cousin at Coventry who is wholly maintained by him and a Female Cousin a Mrs. Herne I forget where to whom he regularly remits 10 pounds a Year, & She is I think his cheapest Dependent. (T, 184–85)

Rousseau appears much more parsimonious than Johnson; moreover, he is also given to mentioning his generosity—for ex-

ample, his little gifts to Mme de Warens, old and in distress. In all
fairness, however, it should be remembered that he regularly sent
money to his aged *mie* Jacqueline, and Bernardin de Saint-Pierre
tells of a school friend who had gone to see her: "Il trouva une
vieille femme qui, en apprenant qu'il avait vu son neveu, ne se
possédait pas d'aise. Comment! monsieur, lui dit-elle, vous l'avez
vu! Est-il donc vrai qu'il n'a pas de religion? Nos ministres disent
que c'est un impie. Comment cela se peut-il? il m'envoie de quoi
vivre. Pauvre vieille femme de plus de quatre-vingts ans, seule,
sans servante dans un grenier, sans lui je serais morte de froid et de
faim! Je répétai la chose à Rousseau mot pour mot. Je le devais, me
dit-il, elle m'avait élevé orphelin."[42]

"J'ai pris en mepris mon siecle et mes contemporains" (1:1135),
writes Rousseau to Malesherbes. As one meditates on Rousseau's
bitterness towards his fellow men, one must keep in mind that much
of his hostility issues from guilt feelings and shame about the fate of
his five children—more so since his domestic tragedy had become
public knowledge through the kind offices of Voltaire. Johnson the
pessimist refuses to speak ill of his age. In 1783, one year before his
death, he tells Boswell: "I have never sought the world; the world
was not to seek me. It is rather wonderful that so much has been
done for me. All the complaints which are made of the world are
unjust. I never knew a man of merit neglected: it was generally by
his own fault that he failed of success. . . . There is no reason why
any person should exert himself for a man who has written a good
book: he has not written it for any individual" (L, 4:172). Johnson's
philosophy, grounded in Christian humility, comes to terms with
the status quo. On the contrary, much of Rousseau's life is devoted to
questioning or sidestepping it. If Jean-Jacques cannot lose himself
in the "pure present," he escapes on the wings of imagination to
inhabit a better world where ideal men and women dwell: "Mon
imagination ne laissoit pas longtems la terre ainsi parée. Je la
peuplois bientôt d'etres selon mon coeur, et chassant bien loin
l'opinion, les prejugés, toutes les passions factices, je transportois
dans les asiles de la nature des hommes dignes de les habiter. Je m'en
formois une société charmante dont je ne me sentois pas indigne. Je
me faisois un siècle d'or à ma fantaisie" (1:1140). He then intensifies

his *rêveries* to the point of achieving a pantheistic ecstasy which
defines the creed and practice of European Romanticism: "Bientôt
de la surface de la terre j'elevois mes idées à tous les êtres de la nature,
au système universel des choses, à l'etre incomprehensible qui
embrasse tout. Alors l'esprit perdu dans cette immensité, je ne
pensois pas, je ne raisonnois pas, je ne philosophois pas; je me sentois
avec une sorte de volupté accablé du poids de cet univers, j'aimois à
me perdre en imagination dans l'espace . . . j'etouffois dans l'univers, j'aurois voulu m'elancer dans l'infini" (1:1141).

It is almost impossible to find an eighteenth-century text as
alien to the thought and sense of Johnson, the thinker and the
man. Immensely self-centered, Rousseau's ego fills the universe.
Such Fichtean projections would have been abhorrent to Johnson,
who always sought to integrate an individual into his society. For
Rousseau, the world is a function of his *moi,* and his character
enables him to love mankind without loving anyone in particular:
"J'ai un coeur tres aimant, mais qui peut se suffire à lui-meme.
J'aime trop les hommes pour avoir besoin de choix parmi eux; je les
aime tous, et c'est parce que je les aime que je hais l'injustice; c'est
parce que je les aime que je les fuis" (1:1144). Just as the universe
exists by virtue of a symbiotic relationship to his ego, the injustice
that pervades the world is proportionate to his concern for mankind; to the degree that members of social orders do not conform to
the needs of his character and ideals, he hates them passionately. In
his fourth letter to Malesherbes, Rousseau gives free rein to his
contempt for royalty and aristocracy:

> Je ne puis vous dissimuler Monsieur, que j'ai une violente
> aversion pour les etats qui dominent les autres, j'ai même tort
> de dire que je ne puis vous le dissimuler, car n'ai nulle peine à
> vous l'avouer, à vous né d'un sang illustre, fils du Chancelier de
> France, et Premier President d'une Cour souveraine; oui
> Monsieur à vous qui m'avez fait mille biens sans me connoitre et
> à qui malgré mon ingratitude naturelle, il ne m'en coute rien
> d'etre obligé. Je hais les grands, je hais leur etat, leur dureté,
> leurs préjugés, leur petitesse, et tous leurs vices, je les haïrois
> bien davantage si je les meprisois moins. (1:1145)

These are hard words, and no writer of the Enlightenment has
matched the tone and intensity of Rousseau's attack against l'An-

cien Régime. Johnson's celebrated letter to Lord Chesterfield affirms his dignity as a man and writer, but it never questions the legitimacy of existing hierarchies. On the contrary, Johnson defends them: "Were I in power, I would turn out every man who dare to oppose me. Government has the distribution of offices, that it may be enabled to maintain its authority" (L, 2:355). Yet, to speak with Hawkins: "although a Tory, he was not so besotted in his notions, as to abet what is called the patriarchal scheme. . . . [H]e seemed rather to adopt the sentiments of Hooker on the subject . . . to look on submission to lawful authority as a moral obligation" (H, 504). He opposes slavery, however, and concurs with Rousseau that men in their original state were equal (L, 2:202).

On September 14, 1773, Johnson and Boswell in the Hebrides dine in the company of Lady MacLeod, mistress of the castle of Dunvegan. After listening to a discussion concerning polygamy and Dr. Cadogan's book on gout, Lady MacLeod asks whether any man was naturally good. "JOHNSON. 'No Madam no more than a wolf.' BOSWELL. 'Nor no woman, Sir?' JOHNSON. 'No, Sir.' Lady M'Leod started at this, saying, in a low voice, 'This is worse than Swift'" (L, 5:211). Clarifying the sense of this postprandial chat after a mere two hundred and ten years, Donald Greene observes that "Johnson, of course, knew his ninth Article of the Church of England: 'Original sin . . . is the fault and corruption of the nature of every man that naturally is engendered of the offspring of Adam, whereby man is very far gone from original righteousness and is of his own nature inclined to evil. . . . ' Lady MacLeod, as Presbyterian, should have known that the Shorter Catechism puts it even more strongly. So should have Boswell, instead of reporting Johnson's remark as if it were an outrageous opinion."[43] Had Jean-Jacques been a *convive* at this memorable gathering (not a farfetched hypothesis, since Boswell had invited him to Scotland), he might have quoted a few lines from his *Discours sur l'origine de l'inégalité:* "N'allons pas surtout conclure avec Hobbes que pour n'avoir aucune idée de la bonté, l'homme soit naturellement méchant. . . . Le méchant, dit-il, est un Enfant robuste" (3:153).

Even a superficial acquaintance with our two authors makes it clear that Johnson had not read Rousseau's works with care or, what is much more likely, that he did not wish to understand him.

Whenever possible, Boswell teases Johnson: "On the 30th of September [1769] we dined together at the Mitre. I attempted to argue for the superior happiness of the savage life, upon the usual fanciful topicks. JOHNSON. 'Sir, there can be nothing more false. The savages have no bodily advantages beyond those of civilized men. They have not better health; and as to care and mental uneasiness, they are not above it, but below it, like bears. No, Sir; you are not to talk such paradox'" (L, 2:73). How differently Rousseau sees his savages! Analyzing the primitive societies and languages in warm climates, he writes in his *Essai sur l'origine des langues:* "Là se formèrent les premiers liens des familles, là furent les premiers rendez-vous des deux sexes. . . . Là se firent les premiers fêtes: les pieds bondissaient de joie, le geste empressé ne suffisait plus, la voix l'accompagnait d'accens passionnées; le plaisir et le désir, confondus ensemble, se faisaient sentir à la fois: là fut enfin le vrai berceau des peuples; et du pur cristal des fontaines sortirent les premiers feux de l'amour" (p. 525). Unaffected by real or imagined objections, Johnson never gives an inch: " 'Lord Monboddo, one of your Scotch Judges, talked a great deal of such nonsense. I suffered *him;* but I will not suffer *you.*'—BOSWELL. 'But, Sir, does not Rousseau talk such nonsense?' JOHNSON. 'True, Sir, but Rousseau *knows* he is talking nonsense, and laughs at the world for staring at him.' BOSWELL. 'How so, Sir?' JOHNSON. 'Why, Sir, a man who talks nonsense so well, must know that he is talking nonsense. But I am *afraid,* (chuckling and laughing), Monboddo does *not* know that he is talking nonsense'" (L, 2:74).

Johnson's chuckles should not deceive us; behind his impatience with Rousseau lurks his unshakeable conviction in the corruption of man. Hawkins comments: "The natural depravity of mankind and remains of original sin were so fixed in Mr. Johnson's opinion, that he was indeed a most acute observer of their effects; and used to say sometimes, half in jest, half in earnest, that they were the remains of his old tutor Mandeville's instructions" (H, 177). Children are not exempt from depravity: "Pity," declares Johnson "is not natural to man. Children are always cruel. Savages are always cruel. Pity is acquired and improved by the cultivation of reason" (L, 1:437). Is it necessary to stress that Rousseau maintains the opposite view? "La pitié, bien que naturelle au coeur de l'homme, resterait éternellement inactive sans l'imagination qui la met en jeu. Comment nous laissons-nous émouvoir par la pitié? En nous transportant hors de nous-mêmes; en nous identifiant avec l'être souffrant. Nous ne souffrons qu'autant que nous jugeons qu'il souffre; ce n'est pas dans nous, c'est dans lui que nous souffrons" (*Essai*, 517). Yet a reader of the *Rambler,* number 60, might point to a passage which seems quite similar to the one by Rousseau: "All joy or sorrow for the happiness of calamities of others is produced by an act of the imagination, that realizes the event, however fictitious, or approximates it, however remote, by placing us, for a time, in the condition of him whose fortune we contemplate; so that we feel, while the *deception* lasts, whatever motions would be excited by the same good or evil happening to ourselves." I have italicized the word *deception,* because it indicates how much Johnson differs from Rousseau in that Johnson derives pity from "the light of revelation." In his book *Samuel Johnson and Moral Discipline,* Paul K. Alkon summarizes this issue:

> Thus, compassion, which seemed inexplicable on rational
> grounds, was treated by Johnson as a divinely irrational
> impulse playing an important social role unique to the
> Christian era by leading to the creation of institutionalized
> philanthropy. The pity which inclines men systematically to
> help their fellows arises not because of what men are, but
> because God . . . has enabled man to transcend his own nature
> at times. It is clear why Johnson, holding this view, found the
> Hobbesian materialistic analysis doubly unsatisfactory, for in
> his opinion it failed to explain charity adequately on the basis
> of its own exclusively rationalistic assumptions, while also
> failing to provide any other explanation.[44]

Johnson's pedagogical theories are consistent with his severe moral views. Often, however, his prescriptions must be taken with a grain of salt. Boswell: "He maintained that a boy at school was the happiest of human beings. I supported a different opinion, from which I have never yet varied, that a man is happier; and I enlarged upon the anxiety and sufferings which are endured at school. JOHNSON. 'Ah! Sir, a boy's being flogged is not so severe as a man's having the hiss of the world against him. Men have a solicitude about fame; and the greater share they have of it, the more afraid they are of losing it' " (L, 1:451). It is enlightening to compare this passage with the episode of Mlle Lambercier's broken comb. Punished unjustly, Rousseau declares: "Ce premier senti- ment de la violence et de l'injustice est restée si profondément gravé dans mon ame, que toutes les idées qui s'y rapportent me rendent ma prémiére émotion" (1:20). Johnson, speaking of Mr. Hunter, one of his first teachers, to Mr. Langton, who asks him how he has come to be the first Latinist of his day, replies in terse words whose sense is the very opposite of Rousseau's declaration: "My master whipt me very well. Without that, Sir, I should have done nothing" (L, 1:45–46). Lest a *rousseauiste,* not at home in Johnson's world, should imagine him to be a taskmaster, two facts need to be brought to his attention. The first is that Johnson was a witty teacher who had but three students: "the celebrated David Garrick, his brother George, and Mr. Offely, a young gentleman of good fortune, who died early" (L, 1:97); the second is Johnson's proverbial kindness—it is almost unimaginable to visualize him flogging a hapless schoolboy. Moreover, Mrs. Piozzi insists that "he had never ceased representing to all the eminent schoolmasters in England, the absurd tyranny of poisoning the hour of permitted pleasure, by keeping future misery before the children's eyes, and tempting them by bribery or falsehood to evade it" (A, 68). The pathetic implications of the phrase "poisoning the hour of permit- ted pleasure" ring like echoes of Rousseau's admonition to be kind to children, so heartrending because of his guilt about his own progeny:

> Aimez l'enfance; favorisez ses jeux, ses plaisirs, son aimable instinct. Qui de vous n'a pas regretté quelquefois cet âge où le rire est toujours sur les lévres et où l'ame est toujours en paix? Pourquoi voulez-vous ôter à ces petits innocents la joüissance d'un tems si court qui leur échape, et d'un bien si précieux dont ils ne sauroient abuser? Pourquoi voulez-vous remplir d'amertume et de douleurs ces prémiers ans si rapides qui ne reviendront pas plus pour eux qu'ils ne peuvent revenir pour vous? Péres, savez-vous le moment où la mort attend vos enfans? (4:302)[45]

In view of Rousseau's tremendous interest in education, which culminates in the *Emile*, it is not possible to compare his complex and innovative theories with the few pedagogical remarks scattered throughout Johnson's works and in the biographies about him. I shall only say that Rousseau, like Johnson, is a theorist (he had but few students) who stresses pragmatic educational principles. The famous question: "A quoi cela est-il bon?" matches to some extent Johnson's precept: "Let the people learn necessary knowledge; let them learn to count their fingers, and to count their money, before they are caring for the classics" (A, 133).

Unlike Jean-Jacques, whose religious experience contains a good dosage of pantheism and mysticism inherited from Fénelon through Mme Guyon and, closer to home, through Maman, Johnson's religious concepts or beliefs seem always orthodox and precise. "His Piety," relates Mrs. Piozzi, "was exemplary and edifying" (T, 183). His prayers, closely modelled on those in the *Book of Common Prayer*, are always propitiatory:

> "O God, giver and preserver of all life, by whose power I was created, and by whose providence I am sustained, look down upon me with tenderness and mercy; grant that I may not have been created to be finally destroyed; that I may not be preserved to add wickedness to wickedness." "O, Lord, let me not sink into total depravity; look down upon me, and rescue me at last from the captivity of sin." "Almighty and most merciful Father, who has continued my life from year to year, grant that by longer life I may become less desirous of sinful pleasures, and more careful of eternal happiness." "Let not my years be multiplied to increase my guilt; but as my age advances, let me become more pure in my thoughts, more regular in my desires, and more obedient to thy Laws." (L, 4:397)[46]

The contrast between Johnson's anguished prayer for salvation and Rousseau's mellifluous *Profession de foi d'un vicaire savoyard* is truly striking. Enlightened by "la lumière intérieure" (4:569),[47] the Vicar expounds at great length the tenets of *la religion naturelle* and concludes his article of faith as follows: "Il est donc au fond des ames un principe inné de justice et de vertu, sur lequel, malgré nos propres maximes, nous jugeons nos actions et celles d'autrui comme bonnes ou mauvaises, et c'est à ce principe que je donne le nom de conscience" (4:598). How Johnson might have censured Rousseau's critique of revealed religion must remain a matter of speculation, inasmuch as he makes no mention of the *Emile*. It is certain, however, that he would have rejected such theology as characteristic of the *infidels* in whose wavering shadows he might have discovered, now and then, his future biographer. Though born a Presbyterian, briefly a Papist, and eventually an Anglican, Boswell was always in need of relaxation from the stern injunctions of any church. Rousseau's faith calms and caresses nervous souls.

The setting of Johnson's prayers is immaterial, whereas Jean-Jacques's *mise en scène* presages Henri Beyle's ecstatic annotation: "Le paysage était un archet qui jouait sur mon âme."[48] In fact, Rousseau's invocation could be termed a pre-text for a *poème en prose:*

> Il me mena hors de la ville, sur une haute colline au dessous de laquelle passoit le Pô, dont on voyoit le cours à travers les fertiles rives qu'il baigne. Dans l'éloignement, l'immense chaîne des Alpes couronoit le paysage. Les rayons du soleil levant rasoient déja les plaines, et projettant sur les champs par longues ombres les arbres, les côteaux, les maisons, enrichissoient de mille accidens de lumiére le plus beau tableau dont l'oeil humain puisse être frapé. On eut dit que la nature étaloit à nos yeux toute sa magnificence pour en offrir le texte à nos entretiens. (4:565)

If one visualizes the Italian Lake Region, one regrets that Johnson was never to fulfill his dream of venturing on an *Italienreise,* that he was never meant to be *ein Taugenichts* like Jean-Jacques, and that his *Maman anglaise* had to find her happiness in the arms of an Italian singing teacher. Soon to die, he writes to Mrs. Thrale who has "betrayed" him with Signor Piozzi: "I have loved you with virtuous affection, I have honored You with sincere Esteem. Let not all our endearments be forgotten, but let me have in this great distress your pity and your prayers. . . . [D]o not drive me from You, for I have not deserved either neglect or hatred."[49] But Jean-Jacques, on the threshold of death, devotes the last page ever written by his hand to an elegy of his Maman. It is as doubtful that the *idylle des Charmettes* ever took place as it is certain that Samuel Johnson could not dare to imagine such sweet regrets: "Ah! si j'avois suffi à son coeur comme elle suffisoit au mien . . . J'engageai maman à vivre à la campagne. Une maison isolée au penchant d'un vallon fut notre azile, et c'est là que dans l'espace de quatre ou cinq ans j'ai joui d'un siécle de vie et d'un bonheur pur et plein" (1:1098-99).

That Rousseau is an ardent believer in Providence will be shown in the next chapter. However, his concern with the afterlife seems quite pragmatic: "Ne me demandez pas non plus si les tourmens des méchans seront éternels; je l'ignore encore, et n'ai point la vaine curiosité d'éclaircir des questions inutiles. Que m'importe ce que deviendront les méchans" (4:591)? After all, certain of his immortality, Jean-Jacques begins his *Confessions* by challenging his fellow men to dare to think themselves better than he is. Johnson's pronouncements on the same subject are among the most delightful ever made:

> The amiable Dr. Adams suggested that GOD was infinitely good. JOHNSON. "That he is infinitely good, as far as the perfection of his nature will allow, I certainly believe; but it is necessary for good upon the whole, that individuals should be punished. As to an *individual,* therefore, he is not infinitely good; and as I cannot be *sure* that I have fulfilled the conditions on which salvation is granted, I am afraid that I may be one of those who shall be damned." (looking dismally.) DR. ADAMS, "What do you mean by damned?" JOHNSON. (passionately and loudly) "Sent to hell, Sir, and punished everlastingly." (L, 4:299).

No one may hope to be spared chastisement: "We do not know that even the angels are quite in a state of security; nay we know that some of them have fallen" (L, 3:200). Concerning eternal bliss, we are told: "The happiness of Heaven will be, that pleasure and virtue will be perfectly consistent" (L, 3:292). As for happiness on earth, Rousseau makes it clear that he cannot partake of it in a city: "Les villes sont le gouffre de l'espéce humaine" (4:277). Only nature offers peace and salvation, and one is hard pressed to make a choice among the many lovely passages illustrating Jean-Jacques's genius for melting his self into a landscape that shimmers like a fata morgana: "Quand l'ardent desir de cette vie heureuse et douce qui me fuit et pour laquelle j'étois né vient enflammer mon imagination, c'est toujours au pays de Vaud, près du lac, dans des campagnes charmantes qu'elle se fixe. Il me faut absolument un verger au bord de ce lac, et non pas d'un autre; il me faut un ami sur, une femme aimable, une vache et un petit bateau" (1:152). Johnson, on the other hand, does not make the smallest effort to assimilate the rhythms of nature or to recapture, upon seeing a periwinkle, long-lost memories; he does write poems in the countryside, but they will be Horatian odes on Sky or odes addressed to the "Thralia dulcis" (see T, 251). Clouds, rain, sunshine do not affect him in any way. "I mentioned," relates Boswell, "a friend of mine who had resided long in Spain, and was unwilling to return to Britain. JOHNSON. 'Sir, he is attached to some woman.' BOSWELL. 'I rather believe, Sir, it is the fine climate which keeps him there.' JOHNSON. 'Nay, Sir, how can you talk so? What is *climate* to happiness?' " (L, 2:195). And, elsewhere, upbraiding his Scottish shadow who is grumbling about very wet days: "Sir, this is all imagination, which physicians encourage" (L, 1:452). Johnson does concede that "some very delicate frames, indeed may be affected by wet weather" (ibid.). Among these, we must surely include Rousseau who—according to Bernardin de Saint-Pierre, his French shadow, whom he eventually succeeds in losing—loves the sun as much as he fears rain: "quand il pleuvait il ne sortait point. Je suis, me dit-il, en souriant, tout le contraire du petit bonhomme du baromètre suisse; quand il rentre je sors, et quand il sort je rentre."[50]

Johnson's theory on the pastoral reveals his lack of sympathy with nature. Like Fontenelle and *le père* Rapin, he pontificates on the most delicate of all literary genres, whereas Rousseau revives the genre simply and genially by living the dream of the Golden Age. I refer, of course, to his *Idylle des cerises* in which Jean-Jacques knows the joy of love "sans mistére et sans honte" (1:138). Johnson cannot and will not have part of it. "No wise man," he informs Boswell, "will go to live in the country, unless he has something to do which can be better done in the country" (L, 3:253). Nothing equals Fleet Street. His comments on urban life beg to be quoted:

"The happiness of London is not to be conceived but by those who have been in it. I will venture to say, there is more learning and science within the circumference of ten miles from where we now sit, than in all the rest of the kingdom" (L, 2:75). And in a more lyrical vein: "Three days I was upon the road, and on the fourth morning my heart danced at the sight of London" (R, 15). Furthermore, a gentleman is safer in town: "He observed that a man in London was in less danger of falling in love indiscreetly, than any where else; for there the difficulty of deciding between the conflicting pretensions of a vast variety of objects, kept him safe" (L, 2:120). Yet, despite his love of London, Johnson never conceives nor even intuits the possibility of transmuting urban experience into poetic myths. For Imlac, the pyramids stand "only" in compliance with that hunger of the imagination which preys incessantly upon life, and must always be appeased by some employment (Ras, p. 145)—the imagination which, for Rousseau, is already what it will be for Baudelaire, *la reine des facultés.*

"Hear me, illustrious philosopher!" Boswell apostrophizes the hermit of Môtiers, before requesting from him extramarital counseling concerning Moma his mistress, la Signora Piccolomini, wife of the *Capitano di Popolo* of Sienna. But is she really married? Is it her duty to sacrifice her finest inclinations:

> I could not answer her arguments, but in my moments of
> virtue and piety I warmly repeated to her the common
> sentiments against adultery. She was very fond of your works, I
> read to her with a grave and serious air the beautiful and
> affecting words of Julie on that terrible vice. I was so moved
> by them that she could not but feel something. But an onrush
> of passion overcame me. I embraced her with a kind of frenzy
> and repeated our criminal ecstasies. She said, *"Voi siete
> precisamente quel Rousseau. Tale quale. Parlate moltissimo della
> virtù, e pero fate il male"* [You are exactly like Rousseau. Just like
> him. You talk a lot about virtue, but what you do is wrong].[51]

Moma—much too good for Boswell—hit the mark. Indubitably, the passage in question may be found in the eighteenth letter of the third part of *La Nouvelle Héloïse,* where Julie describes her marriage to Monsieur de Wolmar: "Je crus voir l'organe de la providence et entendre la voix de Dieu dans le ministre prononçant la sainte liturgie" (2:354)—a letter as unctuous as it is serene. Did Samuel Johnson have the patience to plow through a novel that Immanuel Kant had to read for a second time, so much had he been overcome by its moral beauty during the first reading—a novel which eventually led him to generate the concept of the categorical imperative? It is doubtful, the more so since Johnson jokingly admits to reading only the beginning and the end of books. Yet Rousseau would have subscribed to Johnson's views expressed in his letter to Baretti: "There is, indeed, nothing that so much seduces reason from vigilance, as the thought of passing life with an amiable woman; and if all would happen that a lover fancies, I know not what other terrestrial happiness would deserve pursuit. But love and marriage are different states. Those who are to suffer the evils together, and to suffer often for the sake of another, soon lose that tenderness of look, and that benevolence of mind, which arose from the participation of unmingled pleasure and successive amusement" (L, 1:381). How much more expressive than Johnson's qualms about wedlock is Saint-Preux's tense and poignant exclamation to Julie on being threatened by Claire, "une petite veuve assés piquante" (2:408): "je l'aime trop pour l'épouser" (2:679).

In any case, Johnson's pronouncements on marriage are often influenced by his life with Tetty, so cruelly mimicked by Garrick, whereas Rousseau's disquisitions on the conjugal state are always theoretical, inasmuch as his betrothal to Thérèse takes place very late in his life. Johnson's views on marriage (see *Rambler* nos. 18, 39, 113, 167) run the gamut from gloom to laughter. Unlike Rousseau, Johnson maintains the double standard: "between a man and his wife, a husband's infidelity is nothing . . . the man imposes no bastards upon his wife" (L, 3:406). And elsewhere: "We hang a thief for stealing a sheep; but the unchastity of woman transfers sheep, and farm and all, from the right owner. I have much more respect for a common prostitute than for a woman who conceals her guilt" (L, 3:406). Johnson, however, disagrees with Rousseau's censure of the adulterous ways of aristocratic women with a conviction unmatched in history:

As he was a zealous friend of subordination, he was at all times
watchful to repress the vulgar cant against the manners of the
great; "High people, Sir, (said he,) are the best; take a hundred
ladies of quality, you'll find them better wives, better mothers,
more willing to sacrifice their own pleasure to their children
than a hundred other women. . . . Yes, Sir, the licentiousness
of one woman of quality makes more noise than that of a
number of women in lower stations; then, Sir, you are to
consider the malignity of women in the city against women of
quality, which will make them believe any thing of them, such
as that they call their coachmen to bed. No, Sir, so far as I
have observed, the higher in rank, the richer ladies are, they
are the better instructed and the more virtuous." (L, 3:353)

Despite such divergence in views, Johnson's ideal of a good
marriage is not very far removed from Rousseau's concept of a *liaison
sereine,* such as his friendship with Maman—a liaison which
admittedly, and technically speaking, was not a marriage but
rather a ménage à trois, in fact, the first in European literature:
"Tous nos voeux, nos soins, nos coeurs étoient en commun"
(1:201). Given the Christian-Judaic tradition, it is not surprising
that Johnson downplays the erotic component of a good marriage,
just as Rousseau stresses the affectionate mood of his happiest hours
with Maman: "Je devenois tout à fait son oeuvre, tout à fait son
enfant et plus que si elle eut été ma vraye mére. Nous commen-
çames, sans y songer, à ne plus nous séparer l'un de l'autre, à mettre en quelque sorte toute notre existence en commun" (1:222).
Rousseau swears to have been happy with Maman, and many have
believed him. Johnson, on the contrary, admitting to quarreling
with Tetty, delivers himself on wives in unforgettable terms. With
tongue in cheek, Mrs. Piozzi tells that she heard him once say of a
lady more insipid than offensive: "She has some softness indeed,
but so has a pillow" (A, 118). And when one observed in reply that
her husband's fidelity and attachment were exemplary, notwithstanding this low account at which her perfections were rated,
"Why Sir (cries the Doctor), being married to those sleepy-souled
women, is just like playing at cards for nothing: no passion is
excited, and the time is filled up. I do not however envy a fellow of

one of those honey-suckle wives for my part, as they are but *creepers* at best, and commonly destroy the tree they so tenderly cling about" (A, 118). Conjugal wit of this sort is wanting in Rousseau with the possible exception of a reference to Mme Sabran, in whose company he, still very innocent, journeys to Turin, the lady being "une assez bonne femme, plus tranquille le jour que la nuit" (1:57).

Just as our sages insist upon the sanctity of marriage, they stress that in the state of nature relationships between the sexes are governed uniquely by chance and desire: "les mâles, et les femelles s'unissoient fortuitement selon la rencontre . . . ils se quittoient avec la même facilité" (3:147). And elsewhere: "Quoi donc! avant ce temps les hommes naissaient-ils de la terre? . . . Non: il y avait des familles . . . il y avait des mariages, mais il n'y avoit point d'amour. Chaque famille se suffisait à elle-même et se perpétuait par son seul sang: les enfans, nés des mêmes parens, croissaient ensemble . . . on devenait mari et femme sans avoir cessé d'être frère et soeur" (*Essai*, 525). An accompanying footnote deals with the question of incest; at the beginning, explains Rousseau, siblings married: "Il fallait bien que les premiers hommes épousassent leurs soeurs" (ibid.). However, with the advent of communal life, "la sainte loi" begins to take effect. Johnson's views are quite similar: "Besides, Sir, a savage man and a savage woman meet by chance; and when the man sees another woman that pleases him better, he will leave the first" (L, 2:165). Leave a civilized couple alone, explains Johnson, and nature will take its course: "if you shut up any man with any woman, so as to make them derive their whole pleasure from each other, they would inevitably fall in love, as it is called, with each other" (T, 106). And Mrs. Piozzi adds with much discernment: "In these opinions, Rousseau apparently concurs with him exactly" (T, 108). Johnson, however, deemphasizes the influence of climate and location upon human behavior, whereas Rousseau, a disciple of Montesquieu, proclaims the mildewed commonplace that denizens of the tropics are voluptuaries: "pourvu qu'un Asiatique ait des femmes et du repos, il est content" (*Essai*, 527). Given his Venetian adventure, we may also assume that Jean-Jacques would have approved heartily of Johnson's censure of licensed stews at Rome. And, while on the subject, Boswell continues to prod his man: " 'So then, Sir, you would allow of no irregular intercourse whatever between the sexes?' JOHNSON. 'To be sure, I would not, Sir' " (L, 3:17). And, as if possessed of prophetic power, Boswell then proposes to Johnson a typically preromantic idyll of an English officer meditating "in the wilds of America . . . free and unrestrained, amidst the rude magnificence of Nature, with this Indian woman by [his] side, and this gun with which [he] can procure food when [he] wants it . . . what more can be desired for human happiness?" The answer comes swiftly: "Do not allow yourself, Sir, to be imposed upon by such gross absurdity. It is sad stuff; it is brutish. If a bull could speak, he might as well exclaim,—Here I am with this cow and this grass; what being can enjoy greater felicity" (L, 2:228).

Johnson takes women seriously and respects them for whatever they might achieve intellectually and otherwise: "Of [Mrs. Fitzherbert] Dr. Johnson said . . . that she had the best understanding he had ever met in any human being" (L, 1:83). Miss MacLean's virtues receive even higher praise: "She is the most accomplished lady that I have found in the Highlands. She knows French, musick, and drawing, sews neatly, makes shell-work and can milk cows; in short she can do everything. She talks sensibly, and is the first person who can translate Erse poetry literally" (L, 5:317).[52] At times, his contempt for simple Eves gets the best of him: "She is a very fine woman. But how can you show civilities to a non-entity? I did not think he [her husband] had been married" (L, 2:148). In all fairness, one should add that he also mocks simple Adams. Rousseau is not given to such bantering, not only because his Thérèse is the nonentity par manque d'excellence but also because his feelings about women are hopelessly ambivalent. Saint-Preux's celebrated apostrophe furnishes the perfect antithesis to Johnson's quips: "Femmes! femmes! objets chers et funestes, que la nature orna pour notre supplice, qui punissez quand on vous brave, qui poursuivez quand on vous craint, dont la haine et l'amour sont également nuisibles, et qu'on ne peut ni rechercher ni fuir impunément" (2:676). Yet, in truth, Johnson reveres and perhaps fears the strength of women even more than Rousseau: "Nature has given women so much power that the law has very wisely given them little,"[53] or elsewhere: "Women have a perpetual envy of our vices; they are less vicious than we—not from choice, but because we restrict them."[54] Mrs. Piozzi amplifies: "And yet says Johnson, Woman has *such* power between the Ages of twenty-five and forty-five, that She may tye a Man to a post and whip him if She will" (T, 386). Rousseau shares Johnson's viewpoint: Mme de Warens's domain is a matriarchy and, to some extent, so is Julie's reign over her estate on the shore of Lac Léman; furthermore, Maman's sexual powers surpass his, just as Julie's "baisers âcres et pénetrans" (2:65) overwhelm her lover who confesses: "tu sais mieux aimer que moi" (2:149). When it comes to women who proclaim the gospel, our authors part company. Commenting on a lady Quaker, Johnson exclaims: "Sir, a woman's preaching is like a dog's walking on his hinder legs. It is not done well; but you are surprized to find it done at all" (L, 1:463). I quote this quasi-proverbial remark only to be able to contrast its author with Rousseau, who transforms his Julie, *la tendre amante,* into a *prêcheuse,* beautiful but overflowing with saintly harangues to her docile Saint-Preux and well on the way to becoming *eine schöne Seele:* "Adorez l'Etre éternel, mon digne et sage ami" (2:358).

There exist still other sentimental affinities between our two authors. Both Johnson and Rousseau (the former, the Hercules of Toryism [L, 1:39]; the latter, "the Hercules of Thought"[55]) meet their Queen Omphale in the person of Mrs. Thrale and in the amalgamated characters of Mlles Lambercier (administratrix of the celebrated *fessée*) and Goton, and Mmes Basile, de Warens, and d'Houdetot. Jean-Jacques's analysis remains unsurpassed: "J'ai ainsi passé ma vie à convoiter et me taire auprès des personnes que j'aimois le plus. N'osant jamais déclarer mon gout [*i.e.,* masochism], je l'amusois du moins par des rapports qui m'en conservoient l'idée. Etre aux genoux d'une maîtresse impérieuse, obéir à ses ordres, avoir des pardons à lui demander, étoient pour moi de très douces jouissances, et plus ma vive imagination m'enflammoit le sang, plus j'avois l'air d'un amant transi" (1:17). Meditating on these lines, Johnsonians will think of Johnson's letter to Mrs. Thrale, so well explicated by Bate. "Accordez-moi," reads this let-

ter, "par un petit écrit, la connoissance de ce qui m'est inter-
dit . . . Je souhaite, ma patronne, que vôtre autorité me soit toûjours sensible, et que vous me teniez dans l'esclavage que vous
scavez si bien rendre heureux."[56] The resemblance between these
texts is remarkable; but whereas Rousseau's statement results from
self-analysis, Johnson's letter seems to circumvent the psychological implications of his relationship with his *patronne,* which is not
to imply that he does not understand what ails his soul.

If we compare our authors' views on *les péripatéticiennes de l'amour*
(the expression stems from Thomas de Quincey) we find them at
odds with each other. "Des femmes à prix d'argent" confesses Jean-
Jacques, "perdroient pour moi tous leurs charmes, je doute même
s'il seroit en moi d'en profiter" (1:36). And when he finds the
strength to rise to the occasion, it is in the company of the "bon
Klupffell," chaplain of the Prince of Saxe-Gotha; ashamed and
crestfallen, he leaves Klupffell's kept girl: "Je sortis de la rue des
Moineaux, où logeoit cette fille, aussi honteux que Saint-Preux
sortit de la maison où on l'avoit enivré, et je me rappelai bien mon
histoire en écrivant la sienne. Thérèse s'aperçut à quelque signe, et
surtout à mon air confus, que j'avois quelque reproche à me faire; j'en
allegeai le poids par ma franche et prompte confession" (1:355).
Admonishing her wayward lover, Julie, already married, explains
that all signs of corruption must be avoided: "Ignorez-vous qu'il y a
des objets si odieux qu'il n'est pas même permis à l'homme d'honneur de les voir" (2:301). As for Johnson, there is no incriminating
evidence, save Boswell's sanctimonious insinuations, that he had
carnal relations with prostitutes. But, whereas Rousseau has only
contempt for *les femmes de plaisir* and looks for hidden flaws in order to
justify the contradiction between their beauty and immorality—the
reader will recall his adventure with Zulietta—Johnson performs
acts of charity on behalf of streetwalkers. All his devotees know of
Polly Carmichael, whom he finds lying exhausted in the street and
carries to his home. There, in Boswell's words, Polly becomes an
inmate of his "seraglio" as well as a source of endless complications,
since, according to her host, Polly is "wiggle-waggle" and unwilling
to be "categorical" (T, 184). Perhaps the most intriguing of these
nocturnal encounters takes place with Boswell present: "As we

walked along the Strand to-night, arm in arm, a woman of the town accosted us, in the usual enticing manner. 'No, no, my girl, (said Johnson) it won't do'" (L, 1:457). Rousseau and Johnson agree, however, on the supreme importance of imagination, at least in matters erotic:

> Our conversation to-day, I know not how, turned, (I think for the only time at any length, during our long acquaintance,) upon the sensual intercourse between the sexes, the delight of which he ascribed chiefly to imagination. "Were it not for imagination, Sir, (said he,) a man would be as happy in the arms of a chambermaid as of a Duchess. But such is the adventitious charm of fancy that we find men who have violated the best principles of society, and ruined their fame and their fortune, that they might possess a woman of rank."
> (L, 3:341)

It is doubtful whether this assessment stems from an adventure in Johnson's life. Jean-Jacques, however, covets ladies: "Il me falloit des Demoiselles. Chacun a ses fantaisies" (1:134). Hence he spurns la Merceret, Maman's *femme de chambre,* just as his spiritual son Julien Sorel ignores Elisa's love for the triumph of grasping Mme de Rênal's hand. And as one rereads the great love passages in *La Nouvelle Héloïse,* Johnson's censures sound at times almost as pathetic as they were incomprehensible to Boswell: "[His] violence seemed very strange to me, who had read many of Rousseau's animated writings with great pleasure, and even edification; had been much pleased with his society" (L, 2:12). It should be kept in mind, however, that, disregarding Johnson's deafness to Rousseau's preromantic melodies, his very principles deny one of Rousseau's basic, almost genetic assumptions: that men and women are predestined for each other. "J'étois né pour l'aimer" (1:151), sighs Jean-Jacques, remembering his Maman, and Saint-Preux repeats this fatal belief in elective affinities: "ô toi pour qui j'étois né" (2:547). Johnson, characteristically an eighteenth-century man and, unbeknown to him, in the ranks of such disparate personages as Crébillon-fils, Diderot, de Ponte, and Casanova—the latter met Johnson in London in 1763 and discussed etymology with him—asserts a principle loathsome to Rousseau: "BOSWELL. 'Pray, Sir, do you not suppose that there are fifty women in the world with any one of whom a man may be as happy as with any one woman in particular?' JOHNSON. 'Aye, fifty thousand.' BOSWELL. 'Then, Sir, you are not of the opinion with some who imagine that certain men and certain women are made for each other; and that they cannot be happy if they miss their counterparts?' JOHNSON. 'To be sure not, Sir' " (L, 2:461). That Johnson has in mind married couples is inconsequential; his attitude negates the very basis of *La Nouvelle Héloïse* and, with it, the better part of nineteenth-century novels from *La Chartreuse de Parme* to *Le Lys dans la Vallée* and *Anna Karenina*.

"Des amours de voyage ne sont pas faits pour durer" (1:254), muses Jean-Jacques, while reviewing his liaison with Madame de Larnage. Travelling in a post-chaise to Montpellier, he soon gives in to her charms: "Quand je vivrois cent ans je ne me rappellerois jamais sans plaisir le souvenir de cette charmante femme. . . . Elle avoit ses raisons pour être facile: c'étoit le moyen de valoir tout son prix. On pouvoit la voir sans l'aimer, mais non pas la posséder sans l'adorer" (1:252). Johnson shares Rousseau's pleasure in travelling in mixed company without, however, suffering defeat and conquest by lady travellers. Verging on seventy, he confesses to an inordinate fondness for carriages: "If (said he) I had no duties, and no reference to futurity, I would spend my life driving briskly in a post-chaise with a pretty woman" (L, 3:162). Rather than be a victim, he assumes the role of tormentor. Replying to Mrs. Piozzi's question as to "why he doated on a coach so," he informs her "that in the first place, the company was shut in with him *there;* and could not escape, as out of a room" (A, 151). Jean-Jacques, generally speaking, suffocates in crowds; he is the *promeneur solitaire né,* a wanderer on his way to his dream, in a landscape foreshadowing watercolors of Alpine scenes by English artists of the early nineteenth century, as well as blue valleys by Corot and sunlit meadows by Renoir: "Dès lors je ne vis plus d'autre plaisir, d'autre sort, d'autre bonheur que celui de faire un pareil voyage . . . au bout duquel, pour surcroît, j'entrevoyois Made de Warens, mais dans un éloignement immense; car pour retourner à Genève, c'est à quoi je ne pensois jamais. Les monts, les prés, les bois, les ruisseaux, les villages se succedoient sans fin et sans cesse avec de nouveaux charmes; ce bienheureux trajet sembloit devoir absorber ma vie entiére" (1:99).[57]

Johnson, too, has left records of his travels, the best known being his *Journey to the Western Islands of Scotland*. Also important are fragmentary remarks about trips to Wales and France. I prefer them to his socio-anthropological study of the Western Islands, because these jottings are spontaneous and their incompleteness tempts the imagination:

> We heard lawyers plead.—N. As many killed at Paris as there are days in the year. *Chambre de question.*—Tournelle at the Palais Marchand.—An old venerable building.
>
> The Palais Bourbon, belonging to the Prince of Condé. Only one small wing shown;—lofty;—splendid;—gold and glass.—The battles of the great Condé are painted in one of the rooms. The present Prince a grandsire at thirty-nine.
>
> The sight of palaces, and other great buildings, leaves no very distinct images, unless to those who talk of them. As I entered, my wife was in my mind: she would have been pleased. Having now nobody to please, I am little pleased. (L, 2:393)

Such candor is touching. It testifies to feeling and suggests a *fraîcheur* prized, above all, by Jean-Jacques who would like to recapture the nonmediated experience of walking: "La chose que je regrette le plus dans les détails de ma vie dont j'ai perdu la mémoire est de n'avoir pas fait des journaux de mes voyages. Jamais je n'ai tant pensé, tant existé, tant vécu, tant été moi, si j'ose ainsi dire, que dans ceux que j'ai faits seul et à pied. La marche a quelque chose qui anime et avive mes idées" (1:162). Neither man undertakes voyages to far-off sites, and it is instructive to compare their conception of whither such voyages might lead:

> A journey to Italy was still in his thoughts. He said, "A man who has not been in Italy, is always conscious of an inferiority, from his not having seen what it is expected a man should see. The grand object of travelling is to see the shores of the Mediterranean. On those shores were the four great empires of the world; the Assyrian, the Persian, the Grecian, and the Roman. All our religion, almost all our law, almost all our

arts, almost all that sets us above savages, has come to us from the shores of the Mediterranean." (L, 3:36)

Furthermore, we read that Johnson was thinking of going "to Cairo, and down the Red Sea to Bengal, and take a ramble in India."[58] The halting-places of his itinerary are exotic and presage outlandish expeditions by Kipling's heroes. Rousseau, much more visionary, seems more of a homebody but sends his fictional self around the world. After his return from "les extrémités de la terre," said self describes his *tour du monde* to Mme d'Orbe (unintentional pun): "J'ai vû d'abord l'Amérique méridionale . . . j'ai vû les côtes du Brésil . . . j'ai vû de loin le séjour de ces prétendus géants . . . j'ai vû dans le vaste Océan . . . deux grand vaisseaux se chercher, se trouver . . . j'ai vû l'image de l'enfer" (2:412–14).

As for their appreciation of music and painting, the contrast between our two authors could not be greater. Rousseau rarely mentions painting, though he was an accomplished musicologist and composer. He confides to Bernardin de Saint-Pierre that his little opera and the third volume of the *Emile* constitute his best work: "Mes ennemis ont beau dire, ils ne ferons jamais un *Devin du Village*."[59] Johnson, on the other hand, makes no bones about his dislike of easels and fiddles. Given the inimitable style of his pronouncements, one is led to hope that he does not really mean what he says. But Mrs. Piozzi is quite clear about the matter: "He delighted no more in music than painting; he was almost as deaf as he was blind: travelling with Dr. Johnson was for these reasons tiresome enough" (A, 92). And when urged by Mr. Thrale to admire a landscape, his answer is categorical: "Never heed such nonsense. . . . [A] blade of grass is always a blade of grass, whether in one country or another: let us if we *do* talk, talk about something; men and women are my subject of inquiry; let us see how these differ from those we have left behind" (A, 93).[60]

Indeed, men and women—rather than his own self—are Johnson's subjects of inquiry, whereas Rousseau makes his *moi* the alpha and omega of his quest. Some qualifications, however, are in order. Johnson of course excels in the art of biography, but Boswell stresses also that Johnson's potential as an autobiographer stands unsurpassed—a puzzling assertion, since Rousseau's *Confessions* first appeared from 1782 to 1789. "Had Dr. Johnson written his own life, in conformity with the opinion which he has given, that every man's life may be best written by himself; had he employed in the preservation of his own history, that clearness of narration and elegance of language in which he has embalmed so many eminent persons, the world would have had the most perfect example of biography that was ever exhibited" (L, 1:25). For Johnson a journal fulfills an exclusively private need, and he recommends to Boswell "to keep a journal of [his] life, full and unreserved" (L, 1:433). It must be kept private and burned in case of death, whereas Jean-Jacques's testimony is a gift to posterity. Johnson's criteria of veracity are of the strictest kind, the general rule being "that Truth should never be violated, because it is of the utmost importance to the comfort of life, that we should have a full security by mutual faith" (L, 4:305). The biographer should also furnish us with an honest picture of human nature, concerning which Johnson has written extensively and brilliantly. Rousseau's views on *l'homme de l'homme* and *l'homme de la nature* are equally sophisticated. But, whereas Johnson rarely if ever refers to himself in the development of theories in his essays and biographies, Rousseau frequently abandons the traditional expository manner in favor of analyses based on his *moi* (analyses in which the reader must play an active part), as well as on analyses derived from a fictional construct (*La Nouvelle Héloïse*). In this respect, *Les Confessions, Les Rêveries,* and *Les Dialogues* are of special interest, since these efforts are permeated by his desire to match what has been with what might have been. His purpose is to create, by dint of his autobiographical passion and the quasi-psychoanalytical collaboration of his readers, a true image of himself. Johnson "embalms" his subjects in a kind of literary fluid; Rousseau, no mortician he, to whom spontaneity is everything, grants primacy to life over literature. Following his "chaîne des sentimens" (1:77), his thread of Ariadne, he wishes to lead himself out of a labyrinth of guilt towards an issue luminous with innocence and devoid of shadows. In the words of Marcel Raymond: "C'est qu'il lui est impossible d'accepter, d'assumer sa part d'ombre. S'il paraît en faute, il y a erreur sur la personne" (1:xliv).

Innocent or not, Rousseau creates a style so pure that it renders the very flow of emotions, and his finest pages are comparable in their transparency to a Schubert sonata: "C'est l'histoire de mon ame que j'ai promise" (1:278). If we are to find a thematic equivalent of such a history in Johnson's writings, we have to turn to his prayers, so expressive of spiritual concerns but only partially reflective of the ridiculous and shameful truths of his life, of any life— the *tacenda*, which Rousseau reveals with so much courage. But, are Johnson's prayers characteristic of Johnson, the writer we admire? Can we distinguish them easily from sermons and prayers by various divines of his age? I think not. The Johnson who, according to Boswell, *"offers more bark and steel for the mind"* (L, 1:215) than any other writer, is more modest about his contribution in the conclusion of the *Rambler* than is his biographer: "Whatever shall be the final sentence of mankind, I have at least endeavoured to deserve their kindness. I have laboured to refine our language to grammatical purity, and to clear it from colloquial barbarisms, licentious idioms, and irregular combinations. Something, perhaps, I have added to the elegance of its construction, and something to the harmony of its cadence. When common words were less pleasing to the ear, or less distinct in their signification, I have familiarized the terms of philosophy, by applying them to popular ideas" (R, 3:318–19). Most critics will consider this statement a fair but much too modest evaluation by the man who said, more or less in jest, that "want of money was the 'only motive to writing' that he knew of" (H, 363). His real purpose, adds Johnson, is "to inculcate wisdom or piety," as well as to devote some papers to "the idle sports of imagination" and "to disquisitions of criticism" (R, 5:319).

Johnson, needless to emphasize, excels in prose but rarely rises to the levels of intense power reached by Pascal—an author he admired—who, like Rousseau, also deserves the appellation of poet, if poetry be emotion "compressed" in tranquillity.[61] For Jean-Jacques, however, the key word is "recollected," and it is regrettable that Wordsworth is silent as to what he owes or does not owe to Rousseau.[62] As for Johnson, had he read *La Nouvelle Héloïse* with care, he would surely have reached the conclusion that his definition of "easy poetry" bears some kinship to Saint-Preux's most limpid regrets, in which "natural thoughts are expressed without violence to language" (I, 239). Unfortunately, his comments are limited to "couplets graced only by naked elegance" (I, 242). But, even if Johnson had read *La Nouvelle Héloïse,* he could not have heard or *understood* (in French, hearing and understanding often amount to the same thing) that it was Rousseau who initiated the modern cosmopolitan tradition in France, a recognition which Joseph Texte made the point of departure for his thesis:

> Il est vrai que les romantiques ont déchaîné, si je puis dire, le cosmopolitisme en France, mais le maître de tous les romantiques—et celui de Mme de Staël,—celui dont ils n'ont fait que formuler les aspirations et développer l'influence, c'est Rousseau. C'est bien lui qui a ébranlé, au profit de l'Europe germanique, la vieille hégémonie littéraire de l'Europe latine. C'est lui qui a uni en lui-même, comme le dit Mme de Staël, "le génie du Nord à celui du Midi." C'est du jour où il a écrit, et parce qu'il avait écrit, que les littératures du Nord se sont ouvertes et imposées à l'esprit français. Jean-Jacques, disait encore Mme de Staël, quoiqu'il ait écrit dans notre langue, appartient à "l'école germanique": il a infusé à notre génie national "une sève étrangère."[63]

I should like to amplify Mme de Staël's argument by claiming not only as she does that Jean-Jacques writes in French while belonging to "l'école germanique" (which would explain his tremendous success in Germany) but also that he "sings" in Italian, a language which he loved and whose music he transposes on the French keyboard.[64] Indeed, Samuel Johnson was not meant to appreciate Rousseau, despite the fact that he wrote French passably well, read Italian, and enjoyed a lexicographer's awareness of Germanic roots. Should one conclude that he was too English?

"Madam," said he, "the best part of an author will always be found in his writing" (H, 410). Does this declaration hold true for him who uttered it? Chauncey B. Tinker denies it: "He [Byron], like Johnson, has survived not so much because of a purely literary achievement as by virtue of a remarkable temper of mind, an ardor, an attitude toward life, a force and a fire. What is the secret of his influence?" Tinker's answer, to be sure, is Boswell's *Life.* "The

greatness of Boswell's record," writes Tinker, "is simply Samuel
Johnson, who is not merely the subject, but in the last analysis the
author too. . . . Genius begot genius. The greatest contribution of
Samuel Johnson to English literature was James Boswell."[65] Admittedly, Tinker's viewpoint is no longer fashionable among Johnsonians and Boswellians. Richard Schwartz's conclusion to *Boswell's
Johnson* is a fair summary of contemporary answers to the questions
raised by Donald Greene that are quoted in the first paragraph of
this essay:

> In reading the *Life* we must continually "correct for" Boswell if
> we are to be fair to Johnson, and the result is that we are
> unfair to Boswell's art. The alternative is not appealing: the
> surrendering to Boswell's art with the subsequent falsification
> of Johnson. The best corrective, it seems to me, is to approach
> Boswell from a different direction, to come to the *Life* from the
> *Journal* and private papers, to see the *Life* as essentially a book
> about Boswell, a portion of autobiography. [66]

But, rather than taking sides in the argument about the symbiotic relationship between Johnson and Boswell, I should prefer to
suggest two new lines of inquiry. In the introduction, I have alluded to the first: that Rousseau's narrative style in the *Confessions*
recalls at times the style of Plutarch, who was, in Boswell's words,
the Prince of Biographers; furthermore, that the kinship I perceive
between Rousseau and Boswell may be defined as a similar, enchanting way of telling a marvelous life.[67] The second line of inquiry concerns the possible influence of Rousseau's *Confessions* on
Boswell's masterpiece which appeared in 1794.[68] The first paragraph of the *Confessions* highlights originality of purpose and
uniqueness in execution: "Je forme une entreprise qui n'eut jamais
d'éxemple, et dont l'exécution n'aura point d'imitateur. Je veux
montrer à mes semblables un homme dans toute la vérité de la
nature; et cet homme, ce sera moi." And adds Rousseau: "J'ai dit le
bien et le mal avec la même franchise" (1:5). Does this famous
beginning not call to mind Boswell's proud claim: "I will venture
to say that . . . he will be seen as he really was; for I profess to
write, not his panegyrick, which must be all praise, but his Life;
which, great and good as he was, must not be supposed to be

entirely perfect" (L, 1:30). Like Rousseau, Boswell promises to show a man "as he really was." Unlike Jean-Jacques, who swears to reveal with the same degree of frankness what is good, bad, and ridiculous in his life, Boswell immediately proceeds to hedge his bet by grudgingly admitting that his great and good man was not "entirely perfect." Such a qualification should not be interpreted as a legal or moralistic nicety but as a prudent, if not weary, acknowledgment of what Boswell had to expect—a storm of protest which indeed broke loose when his book appeared. Rousseau, however, having arranged for posthumous publication of his most personal truths, could well afford to be candid about his sins before being buried on the *Ile des Peupliers* at Ermenonville, whence his mortal remains were eventually transferred to the Pantheon in 1794, the year in which Boswell's *Life* saw the day.[69]

Furthermore, similar intentions often engender similar techniques. "I cannot allow any fragment whatever," declares Boswell, "that floats in my memory concerning the great subject of this work to be lost. Though a small particular may appear trifling to some, it will be relished by others . . . I bid defiance to the shafts of ridicule, or even malignity."[70] Does Boswell's need to recover trifling fragments not remind one of Rousseau's obsession to evoke "les moindres faits" of his life in the home of M. Lambercier: "Je sais bien que le lecteur n'a pas grand besoin de savoir tout cela; mais, j'ai besoin, moi, de le lui dire. Que n'osé-je lui raconter de même toutes les petites anecdotes de cet heureux âge" (1:21)? Rousseau continues: "je me rappelle toutes les circonstances des lieux, des personnes, des heures. Je vois la servante ou le valet agissant dans la chambre, une hirondelle entrant par la fenêtre, une mouche se poser sur ma main" (1:21). Is such a tableau not as Flemish as any one of Boswell's intimate scenes? And if these *rapprochements* are only coincidental, if Boswell's biographical portrait of Johnson does not show or betray any conceptual or thematic influences by Rousseau (even though my suspicions are difficult to smother, because Boswell's memory functioned perfectly with almost every acquaintance he sought and every book he read), if James Boswell did not read *Les Confessions* (quite unlikely), then one may still ask whether Rousseau's *mécanique de la vraisemblance*[71] does not bear comparison to Boswell's artful procedure in varying the aesthetic distance between himself and his subject.[72] Pursuing such an inquiry, one could also ask whether Boswell is the equal of Jean-Jacques—not in order to demean the irrepressible and hypochondriac Scot but to shed light on a crucial difference between Rousseau's *Confessions* and Johnson's "autobiography" (that is, Boswell's *Life,* if one assumes Chauncey Tinker's viewpoint). That difference involves honesty beyond the boundaries of good taste, characteristic of *Mon Coeur mis à nu.* Like the *Confessions,* Boswell's *Journals* (supposedly never meant to be published) fulfill to some extent what Baudelaire's words imply; but Boswell is no Rousseau and certainly no Johnson who, if we are to agree with Tinker, left the business of recording his life to someone else.[73] Johnson was fully aware that his surrogate ego would proceed in a manner respectful of his aphoristic genius: "I fancy mankind may come, in time, to write all aphoristically, except in narrative; grow weary of preparation, and connection, and illustration, and all those arts by which a big book is made. If a man is to wait till he weaves anecdotes into a system, we may be long in getting them and get but few, in comparison of what we might" (L, 5:39). Boswell's *Life of Johnson* is indeed "a big book" of aphorisms and anecdotes—almost a hologram of a man, seemingly real, like an apparition at a séance, where life and death achieve a precarious and perfidious equipoise.[74]

"Mort à jamais?" asks Proust after Bergotte's death.[75] Insofar as reading Johnson's works and Boswell's *Life,* as well as other chronicles by Mrs. Piozzi, Hawkins, and Fanny Burney, makes it possible for us to visualize Samuel Johnson, the greatest show in London—to hear him talk, to breathe his *aether,* to imagine his powerful and at times overbearing character, to be dazzled by his wit and intelligence as well as touched by his kindness and compassion, to recognize his loneliness for what it was and is, that of all men—our thoughts about him are those we might have about a man still with us. Johnson's presence will not fade, so it seems, nor will the serene moments of *La Cinquième Promenade* set to music by

Jean-Jacques's heart, beating to the rhythm of waves, as he drifts slowly in a boat near the Isle of Saint-Pierre. *Sont-ils morts à jamais?* Do their thoughts and feelings only whisper in us? Are the lives of Rousseau and Johnson so fully spent that we must acquiesce in the ruthless aside by Diderot's *neveu* that being alive is the only thing that matters?

2 *Candide* and *Rasselas* Revisited

Paris is, indeed, a place very different from the
Hebrides.
—Johnson to Boswell

L'auteur ne sait pas un mot d'arabe, et cependant la
scène est en Arabie.
—*Candide*

"I have heard Johnson say," reports Boswell, "that if they
[*Candide* and *Rasselas*] had not been published so closely one after
the other that there was not time for imitation, it would have been
in vain to deny that the scheme of that which came latest was taken
from the other" (L, 1:342). Much has been written about the resemblance and difference between the Westphalian orphan, very
much at home in France, and his Ethiopian counterpart, the prince
so fluent in English. Unfortunately, however, most of these comparisons stem from Johnsonians whose appreciation of Voltaire's
wit and music seems sadly lacking.[1] Whereas such specialists in-
variably refer to *Candide*, few if any Voltairians have devoted their
attention to *Rasselas*. Thus, André-Michel Rousseau, commenting
on the influence of Voltaire's *conte* in England, limits himself to a
modest observation: "On peut cependant invoquer *Rasselas*, un accident dans la carrière de Johnson, et *Vathek*. Le parallèle du premier avec *Candide*, véritable lieu commun critique, relève de la
comparaison purement formelle."[2] To consider the relationship between *Candide* and *Rasselas* purely formal may or may not be defen-

sible. But to reduce Johnson's masterpiece to an accident in his literary career does not correspond to the facts, since *Rasselas* represents a summary of Johnson's critical, aesthetic, and moral beliefs.

To the best of my knowledge, the only important French critics to concern themselves with Johnson and *Rasselas* are Fréron, Taine, and Cazamian. As early as 1760, Fréron ends his critique of Mme Belot's translation of *Rasselas* with a remark not devoid of truth, at least as far as *Rasselas* is concerned: "C'est un miroir moins révoltant que *Candide,* nous nous y voyons cependant avec toutes nos foiblesses et tous nos malheurs. *Candide* fait d'abord rire l'esprit, et laisse ensuite le désespoir dans le coeur; *Rasselas* nous attendrit, nous fait gémir sur les misères de notre nature; *Candide,* en un mot, nous rend en horreur à nous-mêmes, et *Rasselas* nous fait les objets de notre propre compassion."[3] Cazamian has two anodyne pages on *Rasselas* and concludes that its moral lesson is quite similar to that of *Candide.*[4] Taine, not even mentioning *Rasselas* by its title, launches a bilious attack against "le respectable et insupportable Samuel Johnson," and, in order to facilitate for his countrymen the visualization of this "personnage étrange," asks them to imagine him in a Parisian salon: "On voyait entrer un homme énorme, à carrure de taureau grand à proportion, l'air sombre et rude, l'oeil clignotant, la figure profondément cicatrisée par des scrofules, avec un habit brun et une chemise sale, mélancolique de naissance et maniaque par surcroît." He continues: "Nous demandons aux gens ce qui peut leur plaire dans cet ours bourru, qui a des habitudes de bedeau et des inclinations de constable. On nous répond qu'à Londres on est moins exigeant qu'à Paris en fait d'agrément et de politesse."[5] Is this caricature not reminiscent of Pangloss and, if such be the case, have we not already begun our comparison?

What, then is the relationship between *Rasselas* and *Candide?* Boswell, acquainted with both authors, amplifies Fréron's critique and, it would seem, integrates into his remarks arguments drawn from Rousseau's celebrated *Lettre sur la Providence* (1756), in which Rousseau censures Voltaire's views on optimism as set forth in his *Poème sur le désastre de Lisbonne* (1755)—a letter I shall discuss shortly:

This Tale, with all the charms of oriental imagery, and all the force and beauty of which the English language is capable, leads us through the most important scenes of human life, and shews us that this stage of our being is full of "vanity and vexation of spirit." To those who look no further than the present life, or who maintain that human nature has not fallen from the state in which it was created, the instruction of this sublime story will be of no avail. . . . Voltaire's *Candide,* written to refute the system of Optimism, which it has accomplished with brilliant success, is wonderfully similar in its plan and conduct to Johnson's *Rasselas.* . . . Though the proposition illustrated by both these works was the same, namely, that in our present state there is more evil than good, the intention of the writers was very different. Voltaire, I am afraid, meant only by wanton profaneness to obtain a sportive victory over religion, and to discredit the belief of a superintending Providence: Johnson meant, by shewing the unsatisfactory nature of things temporal, to direct the hopes of man to things eternal. *Rasselas,* as was observed to me by a very accomplished lady, may be considered as a more enlarged and more deeply philosophical discourse in prose, upon the interesting truth, which in his *Vanity of Human Wishes* he had so successfully enforced in verse. (L, 1:341–42)[6]

Boswell's commentary stresses the religious intent which animates *Rasselas* and relates it to *The Vanity of Human Wishes*. Almost always a teacher, Johnson attempts, in the words of Paul Alkon, "to breathe moral instruction into all his works in an effort to make them (as he made the *Rambler*) 'exactly conformable to the precepts of Christianity, without any accommodation to the licentiousness and levity of the present age.'"[7] Regarding Boswell's belief that Voltaire "meant only by wanton profaneness to obtain a sportive victory over religion, and to discredit the belief of a superintending Providence," I can only agree. The sum of these two indeterminate catchall concepts (a nonreligious and nonprovidential view of life) suggests an absurd universe a little à la Camus and a little more à la Beckett. Such is the impression *Candide* makes on me, provided Voltaire's lively, luminous, and "wanton" manner of describing that universe be substituted for the North African's gloomy, and for the Irishman's still gloomier, discourses on it—a change that makes all the difference.[8]

Before analyzing this difference, we should perhaps first listen to the philosophical voices and their echoes which may have been heard by both Voltaire and Johnson before and during the genesis of *Candide* and *Rasselas*. The most distinguished of these philosophers is Leibniz, whose *Essais de Théodicée sur la bonté de Dieu, la liberté de l'homme et l'origine du mal* (1710) is part of an involved debate with Pierre Bayle, his most redoubtable antagonist in matters pertaining to philosophical optimism. Leibniz's epigone Christian Wolf develops the doctrine and, as a result of excessive systematization, both master and disciple are ridiculed by Voltaire.[9] However, philosophical optimism reaches Voltaire not through Leibniz but first by way of Pope's *Essay on Man,* which in turn was written under the influence of William King's *De origine mali* (1702), translated into English in 1731 by Edmund Law, later Bishop of Carlisle. "There can hardly be much doubt," writes Lovejoy, "that it was largely from the original work of King that Pope derived, directly or through Bolingbroke, the conceptions which, rearranged with curious incoherency, served for his vindication of optimism in the First Epistle of the *Essay on Man.*"[10] This work, immensely successful, symbolizes the end of seventeenth-century pessimism (exemplified in Pascal's *Pensées*) and of Cartesian dualism and announces the forthcoming rise of monism (spurred by Spinoza's philosophy), whose artistic correlative finds expression in the baroque world view. Is the author of the *Essay* not comparable to a smithy who fashions a chain of ideas by means of concepts linked together with rhymes, creating thereby a poetic configuration which presages, in terms of its composition and its aesthetic effect, baroque masterpieces of other art forms (for example, a church by Fischer von Erlach or a *concerto grosso* by Händel)?[11]

Compared with *Candide, Rasselas* seems to stand alone and betrays no overt sign of a Popean or a Leibnizian influence, direct or indirect, favorable or unfavorable.[12] Thus, quite original with regard to works by other authors but related to previous works by Johnson (among them, "Seged, lord of Ethiopia" [*Rambler,* nos. 205, 206]), *Rasselas* springs from his powerful intellect which grieves over his mother's fatal illness.[13] That she was then almost ninety years old, and that he had not taken the trouble to visit her for twenty years, does not necessarily indicate a lessening of filial sorrow; on the contrary, this neglected duty may have compounded his grief. In the Victorian words of G. B. Hill: "He would fain sit down and weep. But there was required of him a song and melody in his heaviness. It is little wonderful that the song was a song of sadness."[14]

Boswell furnishes the essential facts concerning the background of *Rasselas,* and G. B. Hill complements them. Of late it has been established that, aside from information drawn from Father Lobo's relation of his experiences in Abyssinia, translated by Johnson, the latter had other sources available to him.[15] For analyses of the various editions of *Candide,* I refer the reader to the critical editions by André Morize, Christopher Thacker (Geneva, 1968), and René Pomeau. Yet neither Morize's nor Pomeau's index makes any mention of Johnson or *Rasselas*—an oversight of which Thacker is not guilty, since he quotes Fréron and Boswell on *Rasselas,* but no one else and nothing more. This oversight seems especially regrettable, because Morize views Pope as the prime philosophical influence in the making of *Candide:* "c'est l'optimisme de Pope, déguisé à l'allemande, masqué de wolfianisme et de leibnitizianisme qui sera l'optimisme de Pangloss: *le Tout est bien* vient des *Epîtres sur l'homme* et non de la *Théodicée.*"[16] Given the importance of England during the intellectual genesis of *Candide,* how is one to account for the Voltaireans' disregard of Johnson, whose opposition against optimism surely equals that of their man? The answer is simple and, we shall see, also explains the neglect of Johnson by Diderot scholars: they have not read him. Surprisingly, according to Morize, *Candide* results from English influences and Voltaire's reaction to them, but it attacks German philosophy: "Car Pangloss est 'le plus profond métaphysicien de l'Allemagne,' et non point de l'Angleterre; et, à travers lui, ce n'est ni Pope ni Shaftesbury que Voltaire veut atteindre, mais Leibnitz et Wolf, les héros de la raison suffisante, des futurs contingents et de l'harmonie préétablie."[17]

Given the plethora of commentaries on *Candide,* there is no use restating what has been written. My introductory sketch seeks only to illustrate by means of a few pertinent quotations the arguments of some of the leading participants in the great debate on optimism, so admirably analyzed by Lovejoy (whose name is not mentioned by Thacker and Pomeau),[18] as well as to situate Johnson *and* Voltaire within the general framework of the debate, taking into account their relationship to Bayle and Rousseau and, of course, to Pope. Furthermore, the sketch has three other functions: first, to set the stage for our comparison of *Candide* and *Rasselas* as works of art; second, to suggest a possible connection between Johnson and Bayle; and third, to show that Voltaire's and Johnson's philosophical opposition to Leibniz is perhaps motivated partially by artistic considerations. What holds true for the artists may also be true for their critics: the theological and philosophical questions concerning optimism and the Great Chain of Being, although of great importance in their respective disciplines, are of secondary and even tertiary value in the literary appreciation of *Candide* and *Rasselas*.[19] Exemplary of what I consider such a shift of the critical focus because of philosophical and moral preoccupations is the unqualified assertion by Richard Schwartz in his *Samuel Johnson and the Problem of Evil:* "The essential difference between *Rasselas* and *Candide* lies in Johnson's psychological orientation with regard to the problem of evil."[20] Such a reduction of artistic differences to the question of evil, such a denial of other valid grounds of comparison, seems (if the critic really means what he says) somewhat one-sided. The masterpieces before our eyes, supposedly a satire and an apologue in the oriental manner, are as far removed from St. Augustine, King, Bayle, and Leibniz as *Phèdre* is from Jansenius. The music of Johnson's and Voltaire's language and the laughter of their minds, ringing within the invisible confines of *Candide* and *Rasselas,* their repressed nostalgia for eros and agapé—these are values that also deserve comparison as they detach themselves fleetingly from the two narratives against the gray background of life "in which much is to be endured, and little to be enjoyed."

Leibniz's *Théodicée* or "doctrine de la justice de Dieu" (p. 57) (*díke,* justice) attempts nothing less than to absolve God of the responsibility for the existence of evil (*innocenter Dieu*) by showing that His acts are based on a profound rational principle. Leibniz defines God as "la première raison des choses," a necessary, eternal fusion of wisdom and infinite goodness. The principle of optimism appears in the eighth paragraph of the *Théodicée:*

> Or cette suprême sagesse jointe à une bonté qui n'est pas moins infinie qu'elle, n'a pu manquer de choisir le meilleur. Car comme un moindre mal est une espece de bien, de même un moindre bien est une espece de mal, s'il fait obstacle à un bien plus grand: & il y auroit quelque chose à corriger dans les actions de Dieu, s'il y avoit moyen de mieux faire. Et comme dans les Mathématiques, quand il n'y a point de *maximum* ni de *minimum,* rien enfin de distingué, tout se fait également; ou quand cela ne se peut, il ne se fait rien du tout; on peut dire de même en matière de parfaite sagesse, qui n'est pas moins réglée que les Mathématiques, que s'il n'y avoit pas le meilleur (*optimum*) parmi tous les Mondes possibles, Dieu n'en aurait produit aucun.[21]

Correlative with the principle of optimism are the principles of plenitude and the Chain of Being, whose source one must seek in Plato's *Timaeus*. Lovejoy has traced their history and interdependence, and I refer the reader to his *Great Chain of Being*. Coexisting with these principles is that of the "sufficient reason"—*la raison suffisante* so "naughtily" defamed by Voltaire. Like many of his puns, it is complex. On the visual level (Cunégonde sees *la chose*), the pun remains wittily obscene; but when we understand *la raison suffisante* in terms of its metaphysical function, we suddenly behold with astonishment a philosophical phallus of cosmic proportions, whence flows a profuse and endless universe. In it (that is, in Leibniz's world) there is no empty space or empty time; every particle of matter contains an infinite number of creatures. The only major figures to disapprove of this plentiful universe, in which pain and sorrow are reevaluated according to a law of universal harmony, are Johnson and Voltaire. The former voices his dissent by applying Zeno's argument to *la chaîne des êtres:* "The scale of existence from infinity to nothing, cannot possibly have being. The highest being not infinite must be . . . at an infinite distance below infinity. . . . And in this distance between finite and infinite, there will be room for ever for an infinite series of indefinable existence."[22] "Johnson's argument," writes a historian of philosophy, "strikes directly at the foundation of the Chain of Being —the principle of plenitude.

Still, with a moment's reflection, we see that it is not really pertinent: the Chain of Being is, so to speak, the cosmological translation of Zeno's paradox, and its fullness is predicated precisely upon the 'fault' Johnson finds with it, namely, that infinite divisibility which affords the insertion between one order and another of 'endless orders.' "[23] A delightful page in Boswell's *Life* specifies Johnson's views on Leibniz; it would be a pity not to quote the following exchange on Tuesday, October 5, 1773, in the Hebrides on the islands of Col and Tyre-yi, parish of the Reverend Mr. Hector M'Lean:

> It was curious to see him and Dr. Johnson together. Neither of them heard very distinctly; so each of them talked in his own way, and at the same time. Mr. M'Lean said, he had a confutation of Bayle, by Leibnitz.—JOHNSON. "A confutation of Bayle, sir! What part of Bayle do you mean? The greatest part of his writings is not confutable: it is historical and critical."—Mr. M'Lean said, "the irreligious part;" and proceeded to talk of Leibnitz's controversy with Clarke, calling Leibnitz a great man.—JOHNSON. "Why, sir, Leibnitz persisted in affirming that Newton called space *sensorium numinis,* notwithstanding he was corrected, and desired to observe that Newton's words were QUASI *sensorium numinis.* No, sir; Leibnitz was as paltry a fellow as I know. Out of respect to Queen Caroline, who patronised him, Clarke treated him too well." (L, 5:286)[24]

The other dissident, Voltaire, less rigorous and more irreverent than Johnson, criticizes *la chaîne des êtres* by pointing to the empty spaces between the gradations in the Catholic hierarchy and, then, between man and ape.[25] Justified or not, the objections of our two authors do not, it seems to me, reflect their real reasons for their feverish opposition to the *plenum formarum.* These may stem instead from an artistic awareness that creators must have their own time- and space-frames in which they themselves and their creatures may breathe fresh air, move about, and fulfill their self-imposed and assigned destinies. But the Leibnizian universe does not allow much room, if any, in which to compose fictional lives; in short, it discourages narrative explorations and flights of lyrical fancy.

It should be noted that Bayle agrees with the German philosopher that God is the source of original sin and that the resulting
evil does not compromise Him. However, he denies any system the
right or the capacity to resolve this paradox. It is a mystery. Pure,
blind faith is his answer. It is also Johnson's answer, who may be
more beholden to Bayle than is generally acknowledged. Yet the
bibliographies on Johnson do not make mention of any article that
relates Johnson to the author of the *Dictionnaire historique et critique,*
a work which he respected and even sought to emulate.[26] The two
men have much in common: encyclopedic minds, an irrepressible
penchant for dialectical combat, hypercritical attitudes coexisting
with deep faith. Nowhere is Bayle's fideism more evident than in
his "Eclaircissement sur les Pyrrhoniens," in which he declares:
"Rien n'est plus nécessaire que la Foi, & rien n'est plus important
que de bien connoître le prix de cette Vertu Théologale. . . . Di-
sons aussi que la Foi du plus haut prix est celle qui sur le témoignage divin embrasse les Vérités les plus opposées à la Raison." Un-
afraid, Bayle goes on to quote St. Evrémond's graceful parody of
his fideistic creed:

> On a donné à cette pensée un air ridicule, & qui vient de main
> de Maître. *Le Diable m'emporte si je croyois rien,* fait-on dire au
> Maréchal d'Hocquincourt. *Depuis ce tems-là je me ferois crucifier
> pour la Religion. Ce n'est pas que j'y vois plus de raison; au contraire
> moins que jamais: mais je ne saurois que vous dire, je me ferois
> pourtant crucifier sans savoir pourquoi. Tant mieux, Monseigneur,
> reprit le Pere d'un ton de nez fort devot, tant mieux; ce ne sont point
> des mouvements humains, cela vient de Dieu. Point de raison, c'est la
> vraye Religion cela, point de raison. Que Dieu vous a fait,
> Monseigneur, une belle grace!* (Bayle's italics)[27]

Untranslatable, this exquisite satire is unanswerable and forces
Bayle to surrender, if only for an endless moment, to the wittiest of
all Frenchmen—that *grand seigneur* who, in his English exile, describes himself as "le gouverneur des canards de Saint-James."
    It gives one pause to compare St. Evrémond's lighthearted,
but ever-so-effective, takeoff to Jean-Pierre Crousaz's enormous and
very impressive *Examen du Pyrrhonisme ancien et moderne* (1733); in

his preface, the Swiss theologian despairs of besting Bayle whose arguments are so intertwined with digressions "si propres à distraire & à détourner la pensée d'examiner"[28] that he compares himself to a man trying to kill the Hydra. That Johnson was well acquainted with Crousaz may come as a surprise to Voltaire scholars, but not to Johnsonians, since Johnson translated Crousaz's *Commentaire sur la traduction en vers de Mr. l'abbé Du Resnel, de L'Essai de M. Pope sur l'homme* in 1739, gracing it with annotations as cursory as they are irascible. Having to agree in principle with Crousaz's orthodox views, he is all the more annoyed with de Resnel's verse translation which is *not always* unfaithful.[29] The abbé's sin looms unpardonable: could it be that alexandrines cannot, dare not, do justice to heroic couplets, since syllabification *à la française* entails only four weak stresses, infinitely less convincing to an English ear than the five strong beats characteristic of the iambic pentameter?

But to return to the master of those who doubt: There are two levels of truth, argues Bayle, which the human mind cannot reconcile—divine wisdom and goodness on the one hand, human suffering on the other: "Si l'homme est l'ouvrage d'un seul Principe souverainement bon, souverainement saint, souverainement puissant," asks a fictitious Zoroaster, "peut-il être exposé aux maladies, au froid, à la faim, à la soif, à la douleur, au chagrin? La souveraine sainteté peut-elle produire une créature criminelle?" Zoroaster concludes with an endorsement of a Manichaeistic credo: "il a fallu nécessairement qu'il y eût dans la nature des choses un Etre essentiellement bon, & un autre Etre essentiellement mauvais."[30] Commenting on these perplexing issues, Lovejoy notes:

> Eighteenth-century optimism not only had affinities with the dualism to which it was supposed to be antithetic, but the arguments of its advocates at times sounded strangely like those of the pessimist. . . . The moral was different, but the view of the concrete facts of experience was sometimes very much the same; since it was the optimist's contention that evil—and a great deal of it—is involved in the general constitution of things, he found it to his purpose to dilate, on occasion, upon the magnitude of the sum of evil and upon the depth and breadth of its penetration into life.[31]

Lovejoy also refers to Soame Jenyns, whose misfortune it was to rouse Johnson's anger, although it should be noted that Jenyns's *A Free Inquiry into the Nature and Origin of Evil* (1757) also deserves laughter: "Thus want of taste and genius, with all the pleasures that arise from them, are commonly recompenced by a more useful kind of common sense, together with a wonderful delight, as well as success in the busy pursuits of a scrambling World." Who but Johnson, quite preoccupied by the threat of insanity, would fault Jenyns so severely when the latter declares, quite possibly tongue in cheek: "Folly cannot be very grievous, because imperceptible; and I doubt not but there is some truth in that rant of a mad Poet, that there is a pleasure in being mad, which none but Madmen know." Jenyns ends his fugue with an admonition to both angels and Houyhnhmns: "doubtless it would be as inconvenient for a Man to be endued with the knowledge of an Angel, as for a Horse to have the reason of a Man."[32] Jenyns is to Johnson what Wolf is to Voltaire. The latter not only ridicules hyperrationalism but also rebels against the sort of pantheistic optimism practiced by the author of the *Essay on Man:*

> Lo, the poor Indian! whose untutored mind
> Sees God in clouds, or hears him in the wind . . .

or elsewhere:

> Know, Nature's children all divide her care;
> The fur that warmed a monarch warmed a bear.[33]

A sensible scheme, known in France as *vendre la peau de l'ours!*

Pope and Voltaire were not only fellow poets but also acquaintances: in fact, Johnson relates with anecdotal relish in his *Life of Pope* that, after Pope had almost drowned in a friend's coach, "Voltaire, who was then in England, sent him a Letter of Consolation. He had been entertained by Pope at his table, where he talked with so much grossness that Mrs. Pope was driven from the room. Pope discovered by a trick, that he was a spy for the Court, and never considered him as a man worthy of confidence."[34] Regardless of the truth of these questionable allegations, the Parisian is closer to his counterpart in Twickenham than to any philosopher of any persuasion: "L'auteur du *Poème sur le désastre de Lisbonne* ne combat point l'illustre Pope, qu'il a toujours admiré et aimé; il pense comme lui sur presque tous les points; mais, pénétré des malheurs des hommes, il s'élève contre les abus qu'on peut faire de cet axiome, 'Tout est bien.'"[35] Above all, Voltaire rejects the idea of a pitiless God who allows the justification of evil through the invocation of eternal laws. Such is the thrust of his poem:

> Aux cris demi-formés de leurs voix expirantes,
> Au spectacle effrayant de leurs cendres fumantes,
> Direz-vous: "C'est l'effet des éternelles lois
> Qui d'un Dieu libre et bon nécessitent le choix?"
> Direz-vous, en voyant cet amas de victimes:
> "Dieu s'est vengé; leur mort est le prix de leurs crimes?"
>   (ll. 13–18)

This poem, which occupies a lesser rank in the official hierarchy of French masterpieces, draws high praise from Pomeau who considers it "une oeuvre hardie sous le classicisme de la forme."[36] Although perhaps daring in regard to content, its prosaic diction sinks at times to a level so pedestrian that Voltaire's call for a friendly deity ("On a besoin d'un Dieu qui parle au genre humain") sounds more like a request for domestic help, perhaps *une femme de chambre,* than an appeal to a deistic God Almighty. But regardless of such differences in valuation, Voltaire plays a diabolical game: on the one hand, he uses the Christian dogma of evil as well as all evidence of suffering in order to destroy systematic optimism; on the other hand, he undermines apologetic optimism which tries to justify our journey through this Vale of Tears. Both moments of his argument stem from Bayle, whose thought he perverts, and no one has taken him to task more severely than Rousseau: "mais croyez-vous de bonne foi, que Bayle, dont j'admire avec vous la sagesse et la retenue en matière d'opinion, eût trouvé la vôtre si démontrée?" Elsewhere in the same letter he affirms:

> Tous mes griefs sont donc contre votre poëme sur le désastre de
> Lisbonne, parce que j'en attendois des effets plus dignes de
> l'humanité qui paroît vous l'avoir inspiré. Vous reprochez à
> Pope et à Leibnitz d'insulter à nos maux, en soutenant que tout
> est bien, et vous amplifiez tellement le tableau de nos misères,

que vous en aggravez le sentiment: au lieu des consolations que j'espérois, vous ne faites que m'affliger. On diroit que vous craignez que je ne voye pas assez combien je suis malheureux; et vous croiriez, ce semble me tranquilliser beaucoup en me prouvant que tout est mal.[37]

What is Johnson's situation in this debate? The answer is complex, and perhaps therefore few answers have been offered. Donald Greene, commenting on Johnson's review of Jenyns's *Free Inquiry*, observes:

> It is interesting to find Voltaire, the avowed enemy of organized religion, and Johnson, the devout 'High Churchman,' joining forces against the Roman Catholic Alexander Pope and the moderately orthodox Anglican Jenyns (at least, he later became so, apparently after a flirtation with deism)—interesting if only to show how little such labels may tell about an individual's fundamental beliefs. Voltaire and Johnson are so hostile to this view [philosophical optimism] because in the first place, as humanitarians, they are appalled by what seems a justification for cruelty and a recommendation to view it with complacency. (GS, 129–30)

Greene proceeds to show that "Johnson's antipathy to the Pope-Jenyns thesis has still deeper roots." Among these, he names Shaftesbury's benevolism, Mandeville's economic theory and, foremost, "the Stoic concept of 'nature,': the idea of the universe, things as they are, as an absolute, a norm, a legislator of moral law" (ibid.).[38] Furthermore, Greene views Rousseau's primitivism as one of the factors contributing to Johnson's opposition to optimism, although he does not take into consideration Rousseau's *Lettre sur la Providence*. This letter makes Rousseau, unbeknownst to Johnson, an ally in his battle against "infidels," if not philosophical optimists.

Also very useful in the clarification of Johnson's *situation* is a short, but thoughtful, book by Robert G. Walker, *Eighteenth-Century Arguments for Immortality and Johnson's Rasselas*. In his introduction, Walker writes: "Central to the meaning of *Rasselas,* I feel, is the relationship between the insufficiency of the world to the spirit of man and the argument from desire for man's immortality. In a sense, then, what follows is an attempt to show that Johnson did precisely what Boswell thought he did in *Rasselas*, that is, from the unsatisfactory nature of things temporal he encouraged the hopes of man for things eternal."[39] This interpretation, to which I subscribe, implies two divergent attitudes, of which the first finds expression in Imlac's discourse on the nature of the soul: "But the Being, said Nekayah, whom I fear to name, the Being which made the soul, can destroy it. . . . He, surely can destroy it, answered Imlac, since, however unperishable, it receives from a superiour nature its power of duration. That it will not perish by any inherent cause of decay, or principle of corruption, may be shown by philosophy; but philosophy can tell no more. That it will not be annihilated by him that made it, we must humbly learn from higher authority" (p. 218). Like Bayle, Johnson seems to resort here to straightforward fideism, and I am tempted to believe that the Savoyard Vicar could have approved Imlac's *profession de foi* and part of what leads to it. However, *Rasselas* also conveys a pessimistic view of life which not only is the point of departure for a Dantesque luminous blessedness but initiates as well a subtle and subversive negativism, pointing to nothing and to nothingness— to a fall into a void, admirably expressed by Góngora's gradual descent from *tierra* to *humo* to *polvo* to *sombra* down to *nada;* to a destructiveness far more devastating than the somewhat superficially discouraging implications of *Le Poème sur le désastre de Lisbonne*. I do not mean to suggest that Johnson lacked faith, but only that powerful personalities like his or Pascal's cause, during moments of sadness or despair, a void infinitely more troubling than do the doubts and griefs which beset ordinary men and women. However this may be, Rousseau disapproves bitterly of those who undermine carelessly, pretentiously, gratuitously, the faith of simple souls: "C'est qu'il y a de l'inhumanité à troubler des âmes paisibles, et à désoler les hommes à pure perte."[40] Yet, given Jean-Jacques's sense of solitude and persecution, would he have dared to censure Johnson for projecting and teaching the disarray of his intimate anguish?

"Oh, how dreadful" exclaimed Fanny Burney, "how terrible is it to be told by a man of [Johnson's] genius and knowledge, in so affectingly probable a manner, that true, real, happiness is ever unattainable in this world!—Thro' all the scenes, publick or private, domestick or solitary, that Nekayah or Rasselas pass, real felicity eludes their pursuit and mocks their solicitude."[41] "Given this irremediable imperfection of things temporal," comments Joseph Wood Krutch, "Johnson's theory of human nature, as condensed in *Rasselas*, rests ultimately upon the desperate assumption that, since man never finds any really self-justifying activity, he must, if life is to be tolerable at all, fill it up with those temporary satisfactions which are gained by the gratification of the easily wearied senses and the parallel gratification of that less easily wearied but still far from limitless appetite for knowledge to which he generally gives no more exalted name than 'curiosity.' "[42]

Candide's disillusioned companion Martin, whose editorial labors in Amsterdam parallel Johnson's years as a hack writer in Grub Street, summarizes the issue once and for all: "Travaillons sans raisonner . . . c'est le seul moyen de rendre la vie suportable" (p. 223). And, as if to prepare his disciple for this morose conclusion, he answers Candide's question about the pleasure one has in faulting everything with a question of his own: "C'est-à-dire, reprit Martin, qu'il y a du plaisir à n'avoir pas de plaisir?" (p. 196). However much Johnson was wont to reject such an insidious question, he could not disavow it entirely when meeting it in Jenyns's treatise: "I am persuaded that there is something in the abstract nature of pain conducive to pleasure."[43] I should add parenthetically that Valéry reformulates this unsettling discovery in aesthetic terms: "Le goût est fait de mille dégoûts." Does Martin's question explain why Rasselas burrows his way out of the Happy Valley—a melancholic Eden where princes live in "blissful captivity" in a palace "built as if [Freud] had dictated the plan" (pp. 10, 11)? Is pleasure in displeasure Candide's "raison suffisante" for leaving Eldorado, or is it only the warm memory of Cunégonde, "haute en couleur, fraiche, grasse, appétissante" (p. 3)? Rarely pleased, often disappointed, the prince and his entourage journey from deception to deception, while Candide and Cacambo stumble from catastrophe to catastrophe, always agitated by "the resistless vicissitudes of the heart" (R, no. 156, p. 69).[44]

As for Johnson's characters, they seem at first glance quite abstract. I say "seem," because in fiction nothing ever really "is." Distant, untouchable, *his* women appear so bodiless that one feels perverse in imagining a palpable Nekayah, Rasselas's sister, strangely and perhaps understandably preoccupied by what Diderot's *neveu* calls "la cohabitation éternelle." Incidentally, we may note that her magisterial utterance, "Marriage has many pains, but celibacy has no pleasures" (p. 119), corresponds in mysterious ways to Paquette's sybilline warning "[qu'il] est dangereux pour une femme acariâtre d'être l'épouse d'un Médecin" (p. 178). As for the men, with the exception of Imlac, Rasselas, the Astronomer, and the Arab, they are pretexts for the illustration of allegorical concepts which, in turn, are colored by feeling and gently satirized. We are shown "the academic life," led by a philosopher who enjoys "the consciousness of his own beneficence" (p. 99), and "the solitary life," embodied by a hermit whose "fancy riots in scenes of folly" (p. 95)—perhaps, a Saint Johnson in the desert? What guides these strange personages? Is it purpose or chance, sexuality or ethics? Professors Bate and Alkon offer answers: the former, noting that Johnson opposed Hobbes's belief "that human motives are determined by a mechanical inner calculus of pleasure" (BA, 144); the latter, that "Johnson was violently opposed to the notion that men are born governed by some 'ruling passion.' Instead, he believed that *'most minds are the slaves of external circumstances, and conform to any hand that undertakes to mould them, roll down any torrent of custom in which they happen to be caught, or bend to any importunity that bears hard against them'* (author's italics)."[45] Does *Rasselas* exemplify its author's theory? Are its protagonists "ever much addicted to women and the pleasures of the table," like Vathek, whose creator William Beckford was born in 1759, the year *Rasselas* and *Candide* were written?[46] The second question answers the first. Indeed, since Johnson believes that all action originates in the mind, he is forced to grant his personae minds of their own which must control their behavior but which also mock the narrator as well as Imlac, his spokesman. Johnson's story—*Rasselas*— tells his story, or does it? Although he knew the grip of the libido, his oriental tale disdains any reference to it. Almost always serious, his characters speak their thoughts . . . or do they? Could it be that their enigmatic behavior results from the sublimation or re-pression of unacknowledged desires?

Voltaire, on the contrary, does not allow for neuroses. Always in charge, he functions like an efficient film director. Bottiglia rightly emphasizes the dramatic nature of his *conte*, "written in a style that calculates an effect of oral spontaneity, that must be heard and visualized to be appreciated, that clearly suggests into-nations and facial expression (even, one [*i.e.*, Bottiglia] might add, gestures)."[47] Brisk dialogues predominate. Unlike Johnson's char-acters, given to engaging in dialogues consisting of lengthy mono-logues, Voltaire's actors often answer questions with questions—a quasi-socratic or talmudic ploy for achieving dialectical superi-ority. Approaching the coast of France, Candide and his friend, "The Last Manichean," debate the nature of man: "Croyez-vous, dit Candide, que les hommes se soient toujours mutuellement massacrés, comme ils font aujourdhui, qu'ils ayent toujours été menteurs, fourbes, perfides, ingrats, brigands, faibles, volages, lâches, envieux, gourmands, yvrognes, avares, ambitieux, san-guinaires, calomniateurs, débauchés, fanatiques, hypocrites & sots?—Croyez-vous, dit Martin, que les éperviers ayent toujours mangé des pigeons quand ils en ont trouvé?" (pp. 144–45).

None of his characters challenges the narrator; none tries to escape him as Jacques, *le fataliste,* tries to escape Diderot. Because of this impression of Voltaire's unrelenting and overpowering pres-ence, his impersonations have often been likened to puppets that fulfill an allegorical purpose: Cunégonde's brother, for example, embodies pride, pederasty, and Teutonic stubbornness. Despite their artificiality, these marionettes seem to come alive and act in a convincing manner, always true to their instructions. Conformists, they obey as Zadig obeys the angel; yet they exude vitality—es-pecially, the women. All are strong: Cunégonde, Paquette and, above all, la Vieille.[48] When the latter begins her story, one laughs; yet, as she relates her calvary through Russia and Eastern Europe, reality seeps into the reader's consciousness, the more painfully so if he has heard similar odysseys of privation from sur-vivors of the War and of the Holocaust.[49] Here is one of the high points in her long history of tribulations: "J'ai vieilli dans la misère

& dans l'opprobre, n'ayant que la moitié d'un derrière, me souve-
nant toujours que j'étais fille d'un Pape: j'ai voulu cent fois me
tuer, mais j'aimais encor la vie. Cette faiblesse ridicule est peut-
être un de nos panchans les plus funestes. Car y a-t-il rien de plus
sot que de vouloir porter continuellement un fardeau qu'on veut
toujours jetter par terre? d'avoir son être en horreur, & de tenir à
son être? enfin de caresser le serpent qui nous dévore, jusqu'à ce
qu'il nous ait mangé le coeur?" (pp. 70–71).[50] Cheered by "the
case of the missing buttock," we are quickly sobered by her discourse on suicide, all the while laboring under an impression of
déjà lu . . . Hamlet's soliloquy reduced to French prose! Voltaire's
control, however, does not preclude infinitesimal modifications in
the behavior of his actors. Attitudes, and the suitable *éclairage,*
shift perpetually, so that each reading reveals unexpected nuances.
For example, Paquette, first meant to be lasciviously obedient, reappears as a rundown strumpet, working the canals of Venice but
ever so ready with a flawless rejoinder: "A peine fut-elle entrée dans
la chambre de Candide, qu'elle lui dit: 'Eh quoi, Monsieur Candide ne reconnait plus Paquette!' A ces mots Candide qui ne l'avait
pas considérée jusques-là avec attention, parce qu'il n'était occupé
que de Cunégonde, lui dit: 'Hélas! ma pauvre enfant, c'est donc
vous qui avez mis le Docteur Pangloss dans le bel état où je l'ai
vû?—Hélas! Monsieur, c'est moi-même, dit Paquette, je vois que
vous êtes instruit de tout'" (pp. 177–78). And, when at last Voltaire tells us that she has become expert in embroidery, we are
flooded with unalloyed pleasure, because that's how life is. The
beast has been found out and its logic bested. All is irony. Like a
good comedienne playing the role of a prostitute, Paquette distances herself from her role; thus, our vision of her changes focus,
and, corresponding to this change, variations occur in the tension
between the role assigned to her and her pure self (the author).

Thus Voltaire, equally adept in choosing *le mot juste* as well as *le
défaut juste,* succeeds in drawing characters more easily recalled
than one's fellow men, for, as Proust has so clearly shown: "Un être
réel, si profondément que nous sympathisions avec lui, pour une
grande part est perçu par nos sens, c'est-à-dire nous reste opaque,
offre un poids mort que notre sensibilité ne peut soulever."[51] The

novelist, Proust claims, creates beings of another sort, spiritual constructs which the reader can assimilate easily instead of being repelled by bodies and emotions which make it irksome or even dangerous to know men, not to speak of women. A splendid example of Voltaire's linear magic (one thinks of Picasso) is his sketch of the governor of Buenos Aires: "Il aimait les femmes à la fureur"; with this foible and virtue in our minds, Voltaire presents his man: "Don Fernando d'Ibaraa, y Figueora, y Mascarenes, y Lampourdos, y Souza, *relevant sa moustache, sourit amèrement,* & ordonna au Capitaine Candide d'aller faire la revuë de sa Compagnie" (pp. 74, 75) [my italics]. A sardonic smile beneath Hispanic whiskers tells more than volumes. A single detail, strong light, no mystery— this is how Voltaire paints.[52] Similarly, Cunégonde, having sprung seemingly only from Voltaire's head, remains as accessible as a quadratic equation. As we participate in her adventures, we are tempted to conclude that she is the most unproblematical tart that ever roamed a book—a simplistic hussy compared to Defoe's Moll, let alone the enthralling Manon.

Whereas *Rasselas* owes its life to a quest for money and salvation (Johnson wrote it in a week to pay for his mother's funeral), *Candide* results from a sportive victory over *la vie vécue,* sticky, messy, deadly. Arouet's enemy is neither God nor *l'infâme,* neither wars nor earthquakes,[53] neither Fréron nor Rousseau, but life, "le serpent qui nous dévore"(p. 71)—in short, *das Dasein* vitiated by an indefinable flaw, a state of affairs for which the Germans have an untranslatable term, *die Unzulänglichkeit des Lebens.* Admittedly, his *conte* tells of feelings; but it is one thing to refer to them and quite another to evoke them. If *Candide* was to be Voltaire's witty answer to life's disasters—a reply for the most part untainted by bitterness and resentment—he had to sidestep his feelings rather than to repress or exclude them. As Bergson observes: "Le rire n'a pas de plus grand ennemi que l'émotion."[54] Indeed, wit and sentiment rarely mix; at best, they turn to humor as in the case of Jean Paul. If satire was ever permeated by good cheer, it has to be in the world of *Candide,* where silhouettes move so swiftly that they leave no shadow. *On y rit de bon coeur et on y triomphe de ses larmes.* Ira Wade's conclusion to his critical masterpiece illuminates this truth:

Certainly no one takes himself too seriously in *Candide*. When the moment of revolt becomes too intense, each person resorts to his wits to save the situation. Thus, wit is not only a means of revolt . . . it is a force, too, a creative effort, an urge to be. Standing face to face with the power of annihilation, impotent to solve either the rationality or the irrationality of things, witness to an impossibly ludicrous cosmic tragedy, *Candide* proclaims loudly, not that "The play is the tragedy Man / And its hero, the Conqueror Worm" but that the play is puny, insignificant, unregenerate man, and its hero an unconquerable, defiant, eternal wit.[55]

Nowhere does Voltaire's defiance assert itself more clearly than in the marvelous recognition scene in which Candide discovers Pangloss and the Baron, chained to their benches, performing as galley slaves: "Quoi c'est Candide! disait l'un des forçats.—Quoi! c'est Candide! disait l'autre.—Est-ce un songe? dit Candide; veillai-je? suis-je dans cette galère? Est-ce là Monsieur le Baron, que j'ai tué? est-ce là Maître Pangloss que j'ai vu pendre?—C'est nous-mêmes; c'est nous-mêmes, répondaient-ils" (p. 207). Their chorus is my favorite moment because it jubilates with happiness and neutralizes the universal doubt that besets all minds: "veillai-je, suis-je dans cette galère?" What a contrast between, on the one hand, this "smooth-sounding" question (phonetically, a master-piece) of which the first part harks back to Brandt's *Narrenschiff* (*Ship of Fools*) and Calderón's *La vida es sueño* and the second part to Molière's *Les Fourberies de Scapin* with its refrain "Que diable alloit-il faire dans cette galère?" (2.7) and, on the other hand, Nekayah's pedagogical concerns! What a contrast between the irrepressible duo, "c'est nous-mêmes," proclaiming the *will to be* and the Prin-cess's final words: "I hope hereafter to think only on the choice of eternity!" (p. 219). Could it be that her earnest manner has so affected Johnsonian interpreters of *Candide* that they have, for the sake of a convenient antithesis, misinterpreted a Mozartian *diverti-mento* for a ribald or ferocious tale?

Concerning the genre of the two works, there is agreement; they are philosophical tales, apologues, etc. Opinions diverge, however, when it is a question of delineating their meaning and historical significance. Thus, W. J. Bate interprets *Rasselas* as a potential *Bildungsroman* that embodies a dialectical progression: "The relevance of Johnson is not simply that he touches directly on so much that we care about. It is especially to be found in the way his thought proceeds, which is like that of experience itself. For his thinking goes first through everything that will not work, minimizing nothing, sharing in the attraction felt by the human heart, and even expressing that appeal memorably. And only gradually, as one thing after another gives way, do we find left a citadel of unshaking results that have withstood the test" (BA, 90). F. M. Keener holds a different view: "Its plot is decidedly not that of a *Bildungsroman* as later writers would develop the form." Jacques van den Heuvel, distinguished editor of Voltaire's *Romans et contes,* makes no mention of *Rasselas* (rare is the Voltairean who does) but classifies *Candide* as "une ébauche d'un roman d'apprentissage."[56] In view of these disagreements among English and French scholars as to the true nature of a *Bildungsroman,* one is justified in tracing its blueprint and superimposing on this outline *Candide* and *Rasselas.* Such a procedure offers, moreover, a way of gathering information concerning the structure of the two works, since it will highlight their thematic characteristics.

It has long been customary among German scholars to consider Goethe's *Wilhelm Meisters Lehrjahre* (1796) as the prototype of all *Bildungsromane,* although *La Nouvelle Héloïse* (1761) also fulfills all the requirements of this supposedly unique German art form.[57] "The first Years are usually imploy'd and diverted in looking abroad. Men's Business in them is to acquaint themselves with what is to be found without; and so growing up in a constant attention to outward Sensations, seldom make any considerable Reflection on what passes within them, till they come to be of riper Years; and some scarce ever at all."[58] Locke's serene observations are almost identical to Dilthey's well-known definition: "I should like to name the novels which belong to the tradition inaugurated by *Wilhelm Meister . . . Bildungsromane.* Goethe's work displays cultural education on various levels and in different characters and epochs of life." *Candide* and *Rasselas* fit easily into these two patterns. The German historian proceeds to refine his prerequisites. "Beginning with *Wilhelm Meister* and *Hesperus* [a novel by Jean-Paul

Richter] they [the *Bildungsromane*] all represent a youth when he enters life at its joyous dawn and seeks sister-souls, meets friendship and love as well as begins to battle with the hard realities of the world, matures as a result of these experiences, finds himself and becomes certain of his task in this world."[59]

Love ranks high among these indispensable characteristics enumerated by Dilthey: "Ich bin gebildet genug, versetzte sie, um zu lieben und zu trauern"[60] (I am sufficiently educated [*gebildet*], she said, in order to love and to grieve). Mignon's words set limits to any complete identification of the two works with the *Bildungsroman*. There is no love in *Rasselas,* and little in *Candide,* or so it seems. Perhaps it would be better to affirm that *Rasselas* circumvents love, if not marriage, whereas *Candide* derides "le consolateur du genre humain" (p. 22) to speak with Pangloss, stung by Paquette. But aside from this condition, both works conform, roughly speaking, to the ideal pattern of the *Bildungsroman,* especially if we relate the two tales to Schiller's definition. On having received the eighth and last book of *Wilhelm Meister,* Schiller wrote to Goethe on July 8, 1796: "Your novel, as it stands, in several instances resembles an epic poem, among other things in this, that it possesses machinery which in a certain sense represents the gods or ruling fate. The subject demanded this. Meister's years of apprenticeship are no mere blind effort of nature; they are a kind of experiment, a secretly-working higher force; the powers of the Tower accompany him with their attention, and, without interrupting nature in her free course, watch and lead him at a distance to an object of which he has and should not have any idea." And after having understood the sense of Goethe's innovative technique of remote guidance control, Schiller continues his analysis by considering the notion of the *Lehrjahre* as such and its correlative of *Meisterschaft:* "But the idea of mastership—which is but the work of ripe and full experience—cannot itself guide the hero of the novel. It can and dare not stand *before* him as his aim and object, for were he to have thought of the aim, he would have attained it *eo ipso;* while guiding him, therefore, it must stand *behind* him. In this way the whole receives a beautiful purpose, without the hero himself having any aim. The understanding, then, finds its work accomplished, while imagination fully maintains its freedom."[61]

Neither *Rasselas* nor *Candide* suggests the presence of a higher intelligence, unless one identifies it with the author. The condition that the guiding spirit lead the hero from behind the wings, as it were, is partially met by Imlac, whereas Martin remains a passive friend, content to say his piece. Spiritually, Pangloss does not matter. *Rasselas* exhibits, to some extent, a beautiful purpose (*eine schöne Zweckmässigkeit*), without the prince's having a specific purpose. In both works, reason and imagination interplay, and the resulting tensions create ironic effects as the Westphalian and the Ethiopian journey through life. They strike up acquaintances with realistic, allegorical, and even utopian figures, as for example, la Vieille, Pococurante and the King of Eldorado, or, in the case of *Rasselas,* the Arab, the Hermit and the sad old man. Mysterious figures, like Mignon or the Harper, who embody the dark powers of destiny, are nonexistent in either work. By the same token, Johnson disregards chance factors, whereas Voltaire relies on them (but only fictionally) in order to stage his recognition scenes: "O Ciel! est-il possible! s'écria le Commandant.—Quel miracle! s'écria Candide.—Serait-ce vous? dit le Commandant.—Cela n'est pas possible, dit Candide" (p. 85). In *Rasselas,* as in England, no one is ever surprised.

Written by mature men, *Candide* and *Rasselas* refer neither to visions of happy childhood, nor to "le vert paradis des amours enfantines," unless one interprets the scene in which Cunégonde drops her handkerchief as a poetic intermezzo. Also missing are portentous dreams, orange sunsets (to be sure, the *castrato* sits beneath an orange tree), swaying wheatfields, and glistening lakes. Hyperconscious, never "suggestive" in the Mallarmean sense of the word, Voltaire and Johnson say what they have to say, always intent on expatiating on the sense or nonsense of life. Similarly, the *Bildungsroman* pays homage to childhood (Wilhelm, in bed with Marianne, bores her with the history of his puppets) but declares the need of adult behavior: "Man ist nicht immer Jüngling, und man sollte nicht immer Kind sein" (One is not always a youth and one ought not always be a child).[62] But maturation implies decay, and no one knows it better than Saint-Preux who, historically speaking, is a fictional coeval of Candide and Rasselas: "Ainsi nous recommençons de vivre pour recommencer de souffrir, et le senti-

ment de notre existence n'est pour nous qu'un sentiment de douleur. Infortunés! Que sommes-nous devenus? Comment avons-nous
cessé d'être ce que nous fûmes?"[63] Sainte-Beuve restates the issue
more simply, if not more lyrically: "Mûrir, mûrir, on ne mûrit
point, on pourrit."[64] *Le temps vécu* is the very fabric of the *Bildungsroman:* Mme Arnoux, graying and—at last, after endless years—
willing, is rejected by Frédéric (*l'Education sentimentale*). The same
happens to Judith, when, a middle-aged *dea ex America,* she faces
her erstwhile admirer (*Der grüne Heinrich*). To be sure, la Vieille
recalls and bewails her youth: "Ma gorge se formait, & quelle
gorge! blanche, ferme, taillée comme celle de la Vénus de Médicis;
& quels yeux! quelles paupiéres! quels sourcils noirs!" (p. 59). But,
she is not *seen* or *felt* aging, nor for that matter is Cunégonde.[65] In
Rasselas, too, time stands still—in respect not to days and weeks
spent travelling but to the wounds it inflicts on body and soul.

Yet, despite the seemingly unimportant role played by love,
destiny (in the sense of *Schicksal*), and time, our *romans philosophiques* exhibit an essential feature of the *Bildungsroman,* namely the
presence of the advisor. "Par pitié," writes Saint-Preux to the
woman he loves: "ne m'abandonnez pas à moi-même; daignez au
moins disposer de mon sort."[66] Similarly, Goethe has his hero exclaim: " 'Ich überlasse mich ganz meinen Freunden und ihrer
Führung,' sagte Wilhelm; 'es ist vergebens, in dieser Welt nach
eigenem Willen zu streben' " ("I abandon myself completely to my
friends and their guidance," said Wilhelm; "in this world, it is
useless to strive according to one's will").[67] Inexplicably, German
readers relish the presence of pedagogues, from Archytas (*Agathon*
by Wieland) and the Abbé (*Wilhelm Meister*) to Settembrini in his
checkered coat and threadbare trousers (*The Magic Mountain*). Like
their German counterparts, Pangloss and Imlac guide or pretend to
guide their charges. But are they superior beings like the members
of Goethe's *Turmgesellschaft* (the Society of the Tower which directs
Wilhelm's steps)? Are they mentors like Pallas Athena, omniscient
in her support of Telemachus and Télémaque? Reflecting on these
questions, one is tempted to believe that *Candide* and *Rasselas* are
satires of the *Bildungsroman* to come, so subtly do they mock the
hopeless roles of guides and teachers who, in the words of Imlac,
"discourse like angels . . . but they live like men" (p. 85).

Other themes make possible a connection between the *Bildungs-roman* and our two works: (1) *The choice of life:* both heroes change their goals. Candide foregoes a dream of love in favor of pulling weeds in Asia Minor, whereas the Prince forsakes daydreaming for visions of a just government. In fact, renunciation (*Entsagung*) is a key concept of the *Bildungsroman:* Pekuah wants to be a prioress; Nekayah, president of a college of learned women; the Prince, a ruler of a little kingdom. All are fully aware that "of these wishes that they had formed . . . none could be obtained" (p. 221). (2) *The experience of guilt:* it is a major theme in *Wilhelm Meister* (Mignon and the Harper), and it assumes a theoretical importance in *Rasselas.* "No disease of the imagination," declares Imlac to the Man of Learning, "is so difficult of cure, as that which is complicated with the dread of guilt" (p. 205–6). Curiously enough, Johnson never analyzes the nature of the Astronomer's crime; perhaps it is the sin of angelism of which Jacques Maritain accuses Descartes—an iniq-uitous but ever-so-desirable assumption of divine control over all matters, including the weather (in short, a form of self-deifica-tion).[68] Nekayah, too, suffers remorse, because she thinks herself the cause of Pekuah's abduction and later because, like Marcel's mother, she is forgetting to grieve. Candide, on the contrary, makes short shrift of crime and punishment; after dispatching Inquisitor and Jew to the hereafter, he quips to his lady-love: "Ma belle Demoi-selle . . . quand on est amoureaux, jaloux & fouetté par l'Inquisi-tion, on ne se connait plus" (p. 52). Small wonder that Dostoyevsky hated Voltaire! (3) *A prevailing sense of earnestness*: Again *Candide* does not fit the bill; *Rasselas,* however, generates moods quite similar to *Stimmungen* in *Wilhelm Meister,* moods often characterized by stately irony and smiling sadness: "Schreitet, schreitet ins Leben zurück!" sing the youths at Mignon's funeral, "nehmet den heiligen Ernst mit hinaus, denn der Ernst, der heilige, macht allein das Leben zur Ewigkeit" (Stride, stride back into life. Take with you what is earnest and sacred, for sacred earnestness alone makes life eternal).[69] (4) *The theme of an ethos, freely conceived, and determined above and beyond passion:* Like self-developing monads, Candide and Rasselas should integrate harmoniously into their lives the love of a woman as well as a useful vocation, if they are to conform to the ideal pattern of the *Bildungsroman. Hors du bureau, point de salut.* "Becoming" or *Werden* is essential to the dynamic progression of a *Bildungsroman.* To be sure, Candide becomes the wise leader of the little band on the shores of the Propontis, yet one would hesitate to describe his maturation as inward because he does not have any "innards." (5) *The importance of the maxim:* Johnson and Voltaire, like Wieland and Goethe, stud their narratives with *sententiae,* although it should be noted that Goethe's *Lebensweisheiten* are warmer than those by Johnson and Voltaire, because they are tinged by the color of the narrative: " 'Ich habe immer gesehen,' versetzte Natalie, 'das unsere Grundsätze nur ein Supplement zu unsern Existenzen sind' " (I have always realized, said Natalie, that our fundamental propositions are only a supplement to our lives).[70] With these differences and similarities in mind, the answer as to whether *Candide* and *Rasselas* are *Bildungsromane* depends on one's interpretation of the structure and significance of the two masterpieces. My answer is forthright: they are and they aren't.

I have stated that *Candide* exemplifies Voltaire's "sportive victory" over life and that the precondition of his triumph is his ability to sidestep his feelings rather than to repress or exclude them from his psyche. Is such a feat possible? By way of an answer, let us recall the end of the eighth chapter, when Cunégonde completes her harrowing history: "Je recommandai à ma vieille d'avoir soin de vous, & de vous amener ici dès qu'elle le pourrait. Elle a très bien exécuté ma commission; *j'ai goûté le plaisir inexprimable de vous revoir, de vous entendre, de vous parler.* Vous devez avoir une faim dévorante, j'ai grand appetit, commençons par souper" (p. 50) [my italics]. I must have read this sentence a hundred times before I appreciated its limpid loveliness, reminiscent not only of Mme de Sévigné's simplicity but also of the most touching of La Bruyère's maxims: "Un beau visage est le plus beau de tous les spectacles et l'harmonie la plus douce est le son de la voix de celle qu'on aime."[71] A lover finds happiness in hearing her voice, his voice. Voltaire intensifies *le plaisir d'entendre et de voir* with the joy of speaking. The one hundred first reading grants new insights. Had the sentence in italics been coordinated by two *et*'s, its meaning and effect would have been conclusive: *je vous ai vu et entendu et parlé, maintenant mangeons.* But, as it stands, its significance is held in abeyance, *suspendue,* as if to prolong through its rhythmic insistence the memory of secret happiness. Is it a coincidence that this key phrase numbers twenty-four syllables—two syncopated alexandrines whose aesthetic and moral values fuse in a sincere and sophisticated harmony? The sexual reference, "Vous devez avoir une faim dévorante; j'ai grand appetit; commençons par souper," is intentionally misleading so as to mask a need of tenderness with a display of *impudeur.* One is reminded of Henri Beyle, shielding his heart with wit, irony, and crude jokes. Who is Cunégonde? To whom is Voltaire speaking in 1759, *malgré lui . . . malgré elle?* The divine Emilie dies in childbirth in 1749, the prospective father being the young Saint-Lambert. Voltaire, attached to his niece Mme Denis since 1745, writes to her on September 10, 1749: "Ma chère enfant je viens de perdre un amy de vingt ans. Je ne regardois plus il y a longtemps madame du Chatelet comme une femme, vous le savez . . . De Cirey je reviens à Paris vous embrasser et retrouver en vous mon unique consolation et la seule espérance de ma vie."[72] Many of his letters to his lady (she was a redhead, with full lips, a snub nose and *le reste*—pure Boucher) bear the imprint of the tertiary rhythm that pulsates in the key phrase, as, for example, this note dated *ce mardy,* 1747: "Venez me voir après l'opéra, je vous attendray, je vous ramèneray. Si vous voulez nous mangerons un poulet." Twenty tinkling syllables about love are sustained by an appetizing afterthought which recurs in *Candide.* Closer still to the key phrase is the other revealing note, also dated 1747: "Mia cara, avro oggi il piacere di vedervi, e di ragionar colla mia musa."[73] This fragment numbers twenty-five syllables and, more significantly, defines Voltaire's manner of living: seeing, discussing and, of course, writing. That Voltaire changed the gender of the speaker is understandable, for when he wrote *Candide* he was over sixty, frail, and chronically ill, while his niece was only in her thirties. What could be more natural than to express his love for Mme Denis through Cunégonde, who transfers it to Candide, young, fair-skinned, and attractive?[74]

What holds true for *Candide*—that its diamond-like surface has a flaw, if love be a flaw—holds true, analogically, for *Rasselas.* If we substitute Johnson's didactic commitment, so severely opposed to "the vanity of human wishes," for Voltaire's shimmering hardness, we shall find that Johnson's commitment is also "flawed." His weakness is not an elusive declaration of love but an ephemeral concession to love and desire as well as to their concomitant complexities and inevitable catastrophes. I have said that it seems almost perverse to envisage the Princess, so highminded and prim, as a woman of flesh and blood; in fact, Nekayah, "wise and aphoristic," seems almost a sister to Goethe's Natalie, whom the German critic Schlechta considers *ein Idealweib* as opposed to the *empirischen Weibe*.[75] (Either term defies translation.) Pekuah, however, is a more spirited damsel; her relationship with her Arab ravisher suggests the outline of a novel, whose plot is the immemorial struggle between a man and a woman, not of the same mind. Johnsonians might demur and point out that his theory on the novel (in his words, "the comedy of romance"[76]) proscribes such fantasies, and that he would have applauded Valéry's refusal to commit *his* intellect to an art form reduced to variations of an insipid theme— "La marquise sortit à cinq heures" or, in our case, "Lady Pekuah rentra à cinq heures," a thought that I find more suggestive. Regardless of posthumous objections, I am convinced that Pekuah's not-so-brief encounter with the Son of Ishmael makes for a fastidious daydream.

Before tracing the articulations of Johnson's fictitious fiction, we should, for a better understanding of his technique, meditate on Pascal's *Pensées,* specifically number 323 entitled "Qu'est ce que le moi."

> Un homme qui se met à la fenêtre pour voir les passants, si je passe par là, puis-je dire qu'il s'est mis là pour me voir. Non; car il ne pense pas à moi en particulier; mais celui qui aime quelqu'un à cause de sa beauté, l'aime-t-il? Non: car la petite vérole, qui tuera la beauté sans tuer la personne, fera qu'il ne l'aimera plus.
>
> Et si on m'aime pour mon jugement, pour ma mémoire, m'aime-t-on *moi?* Non, car je puis perdre ces qualités sans me perdre moi-même. Où est donc ce *moi,* s'il n'est ni dans le corps, ni dans l'âme, et comment aimer le corps ou l'âme, sinon pour ces qualités, qui ne sont point ce qui fait le moi, puisqu'elles sont périssables? car aimerait-on la substance de l'âme d'une personne, abstraitement et quelques qualités qui y

fussent? Cela ne se peut, et serait injuste. On n'aime donc
jamais personne, mais seulement des qualités.

Qu'on ne se moque donc plus de ceux qui se font honorer
pour des charges et des offices, car on n'aime personne que
pour des qualités empruntées.[77]

Action begins in the twentieth chapter when Lui beholds the
qualitative aspects of Pascal's Pekuah: "Illustrious lady . . . My
fortune is better than I presumed to hope; I am told by *my* women,
that I have a princess in my camp" (p. 166) [my italics]. The Arab
owns his women and, when not devoting his efforts to gainful
employment, may be imagined riding his dromedary in the heat of
noon, tempted by a *fata piuttosto inghlese* and bored by intimations
of *déjà eues*. . . . Will he ever, can he have Pekuah as a *personne?*
The answer is never in doubt. Were he to subject her to Clarissa's
fate, he would be left with empty hands, with "des qualités empruntées" (including his sexual pleasure—a lonely experience, because *la dame de compagnie*, unlike Cunégonde, would not be a con-
senting victim). But, even Pekuah willing, Pascal's conclusion
appears unassailable: "On n'aime donc jamais personne, mais
seulement des qualités"; in other words, the Arab may be said to
enjoy *die Eigenschaften ohne die Frau*.

The Arab is greedy, but, unlike Lovelace, he is a gentleman
who knows his etiquette—in short, an Anglo-Arabian *honnête
homme*. Pekuah is not long in making a startling discovery: "I never
knew the power of gold before" (p. 168). Her situation loses its
terror, for "Avarice is an uniform and tractable vice" (p. 170).
"His" women consider her a rival, but, informed that she is "a
great lady detained *only* for [her] ransome" (p. 171), they become
obsequious and reverent [my italics].

The novelist relents and splashes some *couleur locale* on his abstract canvas: "The crocodiles and river-horses are common in this
unpeopled region, and I often looked upon them with terrour,
though I knew they could not hurt me. For some time I expected
to see mermaids and tritons" (p. 172). Apropos crocodiles *and* Pekuah, Wimsatt, the only one to embrace both subjects, quotes
Johnson's preface to his translation from the French of Lobo's *Voyage
to Abyssinia*, originally written in Portuguese: "The Portuguese

Traveller . . . meets with no Basilisks that destroy with their eyes, his *Crocodiles* devour their Prey without Tears, and his *Cataracts* fall from the Rock without deafening the Neighboring Inhabitants."[78] As for Pekuah, Wimsatt shows that the development of her character is an "afterthought," that on the basis of "genetic inferences" *Rasselas* has a "lumpy or bumpy structure," that it is a travel story but "not on the whole, a picaresque story"[79]—a wry understatement, indeed.

The Arab, fond of celestial observations, teaches Pekuah the art of star-gazing. To please her instructor, she feigns interest, for it is better "to observe the stars than to do nothing" (p. 173)—a thought matched more or less by la Vieille: "Je voudrais savoir," she opines, "lequel est le pire, ou d'être violée cent fois par des Pirates Nègres, d'avoir une fesse coupée . . . ou bien de rester ici à ne rien faire?" (p. 218). Concerning the Arab's reaction to Pekuah's pretense, we are told nothing, although the imaginary novelist will devote a lengthy chapter entitled "Pekuah, la prisonnière" to record his frustration and fascination with this impossible woman.

Pekuah's disquisition on the Arab's women deserves attention: "They ran from room to room as a bird hops from wire to wire in his cage. *They danced for the sake of motion*" (p. 174). (The last "verse," which I have italicized, announces Wallace Stevens's "Peter Quince at the Clavier"). And as we listen to Pekuah's tales of life in the harem (to read Johnson is to hear him), we are reminded of Nekayah's description of the women of Cairo: "Their grief, however, like their joy, was transient; every thing floated in their mind unconnected with the past or future, so that one desire easily gave way to another, as a second stone cast in the water effaces and confounds the circles of the first" (p. 106). It is as if Johnson stood between Pascal and Rousseau. Of the former, he illustrates to perfection the dreary truth: "Peu de chose nous console car peu de chose nous afflige." Of the latter, he describes *un état d'âme* which Jean-Jacques has immortalized in *La Cinquième Rêverie du promeneur solitaire*—a serene passage into a timeless present, freed from past and future, categories indispensable for Pascalian and Johnsonian morality.

"How, said Rasselas, can the Arab, whom you represented as a man of more than common accomplishments, take any pleasure in his seraglio, when it is filled only with women like these? Are they exquisitely beautiful?" (p. 175). Pekuah's answer, evasive and to the point, circumvents and centers on sexuality but also implies, ever so faintly, that her captor might have and should have fared better with her: "Whatever pleasures he might find among them, they were not those of friendship or society" (p. 175). In fact, "Pekuah-Johnson" neither condemns nor praises sexual happiness. Whatever its value might be, it cannot, "she-he" implies, be gratifying if it does not exult in its freedom: "as they had no choice, their fondness or appearance of fondness, excited in him neither pride nor gratitude; he was not exalted in his own esteem by the smiles of a woman who saw no other man" (p. 176). The Arab's quandary may well have been Johnson's own, for he was as thirsty for eros as he was hungry for conversation. The Arab procrastinates. Will he fall in love with Pekuah? Once more, I think of Marcel with his captive, feigning indifference and even contempt. It is also noteworthy that the Arab has no rival; there is no cause for jealousy (unless I invest Pekuah "la prisonnière" with Albertine's Lesbian inclinations) and, because of it, the hero succumbs to greed: "The gold, which he would not fetch, he could not reject when it was offered. He hastened to prepare for our journey hither, like a man delivered from the pain of an intestine conflict" (p. 178). There is an epilogue to this pre-Jamesian comedy, and, to the best of my knowledge, no one has referred to it: "Nekayah, having heard her favourite's relation, rose and embraced her, and Rasselas gave her an hundred ounces of gold, which she presented to the Arab for the fifty that were promised" (p. 178). The Prince pays, but it is Pekuah who gives the gold to her captor. Why the extra fifty ounces? I leave the answer to my female readers.

Is it a coincidence that "The History of a Man of Learning" unfolds in the wake of Pekuah's deliverance from the seraglio? She, who would not soothe the Arab, will cure the Astronomer, whose madness relates to Johnson's persistent and tragic fear of losing his mind. Yet his story rings with subdued laughter. Eloquence is no match for cosmic dreams; what is signified overflows the signifiers as the Nile its shores. The Astronomer confides:

> Hear Imlac, what thou wilt not without difficulty credit. I
> have possessed for five years the regulation of weather, and the
> distribution of the seasons: the sun has listened to my dictates,
> and passed from tropick to tropick by my direction; the
> clouds, at my call, have poured their waters, and the Nile has
> overflowed at my command. I have restrained the rage of the
> dog-star, and mitigated the fervours of the crab. The winds
> alone, of all the elemental powers, have hitherto refused my
> authority, and multitudes have perished by equinoctial
> tempests which I found myself unable to prohibit or restrain.
> (p. 183)

Without fail, scholars have stressed the pathology of the case and
have expatiated, justly so, on that short but unforgettable chapter
entitled "The Dangerous Prevalence of Imagination."[80] It abounds
with quotable truths, including the redoubtable disclosure: "Perhaps, if we speak with rigorous exactness, no human mind is in its
right state" (p. 189). However, the Astronomer's delusion not only
illustrates a type of madness but also relates unquestionably to the
history of causality in Western civilization, a history that begins
with the mythopoeic explanation of the change of seasons and the
course of stars by the inhabitants of ancient Mesopotamia and
Egypt. Divine decrees coincide with those that govern society.
Gradually there occurs a depersonalization of the divine regulatory
powers, a development that led to Plato's and Aristotle's concepts
concerning the nature of causation—concepts which held their
own until the advent of David Hume. "The History of a Man of
Learning" vaguely reflects the dilemma which Hume bequeathed
to Kant. Unlike earlier sceptics, "le bon David," as Jean-Jacques
called him for a few months, not only strips the human intellect of
many of its cognitive powers but also denies that it is linked in a
demonstrable manner to the order of the cosmos. Hume's contention is precisely what Johnson's story shows. Logic, argue Hume
and Johnson, is incapable of creating a foundation for causal connection based on reason. We observe nothing, claims the Scot,
except the regular succession of events. Nature is uniform, but our
belief in it is simply a question of expectation and cannot be
grounded in reason. "I sometimes suspected myself of madness,"
admits the Astronomer, "and should not have dared to impart this

secret but to a man like you." "Why Sir, said I, do you call that incredible, which you know, or think you know, to be true?" "Because, said he, I cannot prove it by any external evidence; and I know too well the laws of demonstration to think that my conviction ought to influence another, who cannot, like me be conscious of its force" (p. 186).

It is regrettable that Johnson never laid eyes on Kant's *Critique of Pure Reason* (1781) which appeared before his death. What might have been his reaction? One may assume that it would not have been unfavorable, because the Astronomer's problem relates to the Kantian question: how can we believe something which is neither demonstrated by reason nor evident to the senses? In this respect, the *Critique of Pure Reason* is relevant to the Astronomer's problem because the Copernican Revolution provides for the possibility of a truth which can be grasped by the mind but is demonstrable neither by pure reason alone nor by reference to anything empirical— a truth arising from the inner resources of the mind. Thus, insofar as one may interpret the Astronomer's "despotick fancy" not only as a vaguely Humean dilemma but also as a captivating critique of the Cartesian and Leibnizian concepts of the constitutive power of reason as exercised by God (He creates Being through Reason), Pangloss (who creates truths by way of syllogisms) and the Astronomer (whose reason "governs" over the seasons) may be considered intellectual kin. Voltaire states the problem succinctly in his *Précis du siècle Louis XV:* "Qui croirait que des géomètres ont été assez extravagants pour imaginer qu'en exaltant son âme on pouvait voir l'avenir comme le présent? Plus d'un philosophe, comme on l'a déjà dit ailleurs, a voulu, à l'exemple de Descartes, se mettre à la place de Dieu, et créer comme lui un monde avec la parole; mais bientôt toutes ces folies de la philosophie sont réprouvées des sages, et même ces édifices fantastiques, détruits par la raison, laissent dans leurs ruines des matériaux dont la raison même fait usage."[81]

Furthermore, from a literary point of view, the Astronomer is the uncle of Stendhal's Abbé Blanès. Perhaps the most quixotic of all the personae who move through *La Chartreuse de Parme,* the Abbé, "fou d'astrologie," spends his nights in the belfry of his church in Grianta predicting not only the fall of empires but also the fate of Gina's heart, "cette duchesse toujours si jolie," hope-lessly in love with her nephew Fabrizio.[82] For Samuel Johnson, *la chasse au bonheur* would indeed have been madness. Stendhal does, however, admit in the appendix to *Racine et Shakespeare* that his ideal, equivalent to spending a night with a *catin sublime* (a Milan-ese tart by the name of la Pietragrua) after having listened in her company to Mozart at the Scala, does not favor clear thinking, for "quand on passe sa vie entre les bras d'une femme, tout semble *obscur*."[83] Finally, we should stress that there are no madmen in *Candide;* in fact, French literature, unlike other European liter-atures, features few eccentrics blessed with talent or genius (as for example, Christopher Smart, one of Johnson's acquaintances). Even Sade's monsters reason as if they had studied *La Logique de Port-Royal* and manipulate the imperfect subjunctive with a relish that makes for comic contrasts between pretentious language and gruesome excesses.

But, to return to Pekuah and her Astronomer: She "displayed what she knew" and "her conversation took possession of his heart" (p. 201). Gradually "his thoughts grow brighter," and he begins "to delight in sublunary pleasures" (p. 202). "Fly to business or to Pekuah" (p. 206) fits, with a little twisting, Voltaire's advice to love like a madman when young and work like a devil when old, although on second thought "the Man of Learning" seems to reverse this suggestion. In any case, it is regrettable that Pekuah should end her fictional days as a prioress of a convent, teeming "with pious maidens" (p. 220). She and Johnson's readers deserve better.

"Reste à savoir," comments Taine on Johnson, "quelles idées l'ont rendu populaire. C'est ici que l'étonnement d'un Français re-double. Nous avons beau feuilleter son dictionnaire, ses huit vol-umes d'essais, ses dix volumes de vies, ses innombrables articles, ses entretiens si précieusement recueillis; nous bâillons. Ses vérités sont trop vraies."[84] It would not be hard to find a latter-day John-son to return the courtesy by noting that many of Voltaire's and, a fortiori, Taine's truths are but commonplaces when robbed of style and setting. Few, if any, authors appear original when divested of their ornaments, the exception to the rule being Pascal who re-mains invulnerable because his prose reigns inseparable from its adornments. It cannot be stripped. "We are all naked till we are dressed," wrote an "idler" on Saturday, April 7, 1759 (I, no. 51, pp. 159–60).

Yet the same "idler" might well have agreed with Buffon's adage, *le style, c'est tout l'homme*—an equality (in the mathematical sense) as true as it is useless to the critic, in that both terms *(le style* and *l'homme)* remain ultimately unknowable. Is it therefore not "simpler" to fall back on Baudelaire's advice to transmute *la volupté en intelligence*—to understand at least one's pleasure while eyes glide over Johnson's prologue, as unforgettable as Voltaire's epilogue? "Ye who listen with credulity to the whispers of fancy, and persue with eagerness the phantoms of hope; who expect that age will perform the promises of youth, and that the deficiencies of the present day will be supplied by the morrow; attend to the history of Rasselas prince of Abissinia" (p. 7). These melodious phrases, accompanied by a chorus of sweet English sibilants, cannot but please mind and ear; as one follows the prince's adventures, however, one sympathizes with Chesterton's wish for a little more texture and *couleur locale:* "Johnson could not understand as the medieval illuminator understood, that things are really plainer in gold and purple than in black and white."[85] Be this as it may, it is Wimsatt who offers one of the best analyses of Johnson's idiom which Macaulay describes so scornfully: "a language in which nobody ever quarrels, or drives bargains, or makes love, a language in which nobody ever thinks."[86]

Keeping *Candide* in mind, especially the lesson in experimental physics administered to Paquette, it becomes manifest that Johnson's expository method (instilled with a good dose of irony) could produce speeches reminiscent of those proffered by Doctor Pangloss, whose words and behavior illustrate quite nicely Bergson's explanation of the whys and wherefores of comedy *(du mécanique plaqué sur du vivant).* According to Wimsatt, it is this kind of superimposition of a rigid mechanical system on what is alive that constitutes a typical aspect of Johnson's epistemological and stylistic method:

> [He] matches the physical scale of analogy, but especially the lower, mechanical, and elemental end of it, against the realm of mind. The two halves of experience, the mechanical outer,

the vital, spiritual, and voluntary inner, with their partial resemblances (the mechanics of psychology) are his theme. And as he has the terms of either realm at his command, so he has the terms of the more transparent, algebraic realm where mechanics and psychology and all things else are subsumed. The thoughtful imagery of which Boswell spoke is an imagery of high shadows on the screen of categories, of lengthened metaphysical implications.

And just as Pangloss has a penchant for Latin expressions, so Johnson, according to Wimsatt, "adopts the Latin, when another writer would preserve English idiom by recasting his meaning. . . . Very often what he gains in coherence is more than offset by the intrusion of irrelevant meaning which is concomitant with the unidiomatic. There is an insurgency and agony of language; the emphasis shouts too loud."[87] Wimsatt's reproach, justified or not, could never be leveled against Voltaire, whose lightness of style is proverbial; indeed, the roster of critics who have tried to analyze it reads like an international Who's Who. No one has done it better than Lanson: "Ses petites phrases trottent, courent les unes après les autres, détachées. Voltaire rejette toutes ces lourdes façons d'exprimer les dépendances logiques, et de matérialiser, par des mots-crampons, les rapports des idées. . . . C'est le mouvement endiablé du style qui lie les phrases, qui les emporte ensemble, comme dans une farandole où les danseuses ne se donneraient pas les mains, et garderaient leurs distances seulement en suivant la mesure."[88]

Taking Lanson's estimation at face value, one would be hard pressed to find a common denominator capable of incorporating stylistic values shared by *Candide* and *Rasselas,* the more so since praise of the former almost implies condemnation of the latter. Indeed, Voltaire's style seems to mock Johnson's. Fortunately for all concerned, English is not simply French badly pronounced, as one of the musketeers would have it. Granted, had Addison or even Swift written *Rasselas* the task at hand would be simpler, for "Johnsonese" (a term invented by Macaulay)[89] or "the bugbear style" challenges Voltaire's literary ideal just as do the style and art forms of Shakespeare and Milton. We are told that Voltaire thought

Rasselas reflected "une philosophie aimable" and that it was "très bien écrit."[90] According to Boswell, Johnson felt that *Candide* had more power than "anything that Voltaire had written . . . that he was a good narrator, and that his principal merit consisted in a happy selection and arrangement of circumstances" (L, 3:356). Furthermore, Johnson remarked that French novels compared with Richardson's "might be pretty baubles, but that a wren was not an eagle" (L, 2:125). To be sure, Boswell does not fail to inform us that the two *Salonlöwen* were not always so gentle with each other.[91]

Will we be further advanced in our quest for common stylistic values if we compare an English translation of *Candide* with a French rendition of *Rasselas?* "Translated" to England, Cunégonde's diamonds shed their sparkle, their water clouds, and instead of dazzling us, they resemble rhinestones. The Prince's sallies lose their somber glow and faintly suggest chit-chat in a *Télémaque* rewritten by Fénelon's rival, the great Bossuet who, like Johnson, was a "Christian Tory."[92]

Mais revenons à nos moutons rouges and English mutton. It is a question, I repeat, of juxtaposing Voltaire's and Johnson's styles. To do this, we must make allowances for all that differentiates their respective mother tongues in order to restrict our inquiry to a comparison of effects created by differences in structure and rhythmic energy of which Johnson was well aware.[93] "The conversation now turned upon Mr. David Hume's style. JOHNSON. 'Why, Sir, his style is not English; the structure of his sentences is French. Now the French structure and the English structure may, in a nature of things, be equally good. But if you allow that the English language is established, he is wrong' "(L, 1:439).

Whether it will ever be possible to relate a deep English structure to a deep French structure by virtue of a stylistic transformational grammar is a question beyond the scope of this comparison, although one would like to dream of a Cunégonde lisping in Augustan numbers without offending the shades of Pope and Johnson, or of a Lady Pekuah tripping *à la française* and expiring over mute *e*'s without being faulted by the ghost from Ferney.

Both authors energize their respective messages to the point of defying the law of entropy. Equally intense, they differ in the distribution of their power. Johnson, whose purpose is essentially meditative, neither wants nor needs vulgar action to express his energy in plot, drama, or character but rather seeks to store it in carefully hewn "blocks of thought"—specific masses, which he then balances with incomparable finesse.[94] Voltaire, on the other hand, transmits his electrifying force to his marionettes, forever dodging, escaping, hiding like Montesquieu's Parisian "dans un mouvement perpétuel."[95] There is little, if any, meditation in *Candide*. Ira Wade comments:

> Thus *Candide*'s world is a world of action, varied, tense, contradictory, and paradoxical. It springs from many unknown sources and submerges those upon whom it falls; with constant pounding it beats out life. Whether it comes from forces in nature or in man-made institutions, it crushes and exasperates. Somehow one gets the impression that action produces energy and energy begets force and force is an evil thing. It must be met by another force which springs from another energy derived from counteraction. For the outside action pressing upon the individual brings forth a response which is another action. This naive action takes its source in the will to be. It leaves behind the dead past, traditional action, the absorbed evil action. It pushes forward, young, vigorous, eager, inexperienced, but confident that it can master by struggle, effort, and work the deadly past and the uncertain future. Creation in *Candide* is certainly the answer to universal destruction.[96]

The diction of both narrators remains uniform; the hermit perorates like Imlac, and Paquette narrates as smoothly as la Vieille. Far from being monotonous, such a stylistic consistency engenders amusing effects. Pekuah, on having been abducted, meets her captor, who consoles her in these terms: " 'Misfortunes,' answered the Arab, 'should always be expected. . . . Do not be disconsolate; I am not one of the lawless and cruel rovers of the desart; I know the rules of civil life' " (p. 167). In like fashion, the "Oreillons tout nuds," preparing to cook Cacambo and Candide, shout their delight in the silkiest of French: "C'est un Jésuite, c'est un Jésuite! Nous serons vengés, et nous ferons bonne chère; mangeons du

Jésuite, mangeons du Jésuite" (p. 98). This parallel stress on style and diction does not imply that language is superior to life but that it represents an independent domain, a man-made universe like mathematics, powerless to affect life and death: " 'What comfort,' " murmurs Johnson's philosopher who has lost his daughter, " 'can truth and reason afford me? of what effect are they now, but to tell me, that my daughter will not be restored?' The prince, whose humanity would not suffer him to insult misery with reproof, went away convinced of the emptiness of rhetorical sound, and the inefficacy of polished periods and studied sentences" (pp. 86–87).

Yet this very polish and rhetoric generate most of Johnson's witty effects, often masking subtle self-criticism. Three articles have been devoted to his sense of humor. The first, by C. R. Tracy, envisages Rasselas "as a silly ass, seeking obstinately for absolutes in a world where only relative values are to be found." The second, more penetrating essay, by Alvin Whitely, attempts to show that "*Rasselas* is not formless, but carefully and subtly planned and executed, not lyric but dramatic, not solemn but satiric and ironic." The third article, by Bate, is most to the point and reveals that Johnson, endowed with all the qualities of a great satirist, "had a hatred and fear of satire, which is what led him to be so antagonistic to Swift. To Johnson, Swift [substitute Voltaire] was a frightening example of what not to be, and all the more because of Johnson's own temptations. Against this background, Johnson's lifelong struggle for good humor (a 'willingness to be pleased') and his effort to suppress and check anger suddenly light up. They show that he did not dare to release the satiric impulse partly because it was so strong. But something else is involved—the charity and justice he is always bringing to 'helpless man.' He could not simply watch. He had to participate; and his own willing participation sets a bar to satire."[97] Bate proceeds to illustrate his notion of what he calls a "satire manquée" by analyzing chapter 18 to which I have just referred. In his recent biography of Samuel Johnson, he clarifies the concept under discussion: "It involves a kind of double action in which a strong satiric blow is about to strike home unerringly when another arm at once reaches out and deflects or rather lifts it" (B, 494).[98] However, it is also true that

Johnson could and did write prose satire whose blows are not deflected—for example, his review of Soame Jenyns's *Inquiry* as well as his many political pamphlets. Regardless of Johnson's ambivalent attitude concerning satire, the intensity of one's awareness of Johnson's comic and satiric effects is a direct function of one's capacity to respond to the ironic tension so characteristic of his "polished periods and sentences." Bergson's remark that "le comique s'adresse à l'intelligence pure"[99] bears out this assertion. There is no need to stress that Johnson was a master at creating and exploiting situational humor in literature as, for instance, in his "Dissertation on the Art of Flying" as well as in daily intercourse with his contemporaries. Boswell relates that Garrick had remarked to him: "Rabelais and all other wits are nothing compared with him. You may be diverted by them; but Johnson gives you a forcible hug, and shakes laughter out of you, whether you will or no" (L, 2:231).

Should one regret that Johnson never tried his hand at comic writing beyond the limits of his essays? After all, satire—*réussie ou manquée*—is but one face of comedy. Whatever one's opinion about this matter, *Candide* unquestionably exhibits a subtle, even ideal, balance between stylistic and situational humor, each intensifying the other. Starobinski, referring to Candide as "la victime dont on rit," qualifies him as an archetype.[100] At the risk of committing heresy, we should like to suggest that this aspect of *Candide* (the celebration of the victim who is ridiculed [the *auto da fé*], as well as Voltaire's brilliant manipulation of syllogisms to highlight and illustrate the preposterous logic of life) reminds us of components of Jewish wit whose essence is distilled from a bitter sense of gallows humor: "Hélas! dit le misérable à l'autre misérable" (p. 21).[101] On a superficial level, Voltaire mocks his fellow men, Jews included; but, if we consider his characters as projections of his psyche, then he becomes the butt of his own jokes, whether he knows it or not. André Delattre has laid bare Voltaire's tendency to deride his own feelings: "les rares fois qu'il touche à des sentiments personnels, il transpose aussitôt en ricanements, en quolibets, en bouffonnerie."[102] Such self-mockery seems quite consonant with Theodore Reik's views on the matter: "Yehovah has forbidden the

Jew of our time to express his tragic experiences in a way appealing
to a world that is hostile or, at best, indifferent. But by conferring
upon him the gift of wit, his God has given him the power to
speak of what he *suffers* [italics mine]."[103] Dare one replace the
word *Jew* with François-Marie Arouet, alias Candide? Is there pa-
thos behind his comic façade?

"Hast thou here found happiness at last?" (p. 61), asks Rasselas
of Imlac about his life in the Happy Valley. Imlac's reply could have
been given by the sexagenarian of Ferney: "I know not one of all
your attendants who does not lament the hour when he entered this
retreat. I am less unhappy than the rest, because I have a mind
replete with images, which I can vary and combine at pleasure" (p.
62). In a somewhat dogmatic article, Nicholas Joost affirms that
"on the oneiric level of the preconscious dream . . . *Rasselas* embodies the following experience: . . . man leaves the womb; he
struggles to attain maturity as an individual: defeated by these
struggles, he desires to return to the simplicity and the irrespon-
sibility of the foetal existence, i.e., to the happy valley." Joost
continues: "On the moral level of meaning, the interpretation is
more obvious: *Rasselas* is the story of man's loss of moral innocence,
his discovery of the vanity of all things of the natural life, and his
desire to regain that innocence."[104] Does this psychoanalytic
schema apply to *Candide* "chassé du paradis terrestre"? It is prefera-
ble, we believe, to postpone answering the question of existential
implications by first quoting Freud's conclusion to his *Wit and Its
Relation to the Unconscious:* "The pleasure in jokes has seemed to us
to arise from an economy in expenditure upon inhibition, the pleasure in the comic from an economy in expenditure upon ideation
(upon cathexis) and the pleasure in humour from an economy in
expenditure upon feeling. . . . All three are agreed in representing
methods of regaining from mental activity a pleasure which has in
fact been lost through the development of that activity."[105]

If we remember Johnson's and Voltaire's childhood, Freud's
analysis illuminates the sense of wit and humor in *Rasselas* and
Candide. André Delattre tells us that we know very little of Voltaire's early life; his mother died when he was young, "de même
des zones d'ombre s'étendent sur d'importantes parties de son

moi."[106] There had to be—there was pain in Voltaire's early years just as there was suffering in little Sam's life, physical and psychic torments that were to accompany him until his death. His was a self which "he felt to be unlovable, just as Michael [his father], as far as the son could see, was unlovable."[107] "Not only that," continues Bate, "he was also left completely naked and vulnerable to the cruelest of psychological burdens that he was to face throughout life" (B, 121). It was a burden which Voltaire indubitably shared, a "fierce and exacting sense of self-demand" (ibid.)—in short, the fearful pressure of the superego, merciless companion in any man's life.[108] With all these considerations in mind, the last sentence of Freud's *Jokes and Their Relation to the Unconscious* becomes quite meaningful for anyone trying to understand the implications of Johnson's and Voltaire's wit and humor: "For the euphoria which we endeavour to reach by these means is nothing other than the mood of a period of life in which we were accustomed to deal without psychical work in general with a small expenditure of energy—the mood of our childhood, when we were ignorant of the comic, when we were incapable of jokes and when we had no need of humour to make us feel happy in our life" (p. 236). A short commentary is in order: Freud does not claim that the presence of wit and humor implies that one was or was not happy in childhood, but only that wit and humor indicate that a drive one wanted to suppress was allowed to take its course with the least possible expenditure of psychic energy. It follows that, if one does not have any inhibitions, one does not need humor: *Wer keine Hemmungen hat, braucht keinen Humor.* How all this applies to Johnson and Voltaire seems obvious, especially in the case of Johnson.

But let us turn from Freud to literature. Rather than comparing eighteenth-century literary theories in France and England as well as reviewing the question of Voltaire's influence in England and of Johnson's views on French life and literature (topics outside the assigned limits of this confrontation), I should like to isolate incidents or moments in the two works where they parallel or intersect in literary theory and practice. Imlac's "Dissertation on Poetry" and chapter 22, "Ce qui arriva en France à Candide et à Martin," exemplify such an intersection; it occurs in a Parisian gambling den:

> Quel est, dit Candide, ce gros cochon qui me disait tant de
> mal de la piéce où j'ai tant pleuré, & des Acteurs qui m'ont
> fait tant de plaisir? C'est un mal vivant, répondit l'Abbé, qui
> gagne sa vie à dire du mal de toutes les piéces et de tous les
> livres; il hait quiconque réussit, comme les eunuques haïssent
> les jouissants; c'est un de ces serpents de la litterature qui se
> nourrissent de fange & de venin; c'est un
> folliculaire . . . Qu'appelez-vous un folliculaire? dit Candide.
> C'est, dit l'Abbé, un faiseur de feuilles, un F. (pp. 153–54)

Two remarks are in order. This outburst, as brutal as it is displeasing, shows how hate withers wit, especially when it strikes home (that is, Paris). Voltaire's smile becomes the proverbial rictus.[109] *Rasselas,* to be sure, betrays no trace of venom; its prevailing mood is characterized by sadness, illuminated by moments of cheerfulness. Quite indicative of a nonparallelism, is the reference to F. (Fréron), a writer whom Johnson visited during his trip to Paris in 1775 and to whom he delivered his considered opinion on Voltaire, which according to Donald Greene is "not too unjust": " 'Vir est acerrimi ingenii et paucarum litterarum' (A man of a most keen mind and scanty literature)."[110] Perhaps. If one wished to isolate an intersection between *Rasselas* and *Candide*—to find an artistic moment when one of Imlac's injunctions blossoms in a Voltairean event—one could point to the jolly meeting between Pangloss and a pretty worshipper of Allah:

> Un jour il me prit fantaisie d'entrer dans une Mosquée; il n'y
> avait qu'un vieux Iman, & une jeune dévote très-jolie qui disait
> ses Pate-nôtres: sa gorge était toute découverte: elle avait entre
> ses deux tetons un beau bouquet de tulipes, de roses,
> d'anémones, de renoncules, d'yacinthes, & d'oreilles d'ours:
> elle laissa tomber son bouquet; je le ramassai, & je le lui remis
> avec un empressement très-respectueux. Je fus si longtemps à
> le lui remettre, que l'Iman se mit en colère, et, voyant que
> j'étais Chrêtien, il cria à l'aide." (pp. 211–12)

Let us now review Pangloss's adventure in the light of Imlac's well-known injunctions: "The business of the poet . . . is to examine not the individual, but the species; to remark general properties and large appearances: he does not number the streaks of the tulip" (p. 50).[111] Imlac ends his lecture by emphasizing that the poet's "stile" must "be worthy of his thoughts . . . [that he] must, by incessant practice, familiarize to himself every delicacy of speech and grace of harmony" (p. 51).

One should note *en passant* that the Iman becomes angry not because Pangloss harasses the pretty worshipper but because it takes him so long. Are we justified, though, in relating the tulip in the *décolleté* to Imlac's tulip with or without streaks? Are we considering a meaningful intersection of Voltaire's and Johnson's thoughts, or are we dealing with a coincidence—a literary nul set, so to speak? To be sure, the latter is the case. Does Pangloss's story have poetic virtues worthy of Imlac's critical attention? Indeed it does, although one suspects that Johnson would not have acknowledged in this story, set against a bleak existential background, poetic values which a modern reader cannot fail to recognize: color, fragrance, feeling and, above all, music in the form of a melodious *courante* of vowels. And whereas Pangloss's enumerations before and after this episode are always comically scholastic, this one is lovely. It is Voltaire's voice we are hearing, not Pangloss's, but only for a moment. Beginning with the *oreilles d'ours,* the ensuing *double-entendre* "je le lui remis" safeguards his hopeless desire for youth against ridicule, real or imaginery. Once again, Voltaire has recourse to the same defensive strategy as in the declaration of love to his niece via Cunégonde: the projection of an aura of *impudeur* through a sexual innuendo, itself sterilized by wit. As for Maître Pangloss, does he not represent to perfection Imlac's "species," soon to be relegated to the level of *espèce* by Diderot's *neveu,* and is his final ukase on "stile" not met by Voltaire's proverbial "delicacy of speech and grace of harmony" (p. 51)?

Can we reverse the procedure to see whether Voltairean critical rules in *Candide* find a practical application in *Rasselas?* Unfortunately, Voltaire's two aliases in chapter 22, Madame de Parolignac and "l'homme sçavant de goût," express opinions that neither fit nor do justice to Johnson's achievement in *Rasselas.* The Marquise's exclamation concerning the *Mélanges* of the archdeacon T. curiously resemble Taine's sketch of Johnson: "Ah! . . . l'ennuieux mortel! comme il vous dit curieusement tout ce que le monde sçait comme il discute pesamment ce qui ne vaut pas la peine d'être remarqué légèrement!" (p. 160–61). As for *l'homme de goût,* he pontificates on tragedies of which there is no mention or sign in *Rasselas*. Besides, the apodictic injunction "être grand poëte, sans que jamais aucun personnage de la piéce paraisse poëte" (p. 161) censures Shakespeare and, by implication, Johnson's interpretation of him. In turn, Baretti (Johnson's friend as well as a translator of *Rasselas* into French), denigrates Voltaire's translation of "To be or not to be," affirming that the latter's rendition of the soliloquy has no more value than the translation of Fénelon's *Télémaque* by a "Demoiselle de dix ans dans les Ecoles de filles en Angleterre."[112] Furthermore, Pococurante's denigrations, all tongue-in-cheek, bear no relationship to Johnson's endeavors in *Rasselas*, not even to the chapter "The Wants of Him that wants Nothing," since the Prince's slight bout with *le mal du siècle* in the Happy Valley vibrates with preromantic overtones, while Pococurante's cold strictures lack any kind of feeling: "Oh! quel homme supérieur! disait Candide entre ses dents, quel grand génie que ce Pococurante! Rien ne peut lui plaire" (p. 194).

In truth, Voltaire's concise story has little, if any, kinship with his literary theories and with the neoclassical tragedies which he charged with his hopes for immortality. "No man was ever great by imitation" (p. 48), proclaims Imlac, and Voltaire's achievements illustrate this aphorism. How could he foresee that his *petit conte rococo* was to be his masterpiece? Does *Rasselas* play a similar role in relation to Johnson's other words, notably his essays in the *Rambler, Adventurer,* and *Idler?* One would have to answer in the negative, although Krutch notes that *Rasselas* "is actually more original, or at least more tinged with the color of Johnson's own personality, than seems to have been generally remarked."[113]

Further comparisons engender paradoxes of another kind. In *Rasselas,* so abstract and severe at first sight, "words are [still] the daughters of the earth,"[114] whereas in *Candide,* seemingly so *terre à terre* with its carnal puns, words may be likened to crystal bells, to melodious intellectual signs which are *des signifiants qui finissent par être leurs propres signifiés*.

For the sake of a final paradox, I shall agree with Joseph Wood Krutch who begins his comparison of our authors by declaring: "However antithetical the temperaments of the two men may have been, they find equally absurd the proposition that this is the best of all possible worlds in the simple sense that Pope had proclaimed when he wrote: 'All discord harmony not understood; / All partial evil universal good.'" But I must dissociate myself from Krutch when he *ends* his comparison by maintaining that "Johnson was, in one respect, more of a cynic than Voltaire, because Voltaire believed in the possibility of reform while Johnson did not."[115] For who would wish to offer, by way of consolation, *Candide* to anyone tormented by betrayal, pain, or death? When one suffers, Johnson makes for lighter reading than Voltaire because *Candide* ("une plaisanterie" as Grimm would have it or, according to Mme de Staël, "un ouvrage d'une gaieté infernale") does not sustain him or her who needs help. *Rasselas,* on the other hand, contains a balm, a delicate consolation for men and women no longer able to laugh or even to smile.[116]

If, by way of a conclusion, one had to find an eighteenth-century moralist whose most important article of faith harmonizes with the pietistic sighs that end *Rasselas,* one would have to point a finger at a strange personage promenading through the streets of London in 1762: a pseudo-Armenian seeking exile in England, the one thinker whom Johnson scorned almost as much as Voltaire and whom he thought to be a "very bad man . . . I would sooner sign a sentence for his transportation," he was heard to remark, "than that of any felon who has gone from the Old Bailey these many years. Yes, I should like to have him work in the plantations. . . . BOSWELL, 'Sir, do you think him as bad a man as Voltaire?' JOHNSON, 'Why, Sir, it is difficult to settle the proportion of iniquity between them'" (L, 2:12). Yet, irony of ironies, it is Jean-Jacques, tragic champion of "le plaisir d'être" and powerful antagonist of *les philosophes,* who matches Imlac's hope for an afterlife. Nowhere does Rousseau express it better than in his *Lettre sur la Providence,* a plea so passionate that its conclusion deserves to be quoted in full:

> Je ne puis m'empêcher, Monsieur, de remarquer à ce propos
> une opposition bien singulière entre vous et moi dans le sujet
> de cette lettre. Rassasié de gloire, et désabusé des vaines
> grandeurs, vous vivez libre au sein de l'abondance; bien sûr de
> l'immortalité, vous philosophez paisiblement sur la nature de
> l'ame; et si le corps ou le coeur souffre, vous avez Tronchin

pour médecin et pour ami: vous ne trouvez pourtant que mal
sur la terre. Et moi, obscur, pauvre et tourmenté d'un mal sans
remède, je médite avec plaisir dans ma retraite, et trouve que
tout est bien. D'où viennent ces contradictions apparentes?
Vous l'avez vous-même expliqué: vous jouissez; mais j'espère,
et l'espérance embellit tout.

Rousseau ends his epistle to Voltaire with a magnificent credo that
could have been known to Johnson had he not unfairly branded
Rousseau an infidel and, because of this chronic error, remained
deaf to his voice: "Non: j'ai trop souffert en cette vie pour n'en pas
attendre une autre. Toutes les subtilités de la Métaphysique ne me
feront pas douter un moment de l'immortalité de l'âme, et d'une
Providence bienfaisante. Je la sens, je la crois, je la veux, je l'espère, je la défendrai jusqu'à mon dernier soupir; et ce sera, de
toutes les disputes que j'aurai soutenues, la seule où mon intérêt ne
sera pas oublié."[117]

3 Speculations on Samuel Johnson's *Life of Savage* and Diderot's *Neveu de Rameau*

Le cas de la Reine de Naples était entièrement
différent, mais enfin il faut reconnaître que les
êtres sympathiques n'étaient pas du tout conçus
par elle comme ils le sont dans ces romans de
Dostoïevski qu'Albertine avaient pris dans ma
bibliothèque et accaparés, c'est-à-dire sous les
traits de parasites flagorneurs, voleurs, ivrognes,
tantôt insolents, débauchés, au besoin assassins
— Proust, *La Prisonnière*

Was gehen mich eigentlich meine Schmarotzer an?
—Nietzsche

What, one may ask, does Johnson's melancholic biography
have in common with Diderot's crisp satire? What values might
they share and how might they differ in terms of style and dramatic
structure? To answer these and related questions, we must first
ascertain the degree to which these works embody, each in different
proportions, artistic elements drawn from autobiography, biography, fiction, and satire. Having done so, we may then proceed to
assay the moral truths emanating from the two masterpieces which
occupy unique positions in France and England. However, before
attending to the delicate task of unraveling the four strands from
the fabric of the *Life of Savage* and the *Neveu de Rameau,* we should
make the acquaintance of their subjects, two outsiders so unusual

in character and way of life that their portraits are as unforgettable as they are disquieting.

Jean-François Rameau, mediocre nephew of the illustrious composer of *Les Indes Galantes*, was notorious enough to attract the attention of Mercier and Cazotte, two contemporaries of Diderot, who confirm many aspects of his brilliant portrayal. We meet the *neveu* in the Café de la Régence during a rainy afternoon. After concluding a conversation with Moi, who is and is not Diderot, Lui vanishes, never to be mentioned again by Diderot, who first composed fragments of his satire in 1760 and may have revised it as late as 1782. [1] Johnson's *Life of Savage*, published in 1744, tells the story of the self-styled illegitimate son of the Countess of Macclesfield, a man born in 1697 and deceased on August 1, 1743. Although Savage was ultimately quite successful in convincing his contemporaries of his claim to be the Countess's son by Earl Rivers, three of Johnson's biographers (Hawkins, Boswell, and Mrs. Piozzi) came to doubt his assertions; according to Boswell, Savage left the world to "vibrate in a state of uncertainty" concerning his birthright (L, 1:174).

Johnson knew Savage well. He also loved him. Every page of the *Life* attests to his affection for the extraordinary outsider, one of his companions during those early years Johnson spent in the English capital—lean years that caused Boswell to comment: "it is melancholy to reflect that Johnson and Savage were sometimes in such extreme indigence that they could not pay for a lodging" (L, 1:163). How can one compare the story of a man in whose company the author has subsisted on cold water and stale bread to the history of a man known to his interlocutor only casually in Paris over a period spanning two decades? The intimacy of close acquaintance is, for Johnson, the very precondition for a biography, "for nobody can write the life of a man, but those who have eat and drunk and lived in social intercourse with him" (L, 2:166). Yet, while it is true that Diderot's encounters with Jean-François Rameau were haphazard and surely not sustained by friendship, Diderot knew only too well the poverty that persecuted Rameau during his entire life. Lui reminds Moi in no uncertain terms of those impecunious years when he strolled through the squares of

Paris with straw in his boots: "La, monsieur le philosophe, la main sur la conscience, parlez net. Il y eut un temps ou vous n'etiez pas cossu comme aujourd'hui" (p. 28). And just as Lui expresses many of Diderot's intimate feelings ("ces choses qu'on pense, d'apres les quelles on se conduit; mais qu'on ne dit pas" [p. 93]), so Richard Savage, as recalled by Johnson, is endowed with a Johnsonian aura. Because of this parallelism, one discerns in Johnson's *Life of Savage* and Diderot's *Neveu de Rameau* contrasts and resemblances which, in turn, emphasize meaningful differences and similarities between Denis Diderot, *la girouette* (the weathervane) from Langres, and Samuel Johnson, the pride of Lichfield.

To the best of my knowledge, not even John Morley, equally at home on both sides of the Channel, has pointed to the typological and thematic concordances between the *neveu* and Savage or, for that matter, has linked the author of the *Dictionary*, who reigned over the conversationalists of London, to the editor of the *Encyclopédie*, the most brilliant talker in Paris.[2] This silence seems especially noteworthy, since it is probable that young Diderot, while translating Dr. James's *Medicinal Dictionary* alongside Eidous and Toussaint, may have transposed Johnsonian periods into lissome French.[3] Never does he breathe a word about England's most famous man of letters. This oversight is even more surprising, if one recalls that David Garrick—one of Johnson's few students in Edial, Staffordshire, whence master and pupil left for London on one horse in a scene reminiscent of *Jacques le Fataliste* or *Joseph Andrews*—became a friend to Diderot. The latter in turn wrote *l'Eloge de Richardson*, while the printer-novelist saved Johnson from going to debtors' prison by lending him a few pounds. When Hume and Wilkes, close friends of Diderot, visited Paris in 1763, did they never speak to him of the great Cham of Literature? And what about Gibbon, or Horace Walpole, who was in Paris in 1765 and 1766 and who enjoyed the distinction of being the only Englishman Diderot ever detested. What about *le père* Hoop of whom he was so fond, a gloomy Scot by the name of Hope, who had been a trader, physician, and even a visitor to China? Is it likely that these knowledgable visitors never referred to the author of *The Rambler* (1750–52), *A Dictionary of the English Language* (1755), and *The Idler* (1758–60)? Voltaire, to be sure, knew of *le sieur* Johnson, whose *Rasselas* appeared in 1759, the same year as *Candide*.

Loyalty Cru, author of the delightful *Diderot and English Thought*, expresses surprise that Boswell "was not as eager as Gibbon to seek the acquaintance of Diderot, as he had sought that of Voltaire, Rousseau and many more"[4]—James Boswell, the great interviewer, who in 1766 accompanied Thérèse Levasseur from Paris to Chiswick (all the while making love to her), where Rousseau, lodged at the home of a grocer, was waiting for her. Is it not curious that this extraordinary go-between never dreamt of pitting the greatest of English monologists against *le maître ès dialogue* (in Emile Faguet's opinion "des monologues animés")[5]—an encounter that would surely have been as memorable as the one he planned for Johnson and Rousseau, which to the regret of all never took place. Not once does Boswell mention Diderot. Neither does Johnson. Yet the latter, during his jaunt to Paris in 1775, found it worthwhile to pay his respects to Fréron and to befriend Benedictine monks, while avoiding all haunts frequented by *infidels*, English, French or German.[6] Loyalty Cru concludes his chapter on "Diderot, the Critic," by stressing the incompatibility of Diderot's poetic taste with that of Johnson:

> His favorite English poets were exactly those whom Samuel Johnson was most unwilling or most unable to appreciate: Gray, Young, MacPherson, alias Ossian: It is truly curious to see two men so eminently representative of their respective countries during the latter half of the eighteenth century, and each of whom seems to have carefully avoided mentioning the other by name, judge English poetry from two absolutely opposite standpoints. . . . Johnson harked back to the artistic gospel of the past; Diderot hailed with enthusiasm the inspiration of the future.[7]

Unfortunately, the facts do not bear out all of Cru's antithetical conclusions, for Johnson treats Young's poetry with considerable respect, especially his major works, *The Universal Passion* and *Night Thoughts*.

Although Diderot never wrote nor, it would seem, pro-

nounced the name of Samuel Johnson, he did write a review of a
volume entitled *Histoire de Richard Savage, suivie de la Vie de Thom-
son* (Paris, 1771), which had been translated by the indefatigable
Félicien Prime Le Tourneur, Shakespeare's first French translator:

> *L'Histoire de Savage,* poëte anglais, vient d'être traduite en
> français par M. Le Tourneur. Ce M. Le Tourneur est le même
> qui a traduit les *Nuits d'Young,* poëme du plus beau noir qu'il
> soit possible d'imaginer, et que le traducteur a trouvé le secret
> de faire lire à un peuple dont l'esprit est couleur de rose. Il est
> vrai que cette teinte commence à se faner. M. Le Tourneur
> entend très-bien la langue anglaise, et écrit la nôtre d'une
> manière nombreuse et pure.
>
> Cette *Histoire de Savage* attache; c'est la peinture d'un
> homme malheureux, d'un caractère bizarre, d'un génie
> bouillant; d'un individu tantôt bienfaisant, tantôt malfaisant;
> tantôt fier, tantôt vil, moitié vrai, moitié faux, en tout, plus
> digne de compassion que de haine, de mépris que d'éloge;
> agréable à entendre, dangereux à fréquenter; la meilleure leçon
> qu'on puisse recevoir sur les inconvénients du commerce des
> poëtes, leur peu de principes, de morale et de tenue.
>
> Cet ouvrage eût été délicieux, et d'une finesse à comparer
> aux *Mémoires du Comte de Grammont,* si l'auteur anglais se fût
> proposé de faire la satire de son héros; mais malheureusement il
> est de bonne foi.
>
> Le récit de la vie du malheureux Savage, fils d'Anne,
> comtesse de Manlesfield, qui, pour se séparer de son mari, avec
> lequel elle vivait mal, s'avoua grosse des faits et gestes du
> comte Rivers, est coupé par des morceaux extraits des
> différents ouvrages de Savage, et presque tous fort beaux.
>
> C'est une étrange femme que cette comtesse de
> Manlesfield, qui poursuit un enfant de l'amour avec une rage
> qui se soutient pendant de longues années, qui ne s'éteint
> jamais, et qui n'est fondée sur rien. Si un poëte s'avisait
> d'introduire, dans un drame ou dans un roman, un caractère de
> cette espèce, il serait sifflé; il est cependant dans la nature. On
> siffle donc quelquefois la nature? Et pourquoi non? Ne le
> mérite-t-elle jamais?
>
> La Vie de Savage est suivie de celle de Thomson, l'auteur
> des *Saisons* et de quelques tragédies. Rien à dire de celui-ci,
> sinon que c'était le revers de l'autre; aussi son histoire est-elle
> très-fastidieuse à lire. Il faut, pour le bonheur de ceux qui ont
> à traiter avec un homme, qu'il ressemble à Thomson; pour
> l'intérêt et l'amusement du lecteur, qu'il ressemble à Savage.[8]

How strange: not a word, not a whisper, about the *Neveu de Rameau* (unknown to Grimm and perhaps even to Sophie Volland), whose character is partially summarized in the second paragraph of the book review. Equally reminiscent of the *Neveu de Rameau* is the last sentence of the review which corresponds, roughly speaking, to the sense of an introductory statement by Moi in which he declares: "Je n'estime pas ces originaux la . . . Ils m'arrêtent une fois l'an, quand je les rencontre, parce que leur caractere tranche avec celui des autres" (p. 5). Savage, like the *neveu*, amuses and interests the reader: "c'est un grain de levain qui fermente" (p. 5). Is this similarity in regard to themes a mere coincidence? Are the discrepancies between the two books too harsh to warrant a confrontation?

Admittedly, a glance at the introductory pages of *Le Neveu de Rameau* and the *Life of Savage* scarcely offers a promise of tempting analogies. The English biographer presents us with a "mournful narrative" about a youth who, "born with a legal Claim to Honour and to Riches . . . was in two Months illegitimated by the Parliament, and disowned by his Mother, doomed to Poverty and Obscurity, and launched upon the Ocean of Life, only that he might be swallowed by its Quicksands, or dashed upon its Rocks" (p. 6). Diderot's opening paragraphs, on the contrary, shimmer with sunshine and good cheer. Who can forget Diderot's reminiscence of himself, seated on the Banc d'Argenson by the Palais Royal, musing about this and that and likening his uninhibited reflections to snub-nosed Parisian strumpets plying their trade: "Mes pensées, ce sont mes catins" (p. 3). Yet, despite the numerous contrasts between Diderot's lively dialogue in which Lui challenges Moi and Johnson's sad account of a failure, we shall discover that Savage's life and character dovetail at times with those depicted in the introductory sketch of the *neveu*, whom we meet at the headquarters of the best chess players in town: "C'est un composé de hauteur et de bassesse, de bon sens et de deraison. Il faut que les notions de l'honnete et du deshonnete soient bien etrangement brouillées dans sa tête; car il montre ce que la nature lui a donné de bonnes qualités, sans ostentation, et ce qu'il en reçu de mauvaises, sans pudeur" (p. 4).

Who were the men that served as models or inspiration for our authors? To answer this question, I shall have to cite facts obvious to either Johnson or Diderot scholars but not to both. Most Diderot scholars know little if anything about the *Life of Savage*, and only a few Johnsonians seem to have taken the time to reread *Le Neveu de Rameau*. Thus, what is elementary to the English is news to the French, and vice versa. Yet I hope that the reciprocal illumination, by way of contrast, may redefine sets of orthodox viewpoints concerning the two masterpieces.

Who was Jean-François Rameau?[9] Born in Dijon, this musician, soldier, seminarian, and nephew of the great composer Jean-Philippe Rameau was in Jean Fabre's words "un musicien génial, mais sur un violon ou un clavecin imaginaires; un être abject mais délivré de son abjection par la fierté qu'il en tire ou la conscience qu'il en prend; tout voisin du tragique lorsqu'il bouffonne, jamais plus bouffon que lorsqu'il voudrait être sérieux" (p. xliv). Cazotte, who had been his schoolmate and lifelong friend, remembers him with affection:

> Ce personnage, l'homme le plus extraordinaire que j'aie connu, étoit né, avec un talent naturel dans plus d'un genre, que le défaut d'assiette de son esprit ne lui permit jamais de cultiver. Je ne puis comparer son genre de plaisanterie qu'à celui que déploie le docteur Sterne dans son *Voyage sentimental*. Les saillies de Rameau étoient des saillies d'instinct d'un genre si piquant qu'il est nécessaire de les peindre pour pouvoir essayer de les rendre. Ce n'étoient point des bons mots: c'étoient des traits qui sembloient partir de la plus parfaite connoissance du coeur humain. (pp. 250–51)

Is this expertise in matters pertaining to the heart, practiced by a manifest failure, not reminiscent of Johnson's remark that his troubled hero's chief attainment was "the Knowledge of Life" (p. 136)? Cazotte continues: "Il vécut pauvre ne pouvant suivre aucune profession. Sa pauvreté absolue lui faisoit honneur dans mon esprit. . . . Il a donné en plusieurs occasions des preuves de la bonté de son coeur. Cet homme singulier vécut passionné pour la gloire, qu'il ne pouvoit acquérir dans aucun genre" (p. 251). Similarly, Johnson informs his reader—without irony—that "Compassion was indeed the distinguishing Quality of *Savage*" (p. 41) and that "the great Hardships of Poverty were to *Savage* not the Want of

Lodging or of Food, but the Neglect and Contempt which it drew upon him. He complained that as his Affairs grew desperate . . . his Opinion of Questions of Criticism was no longer regarded, when his Coat was out of Fashion" (p. 101). History relates that the *neveu* ran afoul of the police and was almost exiled to the Antilles or New Orleans—a dismal prospect, reminiscent of Lady Macclesfield's purported plot to rid herself of her son by shipping him off to the American plantations. Furthermore, Savage kills a man during a tavern brawl (one thinks of Villon) yet succeeds in cheating the gallows at Newgate through the intercession of friends, among them Pope. Both men die in confinement: Savage in prison, Jean-François Rameau locked up by his kith and kin in a *maison religieuse* where he, like Savage, conquers the hearts of his keepers.

The discrepancy between the flesh-and-blood Savage who prowled about the streets of London and the life of Savage as filtered through Johnson's imagination seems less noticeable than that between Jean-François Rameau and Diderot's portrait of him. I say "seems" because Richard Savage's *Leben an sich* differs considerably from the story told by his genial and charitable biographer. Such is the view also of Clarence Tracy, who declares in his witty and detailed biography *The Artificial Bastard* that Johnson's *Life,* "though one of the finest works of eighteenth-century biography and a penetrating study of personality, is factually unreliable."[10] Abandoned by his parents, the child is left in the charge of his godmother Mrs. Lloyd, "who while she lived always looked upon him with that Tenderness, which the Barbarity of his Mother made peculiarly necessary" (p. 7). After her death the boy is reared by Lady Mason, who places him in a grammar school near St. Albans where he is called after the name of his nurse without his having "the least Intimation that he had a Claim to any other" (p. 7). On discovering some papers that inform him of his identity, Savage, during the rest of his life, seeks acceptance by his mother who steadfastly rejects his filial overtures. Diderot's comments on the countess's action reveal his concern with the question of *vraisemblance,* and one wishes that he had read Johnson's *Preface to Shakespeare,* in which the latter declares what should have been obvious to Voltaire: "Delusion, if delusion be admitted, has no certain limitation. . . . The truth is, that the spectators are always in their senses, and know, from the first act to the last, that the stage is only a stage, and that the players are only players."[11] To be sure, Diderot questions the verisimilitude of Mother Nature and not that of a drama; moreover, he does so tongue in cheek since, with the exception of Sade, no thinker of the Enlightenment has a clearer premonition of the possibility of monsters and mutants.

Savage is not without friends. Among these is Steele, who tells him that "*the Inhumanity of his Mother had given him a Right to find every good Man his Father*" (p. 13) [author's italics]. Steele even proposes to the "bastard" that he marry his natural daughter, on whom Steele plans to bestow a thousand pounds whenever he can find the money. Savage, however, cannot forego ridiculing his prospective "father-in-law" and is soon banished from his house. Having received financial aid from the actor Mr. Wilks and the beautiful actress Mrs. Oldfield, he devotes his efforts to writing a tragedy entitled *Sir Thomas Overbury* under circumstances quite similar to those evoked by one of Johnson's friends:

> The clock just struck two, the expiring taper rises and sinks in the socket, the watchman forgets the hour in slumber, the laborious and the happy are at rest, and nothing wakes but meditation, guilt, revelry and despair. The drunkard once more fills the destroying bowl, the robber walks his midnight round, and the suicide lifts his guilty arm against his own sacred person. . . . But who are those who make the streets their couch, and find a short repose from wretchedness at the doors of the opulent? These are strangers, wanderers, and orphans, whose circumstances are too humble to expect redress, and distresses are too great even for pity. Their wretchedness excites rather horror than pity. Some are without the covering of rags, and others emaciated with disease; the world has disclaimed them.[12]

Thus writes Lien Chi Altangi, alias Oliver Goldsmith, in his Chinese reportage on "London by Night," an urban scene known only too well to Savage and to his biographer. And lest French readers discount these horrors because of Goldsmith's propensity to be sentimental, it is worthwhile to listen to Hawkins, author of *The Life of Samuel Johnson, LLD.*: "Johnson has told me, that whole nights have been spent by him and Savage . . . in a perambulation round the squares of Westminster, St. James's in particular, when all the money they could both raise was less than sufficient to purchase for them the shelter and sordid comforts of a night cellar" (H, 53). Johnson's *Life of Savage* corroborates this account of extraordinary privation: "He lodged as much by Accident as he dined and passed the Night, sometimes in mean Houses, which are set open at Night to any casual Wanderers, sometimes in Cellars among the Riot and Filth of the meanest and most profligate of Rabble; and sometimes, when he had no Money to support even the Expences of these Receptacles, walked about the Streets till he was weary, and lay down in the Summer upon a Bulk, or in the Winter with his Associates in Poverty, among the Ashes of a Glass-house" (p. 97). Among these "associates," of course, figures Johnson, always poor and giving the little he has to the first-come—be it a blind man or an ailing prostitute. One need not be hypersensitive to understand the awful reality that pervades the rhythm of Johnson's stately prose; for, at the time he is writing the life of his wayward friend, he himself is so destitute that he is obliged to hide from visitors: "Soon after Savage's *Life* was published, Mr. Harte dined with Edward Cave [one of Johnson's editors], and occasionally praised it. Soon after, meeting him, Cave said, 'You made a man very happy t'other day.'—'How could that be,' says Harte; 'nobody was there but ourselves.' Cave answered, by reminding him that a plate of victuals was sent behind a screen, which was to Johnson, dressed so shabbily, that he did not choose to appear; but on hearing the conversation, was highly delighted with the encomiums on his book'" (L, 1:163, n. 1).

Young Diderot too knew want and perhaps hunger but by 1760, the approximate date of the first version of *Le Neveu de Rameau,* had managed to secure for himself a satisfactory degree of bourgeois comfort. As a result, his evocation of the *neveu*'s tribulations represents a narrative that parallels the chronicle of Savage's trials in thought but not in feeling: "La nuit amene aussi son inquietude. Ou il regagne, a pié, un petit grenier qu'il habite, à moins que l'hotesse ennuyée d'attendre son loyer, ne lui en ait redemandé la clef; ou il se rabbat dans une taverne du faubourg ou il attend le jour, entre un morceau de pain et un pot de bierre. Quand il n'a pas six sols dans sa poche, ce qui lui arrive quelquefois, il a recours soit à un fiacre de ses amis, soit au cocher d'un grand seigneur qui lui donne un lit sur de la paille, a coté de ses chevaux. Le matin, il a encore une partie de son matelat dans ses cheveux" (p. 5). Are such thematic coincidences coincidental? Savage descends as quickly as he rises on Boethius's wheel of fortune: "To supply him with Money was a hopeless Attempt, for no sooner did he see himself Master of a Sum sufficient to set him free from Care for a Day, than he became profuse and luxurious. When once he had entred a Tavern . . . he never retired till Want of Money obliged him to some new Expedient" (p. 99). Thus, concludes Johnson: "he spent his Life between Want and Plenty, or what was yet worse, between Beggary and Extravagance; for as whatever he received was the Gift of Chance . . . " (p. 43). Likewise, the *neveu* oscillates between rags and riches: "Aujourdhuy, en linge sale, en culote dechirée, couvert de lambeaux, presque sans souliers, il va la tete basse. . . . Demain, poudré, chaussé, frisé, bien vetu, il marche la tete haute" (p. 4).

Savage and the *neveu* are hangers-on. *Pauvreté oblige.* Lord Tyrconnel is to Savage what Bertin is to the *neveu*—the patron whose wealth "makes right," who has to be flattered, and whose mistress or wife (La Hus or Lady Tyrconnel) must be cajoled with poems and pleased with menial service: "Les bras etendus vers la deesse, chercher son desir dans ses yeux, rester suspendu a sa levre, attendre son ordre et partir comme un eclair" (p. 49). Both spongers know their hour of triumph: "J'étois comme un coq en pate. On me fêtoit. On ne me perdoit pas un moment sans me regretter. J'etois leur petit Rameau, leur joli Rameau, leur Rameau le fou, l'impertinent" (p. 18). Savage also enjoys moments of great popularity: "his Appearance was splendid, his Expences large, and his Acquaintance extensive. . . . To admire Mr. *Savage* was a Proof of Discernment. . . . His Presence was sufficient to make any Place of publick Entertainment popular" (p. 44). Diderot and Johnson go to great lengths to emphasize the tragicomic nature of their "heroes," whose presence constitutes a danger to those who protect them. Commenting on Savage's freedom to observe "the looser moments" and domestic behavior of his masters, Johnson declares: "More Circumstances to constitute a Critic on human Life could not easily concur, nor indeed could any Man who assumed from accidental Advantages more Praise than he could justly claim from his real Merit, admit an Acquaintance more dangerous than that of Savage" (p. 64). Lui states the issue more succinctly: "Quand on se resout à vivre avec des gens comme nous, et qu'on a le sens commun, il y a je ne scais combien de noirceurs auxquelles il faut s'attendre . . . Il y a un pacte tacite qu'on nous fera du bien, et que tot ou tard nous rendrons le mal pour le bien qu'on nous aura fait" (p. 68). Here Diderot states, in essence, the idea expressed in his book review of *La Vie de Richard Savage*: that poets like Savage make dangerous friends—a commonplace in eighteenth-century England and France until the Romantic sanctification of the writer. In any case, Savage's judgments are as merciless as those by the *neveu:* "Of one particular Person, who has been at one Time so popular as to be generally esteemed, and at another so formidable as to be universally detested, he observed, that his Acquisitions had been small, or that his Capacity was narrow, and that the whole Range of his Mind was from Obscenity to Politics, and from Politics to Obscenity" (p. 65).

Shortly after committing homicide, Savage is rescued by Lady Macclesfield's nephew: "Lord Tyrconnel, whatever were his Motives, upon his [Savage's] Promise to lay aside his Design of exposing the Cruelty of his Mother, received him into his Family, treated him as an Equal, and engaged to allow him a Pension of two hundred pounds a Year" (p. 44). Johnson describes vividly some of Savage's misdeeds which cause his fall from grace (selling Tyrconnel's finely bound books and making free of his wine cellar): "He was banished from the Table of *Lord Tyrconnel,* and turned again adrift upon the World, without Prospect of finding quickly any other Harbour" (p. 65). Savage fails to read the handwriting on the wall, and his disgrace surprises him like "a Stroke of Thunder" (p. 66). Indeed, he may have deluded himself like his French double: "il me passa par la tete une pensée funeste, une pensée qui me donna de la morgue, une pensée qui m'inspira de la fierté et de l'insolence: c'est qu'on ne pouvoit se passer de moi, que j'étois un homme essentiel" (p. 65).

The belief that one is indispensable ranks high among childhood illusions, especially when nurtured by family affection; Savage, the bastard, may well have reinforced his ego by inflating it to the point of not being able to "bear to conceive himself in a State of Dependence, his Pride being equally powerful with his other Passions, and appearing in the form of Insolence at one time and of Vanity at another. Vanity the most innocent Species of Pride, was most frequently predominant: he could not easily leave off when he had once begun to mention himself or his Works, nor ever read his Verses without stealing his Eyes from the Page, to discover in the Faces of his Audience, how they were affected with any favourite Passage" (p. 138). The pleasure of performing in front of a captive audience is only too well known to Johnson and Diderot, and Lui's pantomime expresses, albeit in a distorted manner, one of Moi's unfulfilled cravings.

Reflecting on Johnson's biography, one realizes how much his tragic hero is lacking in self-knowledge, which is as harmful as it is beneficial, for one's *coeur mis à nu* can precipitate enduring sadness. What peace could psychoanalytic wisdom have offered a man like Savage, pursuing his mother and bereft of a father?[13] Yet one is tempted to imagine a *dialogue des morts* à la Fontenelle in which Diderot-Moi enlightens Savage with Freudian insights: "Si le petit sauvage étoit abandonné a lui-même; qu'il conservat toute son imbecillité et qu'il reunit au peu de raison de l'enfant au berceau la violence des passions de l'homme de trente ans, il tordroit le col a son pere et coucheroit avec sa mere" (p. 95). Relevant also are the perceptive comments of John A. Dussinger: "Some of the most remarkable passages in this biography are those conveying Savage's obsession with his mother in imagery hinting at the Oedipus complex. The child's dream of union with the mother is projected in Savage's endless wanderings in streets and his frustrations in entering houses, especially his mother's house, which seems to be identified with her personality: '. . . it was his frequent Practice to walk in the dark Evenings for several hours before her Door, in Hopes of seeing her as she might come by Accident to the Window, or cross her Apartment with a Candle in her Hand'" (p. 12). Dussinger goes on to quote what is perhaps the most dramatic passage in *The Life of Savage:* "One Evening walking, as it was his Custom, in the Street that she inhabited, he saw the Door of her House by Accident open; he entered it, and finding none in the Passage, to hinder him, went up Stairs to salute her. She discovered him before he could enter her Chamber" (P. 37).[14] Savage is the "petit sauvage" with the passions of a thirty-year-old man, and Johnson compares his friend to "a Child *exposed* to all Temptation of Indigence, at an Age when Resolution [is] not yet strengthened by Conviction" (p. 75). Diderot's *neveu* knows the reasons for his disaster, if not as a theoretical analyst, at least as a practicing parasite: "Le grand chien que je suis . . . J'ai tout perdu pour avoir eu le sens commun, une fois, une seul fois en ma vie. . . . La sottise d'avoir eu un peu de gout, un peu d'esprit, un peu de raison" (p. 19).

Despite Savage's blindness to his own faults, his dignity does not forsake him. The following episode has often been compared to the well-known anecdote of Johnson's "spirited refusal of an eleemosynary supply of shoes" (L, 1:77). Writes the poor but proud biographer of his proud and poor poet: "He never admitted any gross Familiarities, or submitted to be treated otherwise than as an equal. Once when he was without Lodging, Meat, or Cloaths, one of his Friends, a Man not indeed remarkable for Moderation in his Prosperity, left a Message, that he desired to see him about nine in the Morning. *Savage* knew that his Intention was to assist him, but was very much disgusted, that he should presume to prescribe the Hour of his Attendance, and, I believe, refused to visit him, and rejected his Kindness" (p. 99). The *neveu* has his own brand of pride: "Je veux bien etre abject, mais je veux que ce soit sans contrainte" (p. 46), and he proceeds to elaborate his theory of the immoral and amoral genius whose achievements change "la face du globe" (p. 9). Lui avoids the question of guilt and, in so doing, aligns himself with Bordeu who, after condemning sexual continence, exclaims to Mademoiselle de Lespinasse: "Je veux qu'on se porte bien, je le veux absolument, entendez-vous?"[15] Savage ignores guilt, at least on a conscious level. Brushing away any censure of his works and manner of living, Savage at times resembles a tragic Monsieur Jourdain. The open-minded Johnson never scorns those who delude themselves, be they drunkards in an alley or dispossessed hacks: "He [Savage] was never made wiser by his Sufferings, nor preserved by one Misfortune from falling into another. He proceeded throughout his Life to tread the same Steps on the same Circle; always applauding his past Conduct, or at least forgetting it, to amuse himself with Phantoms of Happiness, which were dancing before him (p. 74). "*Savage, . . .* always able to live at Peace with himself" (p. 73), maintains a philosophical equanimity also characteristic of Lui: "Such were his Misfortunes, which yet he bore not only with Decency, but with Cheerfulness, nor was his Gaiety clouded even by his last Disappointment, though he was in short Time reduced to the lowest Degree of Distress, and often wanted both Lodging and Food" (p. 109). Thus we have the story of Savage, poor though serene, whose life is told in the tragic mood, and the spectacle of Lui, cheerful, destitute, and never missed. The Diogenes of London dies in jail; the one in Paris disappears with a final challenge to posterity: "Rira bien qui rira le dernier" (p. 109).

Gods need not sponge, for customarily ambrosia abounds; when there is a shortage, they visit a Philemon and Baucis. But men are always hungry. Parasites (*para-sitos,* meaning "near grain or food"), like parasitic worms, thrive on hosts, other organisms, and obtain from them victuals in exchange for flattery and other services. Praise of the patron should be subtle and, above all, explains Lui: "il ne faut pas toujours approuver de la meme maniere. On seroit monotone. On auroit l'air faux. On deviendroit insipide" (p. 50). Savage lacks such finesse. "His compliments," writes Johnson, "are constrained and violent, heaped together without the Grace of Order, or the Decency of Introduction: he seems to have written his Panegyrics for the Perusal only of his Patrons" (pp. 29–30). Silky subservience and a deft willingness to play the fool are indispensable prerequisites. Lui's contention, "Il n'y point de meilleur role aupres des grands que celui de fou" (p. 61), rings like an echo of Swift's voice, which in turn echoes that of Erasmus: "He that can with *Epicurus* content his Ideas with the *Film* and *Images* that fly off upon his Senses from the Superficies of Things; such a Man truly wise, creams off Nature, leaving the

Sower and the Dregs, for Philosophy and Reason to lap up. This is the sublime and refined Point of Felicity, called, the Possession of being well Deceived; the Serene and Peaceful State of being a Fool among Knaves."[16]

These lines by Swift remind us of the satirical intention of *Le Neveu de Rameau*, which is to mock and punish as well as to relieve the bile of its author. Johnson's biography, on the other hand, remains uniformly serious in its evaluation of Savage the poet and parasite. Roughly speaking, an inverse function governs the relationship between biography and satire, as, for example, in Proust's evocation of the Baron de Charlus, who is first perceived as an instinctual monster but gradually turns into a person for whom we feel pity. Moi, however, has no compassion for Lui—a lack of sympathy which desensitizes the *neveu*. In the words of Jacques Proust: "Le Neveu, comme la machine à tricoter, est à sa manière un monstre, un prodige."[17] *Von Seele keine Rede.* Georges May states the problem in different terms: "L'effort d'imagination et de lucidité que fait Diderot quand il campe le personnage du Neveu est rendu extrêmement difficile par sa complexité: il est à la fois effort de critique du réel et de recréation de ce réel sous la forme de l'artificiel. En tant que personnage romanesque, le Neveu procède d'un jugement moral porté par Denis Diderot sur Jean-François Rameau et simultanément de la gestation d'un personnage nouveau."[18] Herbert Dieckmann elaborates a similar idea: "Diderot n'est pas auteur réaliste parce qu'il *copie* des personnages réels et vivants; il les comprend dans leur réalité et matérialité, car ils sont en lui à l'état d'idées. Aussi ne décrit-il point ces personnages; il les crée dans et par le dialogue. Ses personnages se manifestent par la parole." Elsewhere he writes, commenting on Diderot's concern with the milieu of any given character: "Il comprenait le Neveu de Rameau comme Rembrandt comprenait les mendiants des rues d'Amsterdam."[19] Here I disagree. If anyone understood beggars as well as Rembrandt, it was Samuel Johnson and not Diderot. To be sure, Diderot was free with his purse and mind when dealing with destitute friends and strangers but not always free with his heart, as attested by his cruel words concerning his former friend Rousseau. Less satire and more *Daseinsnot* might have raised the *neveu* to

Dostoyevskian or Proustian levels of truth. We only need to remember Falstaff to have a measure of Diderot's inadequacy as
creator of a memorable sponger who makes an ineradicable impression on the beholder's consciousness:

> I know thee not, old man. Fall to thy prayers.
> How ill white hairs become a fool or jester!
> I have long dreamt of such a kind of man,
> So surfeit-swelled, so old, and so profane,
> But being awaked, I do despise my dream.
> (*Henry IV*, Pt.2, 5.5.47–51)[20]

The *neveu* occupies, however, a place of honor in Hegel's Pantheon, and few critics have written more felicitously on the philosopher's interpretation of Diderot's satire than Lionel Trilling:
"Hegel represents the Nephew as the exemplary figure of the modern phase of developing Spirit and welcomes his advent with hiero-
phantic glee."[21] But, as everyone knows, concepts concerning existence, whether by Hegel about Lui or by Lui concerning himself,
do not suffice to create a human being in the mind of the reader,
unless these concepts are fleshed out, vivified, *beseelt* by the writer's
magic and skill. "A work," asserts Proust, "in which there are only
theories is like an object which still has the ticket that shows the
price."[22] Trilling is right when he affirms that "Diderot's dialogue
gives us full license to take the Nephew to our hearts and minds,
where he figures not only as an actual person but also as an aspect of
humanity itself, as the liberty that we wish to believe is inherent in
the human spirit, in its energy of effort, expectation, and desire, in
its consciousness of itself and its limitless contradictions."[23] This is
a tall order—the key word being *actual person*—and Diderot is not
artist enough to execute it or, to reverse a Baudelairean adage,
transformer son intelligence en volupté. I understand *le neveu* but do not
feel fully what Trilling gives me license to feel. Something is missing. For all the scintillating chattering and adroit gesticulations,
Lui's callousness makes him appear less "real" than Diderot, whereas Moi does not argue so convincingly as Lui—so, at least, it seems
to me. Johnson's Savage is rarely heard speaking; yet, observes
Frank Brady, "like the grin of the Cheshire Cat, Savage's own

voice—in indirect conversation, in his speech at the trial, in poems, and in letters—erupts and fades throughout the story."[24] His last words are as ambiguous as his life: "The last Time that the Keeper saw him was on *July* 31st, 1734; when *Savage* seeing him at his Bed-side said, with an uncommon Earnestness, *I have something to say to you, Sir,* but after a Pause, moved his Hand in a melancholy Manner, and finding himself unable to recollect what he was going to communicate, said *'Tis gone.* The Keeper soon after left him, and the next Morning he died" (p. 135).

It is Savage's very soul which is at stake. Because no satirical detail, however skillfully conceived, has ever revealed or betrayed the presence of a soul, Johnson refuses the satire and realism practiced by Defoe, Gay, Richardson or, for that matter, Diderot, always preoccupied with distinguishing marks, like his "verrue à la tempe."[25] Whereas Boswell's *Life* illuminates the innumerable "warts" of his idol, by and large the idol disregards specific blemishes of Savage, of whom we are only told: "He was of middle Stature, of a thin Habit of Body, a long Visage, coarse Features, a melancholy Aspect, of a grave and manly Deportment, a solemn Dignity of Mien, but which upon a nearer Acquaintance softened into an engaging Easiness of Manners. His walk was slow, and his Voice tremulous and mournful. He was excited to Smiles, but very seldom provoked to Laughter" (pp. 135–36). Other contemporaries recall a man of a livelier sort. Tracy relates that "Mrs. Thrale has left a vivid impression of his personality, which though acquired at second hand—for she was only three at the time of his death—shows that Savage became a legend of captivating charm."[26] The rest of Johnson's biography concentrates on events, attitudes, and meditations in the sublunary transit of Savage. Johnson writes the biography of a man who has just died, and his quill traces baroque sentences against the background of the companion's palpable absence, *une absence épaisse,* to speak with Valéry. To the best of my knowledge, none of the legion of Johnsonians has remarked that Samuel Johnson's biography of his friend—one is tempted, at times, to grant him either the status of a *saint virtuel* or a *Satan manqué*[27]—never alludes to the question of his salvation or his afterlife. The whys and wherefores of this silence remain to be answered. For that matter, does Johnson ever refer to the theme of salvation in his *Lives of the English Poets?*

To return to Diderot's *verrue,* surprisingly there is no wart on the *neveu*'s face, no substance to his body, no fullness so inviting as that of the hostess of the *Grand Cerf:* "une femme grande et replète, ingambe, de bonne mine, pleine d'embonpoint, la bouche un peu grande, mais de belles dents, des joues larges . . . les bras un peu forts, mais les mains superbes, des mains à peindre ou à modeler."[28] What a pity that she is an exception among Diderot's portraits of men and women, for the most part reduced to ideological or linguistic impressions. Compressed in the *hic et nunc,* the *neveu* performs on the stage of life where he pops up, as if in a Punch and Judy show, in the gardens of the Tuileries. Commenting on his pantomime, Elisabeth de Fontenay interprets it as a critique of Idealism and Spiritualism: "Le métaphysicien fait l'Arlequin, pour mieux jouir de ce avec quoi il joue, pour mieux retrouver ce que le passé a permis et que l'avenir—criticiste, positiviste—interdira. Diderot, le Neveu de Rameau sont des pervers, mais sa perversion est aussi une arme de la critique, et troubler vaut bien détruire." The nephew just is, never was, never will be. Roger Kempf puts it succinctly: "Les personnages de Diderot sont sans avenir;" and James Doolittle amplifies this impression: "in this work the demands of chronology receive very short shrift. Objective time is used in it, but only on occasion; it is subordinated and often sacrificed completely to the creation, brought about in part by the use of evocative symbols, of illusory characters moving in an imaginary world." Walter Rex perceives the *neveu* as "careening . . . from moment to moment, constantly abolishing his past . . . creating one after another intensities," demanding total attention from the "reader-listener," as does music.[29] We catch a glimpse of Lui during an afternoon that never knew a morning, that will not fade at dusk, whereas Savage, beyond time, has crossed the vanishing point of mortal perspective. And Johnson would have to have been the poet he was not to have immortalized a Savage graying in time, like Saint-Preux, oblivious of days, weeks, and months. Yet, despite Johnson's patent disregard of the laws of mimesis and novelistic techniques practiced by the author of *La Nouvelle Héloïse,* we sense nonetheless the presence of Time the Destroyer:

> He was always full of his Design of returning to *London* to bring his Tragedy upon the Stage . . . [and] thus spending the Day in contriving a Scheme for the Morrow, Distress stole upon him by imperceptible Degrees. His Conduct had already wearied some of those who were at first enamoured of his Conversation; but, he might, perhaps, still have devolved to others, whom he might have entertained with equal Success, had not the Decay of his Cloaths made it no longer consistent with their Vanity to admit him to their Tables, or to associate with him in publick Places. He now began to find every Man from home at whose House he called; and was, therefore, no longer able to procure the Necessaries of Life, but wandered about the Town slighted and neglected, in quest of a Dinner, which he did not always obtain. (p. 119)

Hours are only known by their effects—*omnes vulnerant, ultima necat*—and the impression made on me by Johnson's compassionate portrayal of decay is analogous to feelings released by Rousseau's story of Mme de Warens. Victim of her own harebrained schemes and the confidence men who take advantage of her, she presents a sorry picture of a matron, bankrupt and amoral—she who had been his lovely Maman: "Déjà le sentiment de sa misère lui resseroit le coeur et lui retrecissoit l'esprit . . . quel avilissement! que lui restoit-il de sa vertu prémière? Etoit-ce la même Mad^e de Warens jadis si brillante à qui le Curé Pontverre m'avoit adressé? Que mon coeur fut navré."[30]

Diderot tells us so much, yet so little, about the *neveu,* who spills out his story without shame or compunction, taking pride in his lack of scruples: "On est dedommagé de la perte de son innocence par celle de ses prejuges" (p. 59). And what he affirms is often genial. Nonetheless, Lui strikes me as unreal—unreal perhaps also to anyone who has known closely one of those restless and starving intellectuals who, after the Second World War, used to wander up and down the Boulevard St. Germain or along Christopher Street in Greenwich Village, until such sites became so expensive that these godforsaken outsiders could no longer survive *d'expédients. La*

Raméide seems far more human than *Le Neveu de Rameau* because its wretched alexandrines proclaim a wretchedness no less authentic than the artistically modulated despair in modern fiction. In literature, perfection of form always redeems pain and sorrow, and it is the anodyne mediocrity of *La Raméide* which vouchsafes authenticity: "Il me semble que le Ciel m'ait fait pour les revers / Connaissant mon devoir, je les ai tous soufferts."[31] I have already referred to Diderot's doubts concerning the likelihood of Lady Macclesfield's rejection of her child: "On siffle donc quelquefois la nature? Et pourquoi non?" Why did the author of *Ceci n'est pas un conte* limit himself to talking about "la tribulation de ses intestins"[32] rather than suggesting, by way of art, the sensation of hunger? The answer is that he, not unlike Sartre with whom he has much in common (materialism, sociological insight, polemical genius, and a dreadful quarrel with a friend), mistook talking about a sensation for the artistically engendered effect of the same sensation. No one has better defined the challenge of rendering or even capturing a sensation than Rousseau, when he seeks to evoke the fleeting moments that give him the right to say that he has lived: "Encore si tout cela consistoit en faits, en actions, en paroles, je pourrais le décrire et le rendre, en quelque façon: mais comment dire ce qui n'étoit ni dit, ni fait, ni pensé même, mais goûté, mais senti" (1:225).

Trilling's commentary illustrates an error committed by many historians of ideas and of literature: the identification of a personified concept (Hegel's *neveu*) with an authentic literary character in whom one believes because he is true to life: "The Nephew deserves admiration, Hegel says, because through him Spirit is able to pour 'scornful laughter' on existence, on the confusion pervading the whole and on itself as well." Trilling then juxtaposes *le neveu* to Werther: "Werther is incapable of embodying the Nephew's cosmic wit; irony is beyond his comprehension."[33] Unfortunately, Hegel's hero is, and always will remain, a construct within his dynamic system, and no one has ever believed in the reality of his *Neffe* to the point of committing suicide. Werther, however, has had his imitators. To return to the *neveu* and Savage, the former is *pensé sur le vif;* the latter, *aimé dans la mort.*

Life mocks Savage; *Lui* mocks *Moi* as well as *Nous*, us the readers, who are often helplessly drawn into the vortex of his irony. To read *Le Neveu de Rameau* is to be with him intellectually, if not emotionally. One is overwhelmed, shocked, and often amused. "En créant l'illusion d'une véritable conversation d'où naît le récit d'événements actuels," declares Dieckmann, "Diderot supprime la conscience de la distance. Il réussit à nous communiquer la chose même."[34] Perhaps *la chose,* but not the impression of its opposite *un homme,* a creature forever dispersed in time. Diderot offers us what is missing in Johnson—the brittle present, analyzed by Leo Spitzer. Johnson avoids it. In the words of Frank H. Ellis: "Savage remains faceless and voiceless."[35] Such, indeed, is the appearance of the dead beyond the wall of sadness, whose shadow falls on Everyman. The *Life of Savage* is an allegory as well as a biography, for every life reveals ontological constants: "There is such an Uniformity in the Life of Man," asserts the author of the *Rambler,* "if it be considered apart from adventitious and separable Decorations and Disguises, that there is scarce any Possibility of Good or Ill, but is not common to Humankind. . . . We are all prompted by the same Motives, all deceived by the same Fallacies, all animated by Hope, obstructed by Dangers, entangled by Desire, and seduced by Pleasure" (R, no. 60, p. 320). Johnson offers an object lesson which he suspects, he knows, he deplores, will not be heeded.

Commenting on the *Life of Savage,* Professor Bate discerns an unpredictable combination of tendencies usually found in more specialized and restricted forms: (1) the high-minded Plutarchan ideal that example is the best teacher; (2) the new realistic fiction which, if applied to biography, Johnson prizes to the extent that it can "exhibit life in its true state," provided that all incidents be factually true; (3) the eighteenth-century interest in criminal biographies; (4) the moral essay; (5) the profoundly original idea of a critical biography that relates the life of an author to his writings (BA, 222). One need only apply this set of criteria to *Le Neveu de Rameau* to appreciate the distance separating the works under discussion. Diderot satirizes Plutarch's ideal through the *neveu's* contempt for teachers and pupils alike; he stresses realistic effects almost obsessively in his would-be biographical sketch of *le neveu* which, in fact, does not correspond to the truth of Jean-François Rameau; he elaborates the tale of the renegade of Avignon and the story of the Jew of Utrecht—anecdotes that glorify criminals; he expounds, at least in *Le Neveu de Rameau, la morale* of the amoral and immoral artist; and finally, he paints "the portrait of the nephew as a young hack and sycophant." In so doing, he elaborates and somewhat "perverts" a literary genre invented by Johnson, the critical biography of a poet, parasite and failure but still a poet[36]— a genre eventually metamorphosed by Rousseau and Goethe into the critical autobiography of the artist, *Les Confessions* and *Dichtung und Wahrheit*. These in turn lead to *A la recherche du temps perdu, Portrait of the Artist as a Young Man,* and *Tonio Kröger*.

I have stressed Diderot's obsession with, and confinement in, the present. Nowhere does he succeed in conjuring up so skillfully a sense of *le présent vécu* as in his evocation of *l'Auberge du Grand Cerf* (*Jacques le Fataliste*), governed by *l'hôtesse* who relates, between toasts to her *curé, l'Histoire de Mme de la Pommeraye*. In it, voices echo and create an impression of space in the minds of Diderot's readers who in truth are, first of all, listeners. I think that this imagined dimension appears less open in *Le Neveu de Rameau* perhaps because of the essentially ideological nature of the work. Ideas by themselves do not generate artistic space, only mathematical dimensions. Voices are shrill; the excitement intense; the decor sketchy, colorless, devoid of nuances in shade and light. Georges May agrees and disagrees with my impressions: "Dans *Le Neveu de Rameau* Diderot n'a aucune aventure à nous raconter et ce roman sans intrigue parvient à être un chef-d'oeuvre, grâce aux idées exprimées sans doute, mais surtout grâce à leur orchestration. Sans les portraits magistraux des deux interlocuteurs, sans le fond de tableau du Café de la Régence, et, derrière lui, du Paris de 1760, le livre non seulement ne serait plus un roman, mais serait peut-être aussi insupportable que *Le fils naturel*."[37]

Two plays have been based on *Le Neveu de Rameau*, an adaptation by P. Fresnay and J. H. Duval performed at the Théâtre de la Michodière and one by Elisabeth de Fontenay entitled *Diderot à Corps Perdu*.[38] Furthermore, the *Satire II* could also be turned into a screen play, entitled "Dinner with Rameau." Dare one imagine a film called "Richard Savage"? Yes, provided that it be made in the style of Rossellini, as in the cinematographic masterpiece by Claude Goretta called "Jean-Jacques Rousseau—Les années d'exil." In this film, a living present harmonizes with an irrevocable past, while one hears and sees Jean-Jacques, admirably played by François Simon, whose features bear a haunting resemblance to Rousseau's death mask. Rousseau wrote his own "screen-play," whereas Savage did not and could not. Such a film would therefore have to consist of contrapuntal effects between the majestic voice of Johnson and dreamlike appearances of Savage moving against a Hogarth background of eighteenth-century London. But such a fanciful project already suggests the universe of Dickens and Balzac, the *tableaux* of Flaubert, the moody and forlorn landscapes of Hardy.

It is noteworthy that neither Johnson nor Diderot, both inveterate city-dwellers, makes any special effort to suggest a poetic or psychological relationship between their heroes and their urban settings. To be sure, Diderot initiates his satire with a precise reference to the Palais Royal and the Café de la Régence and, during the course of the dialogue, the *neveu* mentions Cours-la-Reine as well as the boulevards and the Tuileries where he displays his better half, the most precious possession of a husband pimping for his wife: "Quand elle traversoit la rue, le matin, en cheveux, , et en pet-en-l'air, vous vous seriez arreté pour la voir, et vous l'auriez embrassée entre quatre doigts sans la serrer. Ceux qui la suivoient, qui la regardoient trotter avec ses petits piés; et qui mesuroient cette large croupe dont les jupons legers dessinoient la forme, doubloient le pas; elle les laissoit arriver, puis elle detournoient prestement sur eux, ses deux grands yeux noirs et brillants qui les arretoient tout court" (p. 109). There is no such passage in the *Life of Savage* and, furthermore, no suggestion of any erotic activity by the hero. He makes a point of insisting on his chaste relations with Mrs. Oldfield, the actress "touched with his Misfortunes" who "allowed him a settled Pension of fifty Pounds a Year, which was during her life regularly paid" (p. 19). The kindhearted biographer continues: "it is proper to mention what Mr. *Savage* often declared in the strongest Terms, that he never saw her alone, or in any other Place than behind the Scenes" (p. 19). When his patroness dies,

Savage wears mourning as for a mother, writes an elegy in her memory, and publishes it anonymously, contrary (Tracy says) to "his almost invariable custom of flaunting his name on his title-pages." Moreover, he goes out of his way to justify his excessive discretion regarding the deceased. Tracy concludes: "It is indeed hard to avoid the conclusion that Savage's connection with Anne Oldfield was more intimate than a professional back-stage acquaintance or than the relation of patroness and pensioner."[39]

Savage's modern biographer also evokes wittily a Savage caught between two hysterical females. The first was Mrs. Haywood, formerly married to the Reverend Valentine Haywood, "a strange mate for one of her propensities." Tracy goes on to relate that her novel *Love in Excess* (1719) occasions her meeting with Savage, who addresses a poem to the lady. "His lines to her are fulsome in their flattery, likening genius to the eagle gazing undazzled at noon-day sun." "Like Disraeli," chuckles Professor Tracy, "Savage thought he knew how to handle women." We are also told that she produced a comedy called *A Wife to be Lett* (1723), a title Savage borrowed for his satire. Eventually, they quarrelled over Savage's other mistress Martha Fowke Sansom, "a big-bon'd, buxom, brown woman," with morals that leave ·little—or a great deal—to be desired.[40] When, according to his forebearing biographer, Savage happens to meet the now-destitute whore who testified against him during his trial for manslaughter, he reproves "her gently for her Perjury, and changing the only Guinea that he has, [divides] it equally between her and himself" (p. 40). Johnson concludes the episode in terms which foreshadow de Quincey's vision of "stony-hearted Oxford Street":"This is an Action which in some Ages would have made a Saint, and perhaps in others a Hero, and which, without hyperbolical Encomium, must be allowed to be an Instance of uncommon Generosity, an Act of complicated Virtue" (p. 40). Lest Diderotphiles be misled by these saintly implications, I ought to quote a well-known paragraph from Boswell's *Life* which casts a few shadows:

> I am to mention, (with all possible respect and delicacy, however,) that his conduct, after he came to London, and had associated with Savage and others, was not so strictly virtuous,

in one respect, as when he was a younger man. It was well known, that his amourous inclinations were uncommonly strong and impetuous. He owned to many of his friends, that he used to take women of the town to taverns, and hear them relate their history. In short, it must not be concealed, that, like many other good and pious men, among whom we may place the Apostle Paul upon his own authority, Johnson was not free from propensities which were ever "warring against the law of his mind," and that in his combats with them, he was sometimes overcome. (L, 4:395–96)

Whether Johnson suffered such defeats will never be known, or shouldn't, inasmuch as his profligate biographer may have mistaken his own shadow for that of his subject.

Thus, the city is but a background for considerations about men and women for whom any other setting suggests defeat: "No Sir, when a man is tired of London, he is tired of life" (L, 3:178)[41] and "Fleet Street has a very animated appearance; but I think the tide of human existence is at Charing Cross" (L, 2:232). Johnson never refers to the territory where Savage was wont to roam, whether it be the Strand or Grub Street, St. James's Park or the Mall, Vauxhall or Ranelagh, where the likes of Savage could stroll about, dine, and flirt with sundry ladies. Never does he write about the humbler pleasures to be found at Marylebone or at Cuper's Garden; never does he show us Savage on a boat trip cruising on the ebbing tide from Whitehall Stairs to Wapping. The town is a fixed and implicit reality from which any departure is tantamount to disappointment as, for example, is Savage's plan to retire to the country: "he could not bear to debar himself from the Happiness which was to be found in the Calm of a Cottage, or lose the Opportunity of listening without Intermission, to the Melody of the Nightingale, which he believ'd was to be heard from every Bramble" (p. 111). On reading these comments steeped in irony, students of French literature cannot help recalling similar schemes nurtured by des Grieux after his first disappointment with his *chère Manon:* "Je formai là-dessus, d'avance, un système de vie paisible et solitaire. J'y faisais entrer une maison écartée, avec un petit bois et un ruisseau d'eau douce au bout du jardin."[42] Did L'abbé Prévost ever meet Savage when he first appeared in London in 1728, before his infatuation with Lenki, the adventuress from Holland or Hungary (Lenki—Ilonka)?[43] The question is not inane, since both men were born during the same year (1697) and, what seems more significant, lost their hearts to Mrs. Oldfield, who lost hers to Savage. Prévost's *L'Homme de qualité* draws her portrait: "Cette comédienne étoit aimée du brigadier Churchill, frère ou neveu du feu duc de Marlborough, et gouverneur de Plymouth. Elle vivoit avec lui comme sa femme; elle en avoit même quelques enfans, qu'il avoit fait baptiser sous son propre nom. . . . Les dames de la plus haute distinction se faisoient un honneur d'être en liaison avec elle. . . . Il faut convenir, en effet, que c'étoit une fille incomparable. Elle m'a fait aimer le théâtre anglois."[44] Indeed, it is not improbable that, during his first visit to London (1728–30), Prévost espied or even met Richard Savage, "shoeless and shirtless . . . a scarlet cloak elegantly about his naked shoulders, and so accoutred . . . greeted with respect in good society" (T, 764). As for the *neveu*, he eschews pastoral pleasures and, if he sleeps beneath the stars of the Champs Elysées—green fields in those days—it is for want of a comfortable bed. Neither Diderot nor Johnson intuits the poetic potential of cities. The former waxes lyrical over landscapes with ruins, silvery with moonlight—preferably on a canvas by Hubert. The latter condenses his account of his French tour in a terse reply to Boswell: "Sir, I have seen all the visibilities of Paris, and around it" (L, 2:401).

During his prosperous years in the home of Lord Tyrconnel, Savage wrote *The Wanderer* (1729, a long poem not relevant to the issues under discussion) and a pamphlet called *An Author to be Lett* (1729), in which he introduces Iscariot Hackney, a prostitute scribbler. The booklet contains a surprising number of statements quite similar to affirmations made by the *neveu*. It is divided into "The Publisher's Preface" and "A Proposal to Knights, Esquires, etc.," the first part roughly corresponding to the role enacted by Moi and the second part to the role played by Lui the amoralist, blessed and cursed with good taste. Savage's satire does not make use of dialogue; however, the narrative voice of "the publisher" addresses a number of literary figures, all enemies of Pope and Savage (Dennis, Norton, Theobald, whose names will reappear in Palissot's preface to *La*

Dunciade, 1764), while Hackney's voice speaks to the world at large. The first voice (one could dub it Savage's Moi) intones: "It is with much Glee that I have mark'd the Herd bellowing against the *Dunciad* for Indelicacies . . . composed, for the most Part, of Authors, whose Writings are the Refuse of wit, and who in Life are as the very Excrement of Nature. Yet even here Mr. Pope shews himself a Master. It is true that he has used Dung; but he disposes that Dung in such a Manner, that it becomes rich Manure, from which he raises a Variety of fine Flowers. He deals in Rags, but he deals with them like an Artist" (preface). Lui's question, "A quoi bon la mediocrité dans les genres" (p. 7), is answered by the publisher who asserts that Pope's enemies, "tho' they are sad writers, might have been good Mechanicks." He goes on to ask, "Had it not been an honester and more decent Livelihood for Mr. N—rt—n (Daniel's Son of Love, by a Lady, who vended Oysters) to have dealt in a Fish-Market, than to be dealing out the Dialects of Billingsgate" or, "Should not Mr. R—ch—rd M—rl—y rather have been blacking Shoes at the corner of Streets . . . than black'ning Reputations"?

The publisher's voice soon gives way to Iscariot Hackney, who announces Diderot's Lui: "To be inoffensive is a puritanical Spirit, and will never succeed in a free-thinking Age. . . . You must know when my Mother was pregnant of me, she once dreamt she was delivered of a Monster" (p. 2). Such a self-characterization invites comparison with the *neveu*'s exclamation that he is a man botched by Mother Nature: "Quand elle [la nature] fagota son neveu, elle fit la grimace" (p. 96). Already at school, Iscariot discovers a "promising Genius for Mischief" (p. 2) carrying tales from one boy to another in order to set them up fighting. He concludes: "Now I understand to be a great Wit, is to take a Pleasure in giving every Body Pain" (p. 2), a self-realization echoing the *neveu*'s command: "Qu'on me dechire les honnêtes gens" (p. 38). And does Hackney's self-portrait not suggest traits of the *neveu*'s character? "I have naturally a Sourness of Temper, a droll Solemnity of Countenance, and a dry Manner of joking upon such Accidents, as Fools who value themselves upon Humanity, would be apt to be compassionate. I have also a Propensity to sneer upon all Mankind, and particularly upon those who fancy they can oblige me" (p. 3). The *neveu* repeats the same thought: "La reconnoissance est un fardeau; et tout fardeau est fait pour etre secoué" (p. 40). Hackney glides in and out of antechambers in a manner that presages the pirouettes of the *neveu*, at the beck and call of the couple Bertin-Hus: "I was admitted while her Ladyship was *shifting;* and on my Admittance, Mrs. *Abigail* was order'd to withdraw. What passed between us, a Point of Gallantry obliges me to conceal" (p. 3). Hackney plies many trades: "I abridg'd Histories and Travels, translated from the French, what they never wrote . . . and when a notorious Thief was hanged, I was the Plutarch to preserve his Memory" (p. 4). Similarly, the *neveu* is the historian of the *renégat d'Avignon,* not to mention the *juif d'Utrecht.* Like his counterpart at the Comédie Française, Hackney applauds and hisses at "the first Night of any Drury Lane Performance" (p. 5). Furthermore, he is also a tutor, knowledgeable where "good Wine, good Beds, buxom Girls, and tall Steeples" (p. 9) might be found. His ambitions match the *neveu*'s talents: "I wou'd have spirited my Pupil to run away with a Nun; and, if he aimed at smaller Game, not scrupled being a Pimp" (p. 9). Like the *neveu,* fantasizes about being wealthy: "Who knows but I might have married some rich Widow by securing my Pupil for one of her Daughters? I wou'd have contrived he shou'd have stolen the young Lady to avoid paying her Fortune" (pp. 9–10). Could a Denis Diderot not turn such prosaic prose into an enchanting intermezzo, entitled "la scene du proxénète et la jeune fille" (p. 24)? In one respect, however, Iscariot Hackney's daydreams reach heights unequalled by Lui but realized thirty-odd years later by François Marie-Arouet and, eventually, not only by the Romantics but also by revolutionaries of every persuasion, including Lenin. "Thus," daydreams Hackney, "tho' I had but a hundred a Year, and for no more than two, or three Years Service, I could retire to Swisserland . . . with about Fifteen Hundred Pounds in my Pocket, and an Anuity of fifty Pounds *per Annum* for Life" (p. 10). Hackney ends his dour ruminations by exclaiming: "In short, I am the perfect Town Author: I hate all Mankind" (p. 11), an epilogue matched by the *neveu*'s epigram: "Il vaudroit presque autant que l'homme ne fût pas né" (p. 24).

What is missing? Foremost, one regrets the absence of dialogue, pantomime, discussions about music—in short, the ineffable charm of Diderot's personality and of his intellectual curiosity. The informative preface by James Sutherland to Savage's satire summarizes the literary history of *An Author to be Lett*. Given the intricacies of the times, I shall quote from it at length so as to enlighten the Diderotphiles who may not be familiar with that period of English literature. Professor Sutherland relates that Savage's pamphlet is a by-product of Pope's war with the dunces. There is firm evidence that the two men knew of each other in December 1727, when Pope sent Savage (in Newgate under the sentence of death) five guineas through Edward Young and that, after Savage's release, the latter may have become a source of gossip for Pope:

> In the *Dunciad* of 1728, however, there is comparatively little that would require a knowledge of the sort of literary gossip in which Savage specialized. It was not until Pope went to work on *The Dunciad Variorum*, with its detailed biographical documentation and its further denigration in prose of those who had already been satirized in his verse, that Savage's first-hand knowledge of Grub Street must have become really useful, even indispensable. . . . At all events, it was generally held by Pope's victims that Savage was his main source of information. The charge was made by Orator Henley in *The Hyp Doctor*, April 29, 1735:
>
>> *Richard Savage,* Esq; was the *Jack-all* of that *Ass* in a *Lyon's Skin,* he was his *Provider:* Like *Monmaur,* the *Parasite of Paris,* he rambled about to gather up *Scraps of Scandal,* as a Price for his *Twickenham Ordinary;* no Purchase no Pay; no Tittle-tattle, no Dinner. (preface, ii)

Professor Sutherland then proceeds to offer a critical estimate of Savage's satire: "In *An Author to be Lett,* however, although he glances from time to time at individuals, Savage was more concerned with drawing the picture of a typical Grub-Street author. Iscariot Hackney is clearly a composite portrait, to which Concanen, Cooke, John Durant Breval (the travelling tutor), Eliza Haywood, James Moore Smythe, and many others may have contributed something. Iscariot's literary activities include most of those parcticed by the various authors whom Pope had satirized in *The Dunciad"* (p. iii). Sutherland concludes his preface by quoting Johnson: "Of his exact Observation on human Life, he has left a proof, which would do Honour to the greatest Names, in a small pamphlet called *The Author to be Lett"* (p. 45), and he goes on to write:

> To most readers, Johnson's praise of this lively little work must seem excessive. When he wrote those words he was probably relying, as he seems often to have done on other occasions, on the memory of many years; and if he had glanced at the pamphlet again he might have been inclined to make the same observation as he made on his own *Irene* [Johnson's tragedy, produced by Garrick in 1749]: "Sir, I thought it had been better." Yet Savage's pamphlet is well written, and the first two paragraphs especially, in which he describes the childhood of the young Iscariot, compare very favorably with anything else written in the Martinus Scriblerus vein. (p. ii)

The background of *An Author to be Lett* bears comparison with the urban jungle which *Le Neveu de Rameau* describes three decades later. Again we turn to Jean Fabre for a pithy sketch of the Parisian literary scene, crowded with supernumeraries who are all but forgotten today:

> Dulaurens et Chevrier détestent tous deux Fréron et le traitent d'âne, à qui-mieux-mieux, mais, pour Dulaurens, *le Colporteur* n'en est pas moins l'oeuvre d'un "écrivain sans génie," un plagiat éhonté de Straparole, tandis que pour Chevrier, *Imirce* ne vaut pas davantage. Palissot [author of the satirical comedy *Les Philosophes* (1760), which ridicules Rousseau and Diderot] insulte et calomnie tout le monde, sauf Voltaire, et Voltaire, lui-même, rit sous cape des croquignolles que Palissot distribue si généreusement à ses amis. Vue de près, la bataille philosophique n'a pas la belle ordonnance qu'on serait tenté de lui prêter . . . et Diderot n'a pas dû forcer beaucoup les choses pour s'annexer Rameau et en faire l'exécuteur de ses vengeances. (pp. liv–lv)

With this situation in mind, Georges May has carefully illuminated, and commented upon, the anguish experienced by Diderot after the failure of his play *Le père de famille* (1761), qualified by Palissot as "une sodomie théâtrale" (Fabre, lxxi): "il n'est pas douteux que l'angoisse de l'échec . . . sans doute engendrée en partie ou tout au moins accentuée par la gloire posthume de Richardson, soit un des sentiments présents dans la conscience de Diderot, au moment où il se met à écrire son chef-d'oeuvre. On est même conduit à se demander si ce sentiment d'inquiétude lancinante n'est pas aussi une des sources intérieures profondes et cachées du *Neveu* de Rameau."[45] Thus, from a French vantage point, Iscariot Hackney takes on special interest because he, along with his creator Savage, not only foreshadows Lui and Moi but also creates by their polemical roles concerning Pope's *Dunciad* a situation which will be repeated in Paris after the furor caused by the performance of Palissot's *Les Philosophes* in 1760, and after the publication of his *Dunciad* in 1764.

Further complicating the varied analogies that link *An Author to be Lett* to *Le Neveu de Rameau* is the fact that *La Raméide* (1766), Jean-François Rameau's pitiful mock epic, contains themes illustrated in Savage's life as he depicts it in his poem *The Bastard* (1728), as well as in Johnson's *Life of Savage*. Thus Rameau, illustrious composer as well as champion of *la basse fondamentale*, rejects his nephew with an indifference reminiscent of Lady Macclesfield's cruelty to her putative son:

> J'attendais de cet Oncle, au moins un peu d'aisance,
> Par pur égard au tems de trente ans de constance,
> A lui faire la cour à l'example des miens,
> Mais tout à son talent, il voyait peu les siens.
> Très souvent, toutefois approuvant sa doctrine,
> Aux jardins on le vit me faire bonne mine:
> Des heures se passaient tous deux à discourir,
> Mon art à l'écouter sçavait le retenir,
> Surtout à ce grand mot, *basse fondamentale.*[46]

Savage does not mince words but, like Shakespeare's Edmund, exults in being *un enfant de l'amour*.

> Blest be the *Bastard*'s birth! through wondr'ous ways,
> He shines eccentric like a Comet's blaze.
> No sickly fruit of faint compliance he;
> He! stampt in nature's mint of extasy!
>
> . . . .
>
> O *Mother*, yet *no* Mother!—'tis to you,
> My thanks for such distinguish'd claims are due.[47]

Whether Samuel Johnson overestimated the value of *An Author to be Lett* remains to be seen. Although Professor Sutherland judges the little satire from an English viewpoint, nothing prevents a Diderotphile familiar with English from considering it, as well as its author's life, as potential blueprints of *Le Neveu de Rameau.* Could it be Samuel Johnson was right when he claimed that Savage's observations would do honor to the greatest names? Did he intuit in that little pamphlet values instantaneously recognized by Schiller and Goethe in *Le Neveu de Rameau?* And how, we may ask ourselves incidentally, could such a discrepancy between the modern English critical estimate of *An Author to be Lett* and Samuel Johnson's opinion of it develop? An answer to this question would have to refer not only to changing literary values but also to prevailing Anglo-American views on satire which have prevented modern critics from interpreting Savage's pamphlet *à la française.* Such an answer would have to stress the fact that the great satirists of the late seventeenth and eighteenth centuries all wrote their masterpieces in verse: Dryden, *Mac Flecknoe* (1684); Pope, *The Dunciad* (1728); Johnson, *London* (1738) and *The Vanity of Human Wishes* (1749). The notable exceptions to the rule were Swift and Gay. Even more significant is the fact that none of these authors, except Swift, defiled himself—directed his satire against himself. Only Swift sends his barbs (somewhat dulled by apologetic implications) against his own person, arrows exclusively in verse, like "The Life and Character of Dean Swift" (1733) and "The Death of Dr. Swift, D.S.P.D. occasioned by reading a Maxim in Rouchefoucault" (1739). Successful satire in verse, even if aimed at the author or at his narrative voice, defeats or neutralizes the masochistic intent by virtue of its inherent rhythm.[48] Swift was too skilled a musician to strike a note fatal to himself. Thus, all things considered, the satirist cannot satirize whom he seeks to satirize, because satire dehumanizes its victim—be it Leibniz, turned into Pangloss, or Jean-François Rameau, into Lui. As a result, the satirist must content himself with mocking the appearance of his victim which, to be sure, may harm the victim—shadow-boxing, as it were, rather than clawing at his essence, unless, like Swift, the satirist attacks his own shadow in verse, an enterprise bound to fail

if the satirist is a good poet. Prose, however, offers a greater potential for self-flagellation, a truth borne out by *Le Neveu de Rameau*
and *Notes from the Underground,* as well as by *An Author to be Lett.*
The latter, if interpreted with Diderot, Hegel, and Dostoyevsky in
mind, may indeed have deserved Johnson's praise and must also be
reckoned as a challenge to the rule that failures cannot—or should
not—succeed in defining their own failure.

However this may be, the genre chosen by an author not only
is a function of his education, personality, and intimate dreams but
also, by way of traditional literary patterns, delineates the scope of
his intentions. Curtius was the first to show the degree to which
classical satire, specifically Horace's *Seventh Satire,* has affected the
thematic content of *Le Neveu de Rameau.* After quoting pertinent
passages, Curtius declares:

> Such is the structure of Horace's satire. If we call to mind the
> content of the *Neveu de Rameau,* the inner connection is
> apparent at once. We see the resemblance between the slave
> Davus, who takes advantage of the fool's licence granted
> during the Saturnalia, and the parasite Rameau, whose
> *inaequalitas* is emphasized as the chief trait of his character at
> the very beginning: "c'est un composé de hauteur et de
> bassesse, de bon sens et de déraison . . . Quelquefois il est
> maigre et hâve . . . Le mois suivant, il est gras et
> replet . . . Aujourd'hui en linge sale . . . Demain poudré,
> chaussé, frisé . . . " Compare this with Horace's
> characterization of the singer Tigellius (Sat., I, 3). Of him we
> read (1. 17 f.) "nil fuit unquam sic impar sibi"; of Rameau's
> nephew: "rien ne dissemble plus de lui que lui-même."
> Perhaps Diderot also had in mind the idea of *inaequalitas* in
> composing the following remark addressed to Rameau: "Je
> rêve à l'inégalité de votre ton tantôt haut, tantôt bas." But this
> resemblance between Davus and Rameau is not all. More
> important, I think, is the fact that the basic theme—contrast
> between the fool, enslaved by want, necessities, lusts, and
> passions, and the self-sufficient and therefore only free man,
> the sage—is identical in the two works.[49]

The analogies noted by Curtius correspond to the ones we perceive
between Johnson's *Life* and Diderot's *Neveu de Rameau.* Does Johnson not also stress the spurious contrast between Davus (that is,

Savage and his "associate in poverty"), wretched and almost mad
with poverty, and those who are rich and smug? "Those are no
proper Judges of his Conduct who have slumber'd away their Time
on the Down of Plenty, nor will a wise Man easily presume to say,
'Had I been in Savage's Condition, I should have lived, or written,
better than Savage'" (p. 140). Furthermore, the relative distance
between the slave, chained by his passions, and the wise man
(Horace) is created by the opposition between Savage and his biographer who, although "an associate in poverty," assumes the role of
the tolerant sage, just as Moi establishes a judgmental distance
between himself and *le neveu*.

What then is the dosage of satire in the two works under discussion and what is the role of satire in Johnson's poetry? "Without
London and the *Vanity of Human Wishes*," writes E. L. McAdam,
"both imitations of Juvenal, Johnson's poetry would be little read
today. The first was much more popular in Johnson's time than was
the second. . . . This difference is not difficult to understand. *London* was a timely poem. Imitation though it is, it presents a sharp
attack on the Walpole administration, on the French and the Spanish, and on various vices of the day" (P, xvii–xviii). McAdam goes
on to stress the "academic quality" of *London*, a flaw almost absent
from the *Vanity of Human Wishes:* "The emotion is deeper, because
Johnson is criticizing not one city or one people, but human life
itself. . . . His religion was founded on the great tradition of historical Christianity, that life on earth is essentially a conflict and on
the whole unhappy, that its purpose is preparation for the world to
come. This feeling did not, to be sure, engulf Johnson, for his was
a highly social nature; but it was basic in him, and he did not try,
either by dissipation or by self-delusion, to escape it" (ibid.). Now,
although Diderot's favorite poet was Horace, many themes in *Le
Neveu de Rameau* strike me as Juvenalian in mood. This impression
is less justified in the case of Diderot's *Satire I,* also written under
the auspices of Horace (one could make a case for the influence of
Persius as well). Sharp, disjointed, even cutting, this short work
offers speculations on varieties of temperament: "il y a l'homme
loup . . . l'homme taupe . . . l'homme ours qui ne me déplaît
pas," as well as maxims about professional deformation: "L'homme

qui est tout entier à son métier, s'il a du génie, devient un prodige," a remark prophetic of Rameau's uncle.[50] Regardless of the
relative importance of Horace or Juvenal in the literary heritage of
Johnson and Diderot, the main point to keep in mind is that Diderot was an atheist and a materialist who, in the twentieth century, would have been an ardent supporter of quantum theory with
its probability waves, not to speak of theories about DNA. Johnson, on the other hand, was a devout Christian who could not
bring himself to compose a satire about a man of whom he had
been fond. This reluctance to be witty at the expense of a dead
friend is, in fact, his strength, for *caritas* is a prerequisite for any
biographer who records "the history of a soul"—this expression
having been coined, it should be mentioned, by Rousseau: "C'est
l'histoire de mon ame que j'ai promise."[51]

Few would dispute the excellence of Jean Fabre's introduction
to *Le Neveu de Rameau*. It teems with insights and raises questions,
some perhaps now answerable with our speculations in mind.
Commenting on Goethe's attempt to define Diderot's intentions,
Fabre writes:

> En désespoir de cause, Goethe isole un noyau qu'il
> considère comme primitif: le scandale occasionné par la
> comédie des *Philosophes,* cherche à définir une intention
> première: la polémique contre Palissot et ses pareils, puis, rend
> compte de tout le reste par la théorie des révisions ou des
> rédactions successives. Avouons franchment, qu'après un siècle
> et demi d'exégèse, la critique du *Neveu de Rameau* procède
> toujours de la même méthode et n'est guère plus avancée.
>   Il serait naïf de s'en étonner. Comme Goethe, le lecteur de
> 1950 en est réduit à interroger l'oeuvre elle-même. Aucun
> témoignage portant directement sur elle n'est remonté du
> XVIIIᵉ siècle pour l'éclairer. Autour du *Neveu de Rameau,*
> replacé en son temps, c'est toujours le vide et le silence. Si
> parfaits que, comme le fondu du manuscrit, ils pourraient bien
> avoir, eux aussi, une valeur d'indices ou de signes. On
> n'imaginait pas Diderot si mystérieux. Mais cette vie si
> répandue, si bavarde, si outrageusement exempte de secrets
> eut, peut-être, tout de même son secret: ni Mlle Volland, ni
> Mme de Meaux, ni la bonté, ni la haine, ni la tsarine, ni Dieu,
> mais seulement le *Neveu de Rameau*. Tout paraît s'être passé

comme si Diderot, au lieu d'écrire pour la foule ou pour les
"happy few": les hôtes du Grand Val, les abonnés de Grimm,
avait écrit, une fois, pour lui seul. On attend toujours
l'apparition, toujours possible, du document qui viendra
démentir cette impression. Mais le secret paraît avoir été
jalousement gardé et, beaucoup plus que l'histoire romanesque
du manuscrit, c'est là le vrai mystère du *Neveu de Rameau*. (pp.
xxviii–xxix)

With Fabre's remarks in mind, we should take a second look at
Diderot's book review of *La Vie de Richard Savage:* "Cet ouvrage eût
été délicieux, et d'une finesse à comparer aux Mémoires du Comte
de Grammont, si l'auteur anglais se fût proposé de faire la satire de
son héros; mais malheureusement il est de bonne foi." The adjec-
tive *délicieux* seems out of place, given Johnson's somber account of
Savage's life and death. Why would Diderot who, according to his
daughter Angélique, was more than generous to impoverished authors and enjoyed sobbing over familial misfortunes, characterize
this chronicle with such a whimsical word? Could he have read the
Life without thinking about his *neveu?* Hardly. If so, the third
paragraph couches a private joke; we may surmise that he wrote it
tongue in cheek, thinking of his *manuscrit délicieux* (alas unknown
to his friends and the public at large) and waiting for the approval
of posterity. The final words, "mais malheureusement il est de
bonne foi," seem perplexing unless one assumes that a satirist must
necessarily be *de mauvaise foi* when he sets out to evoke "un homme
malheureux, d'un caractère bizarre, d'un génie bouillant; d'un in-
dividu tantôt fier, tantôt vil; moitié vrai, moitié faux, en tout, plus
digne de compassion que de haine, de mépris que d'éloge; agréable
à entendre, dangereux à fréquenter." Save for the qualification "tantôt bienfaisant," Diderot's interpretation of Johnson's Savage is,
roughly speaking, identical to his perception of *le neveu*—I say *his*
interpretation, because the real nephew Jean-François Rameau was
also kindhearted. If, by a leap of critical fancy, one imagines that
Johnson had taken it upon himself to write the *Life of Jean-François
Rameau,* his biography might have resembled that of Savage; likewise, Diderot in London would have produced a Savage with the
foibles, tics, and words of *le neveu*, an eccentric and poverty-stricken

English parasite, frequenter of coffee houses and taverns, a *minus habens* with pretensions to nobility.[52] As for Diderot's implicit comparison of *La Vie de Richard Savage* to *Les Mémoires du comte de Gramont* (1713) by Anthony Hamilton, I do not know what to make of it. Diderot could not have perceived a relationship between Hamilton's lively and elegant evocation of the comte de Gramont and Johnson's Savage, unless he was so preoccupied with the satirical aspects of English nobility, as described respectively by Hamilton and Johnson, that he juxtaposed the two works without giving the matter too much thought. Or dare we speculate that the remark is but a red herring, meant to mask a possible indebtedness of Diderot to Samuel Johnson's *Life of Savage* and to Savage's *An Author to be Lett?*

If we assume that Diderot was thinking of his *Neveu de Rameau*—in a fragmentary state or almost completed—when he wrote the book review, two conclusions emerge. The first is that Diderot, at home in English literature, had read the original version of Johnson's *Life of Savage* in 1744, or at some later date (Johnson's biography continued to reappear in 1748, in 1767, and in 1769). His appetite whetted, he may have procured for himself Savage's *An Author to be Lett*. These two works may then have inspired him to write his second satire, just as the works of Shaftesbury, Sterne, and Richardson had fired his creative potential. This hypothesis is not unreasonable, in view of the fact that in 1762, when the first versions of *Le Neveu de Rameau* most likely were beginning to take shape, Samuel Johnson was England's most famous man of letters as well as the recipient of a royal pension from George III. Could Diderot have known of Savage's pamphlet without reading about it in Johnson's *Life of Savage?* Indeed, as early as 1735, Prévost's *Le Pour et Contre* features in volume 7 a disquisition on bastards, followed by disquieting questions: "Qui peut se vanter parmi les Hommes de n'être pas le fruit d'un amour criminel? . . . Est-ce un crime si rare que l'infidelité dans une Epouse? . . . Tel qui reproche sa naissance au fils d'une amante foible et crédule . . . est souvent plus méprisable que celui qu'il croit outrager. Il lui fait une honte de devoir le jour à la fornication, et lui-même ne le doit peut-être qu'à l'adultère, qui est un crime beaucoup plus odieux." Prévost then proceeds to tell his own version of the story of Savage, who, facing the gallows for having committed homicide, turns to the Muses to save his neck: "Il devint Poëte en un mot, le veille de son supplice." Savage gains the esteem of all who know him, even his enemies: "Rien n'est si tendre et si naturellement exprimé que son repentir. C'est en faire bien l'éloge que d'assurer sur le témoignage de mon Correspondant que sa Pièce a fait verser des larmes, et que les Parens mêmes de celui qui est mort de sa main ont consenti à le voir et à se réconcilier avec lui."[53] We know that Rousseau and Diderot thought highly of Prévost's novels and, George Havens informs us that "it is quite probable, especially in the case of Diderot, that they were also readers of the *Pour et Contre.*"[54] The melodramatic story of the bastard must have caught Diderot's attention, for is Savage not a *fils naturel?* And, if we assume Diderot's early acquaintance with Prévost's Savage, it stands to reason that Diderot, curious among the curious, should have made it a point to read *An Author to be Lett,* the more so since Johnson praises it to the sky.

However, there is another connection, though indirect, be-tween this little pamphlet and Diderot. In 1764 Palissot, author of *Les Philosophes,* published *La Dunciade ou la Guerre des Sots.* Its pref-ace is quite relevant:

> La Dunciade, lorsqu'elle parut à Londres, fut l'époque d'une
> révolution très avantageuse pour les lettres; révolution dont les
> suites se font encore sentir en Angleterre. On sait combien la
> gloire des nations est liée à celle d'un petit nombre de génies
> rares qui les rendent respectables par leurs travaux. Les noms,
> aujourd'hui obscurs, des Dennys, des Ralph, des Théobald, des
> Norton, des Cibber, des Blackmore, ayant été livré au ridicule
> qu'ils méritaient, la justice que l'on devait à leurs célèbres
> adversaires fut plus prompte . . . on ne prononça plus sans
> respect les noms des Dryden, des Addison, des Swift, de Pope
> lui-même; et le génie fut vengé.[55]

Savage's preface also mentions Dennis, Theobald, and Norton. What prevents us from supposing that, while Palissot was doing thorough research on Pope's *Dunciad,* which he imitates closely, he found the pamphlet by Pope's purveyor of gossip Richard Savage?

Furthermore, what keeps us from supposing that Diderot, thirst-
ing for revenge, obtained the pamphlet through a disloyal acquaintance of Palissot? Usually, the best ammunition against one's enemies comes from them, and Diderot was devious enough to resort
to counterespionage.

The second possibility is that Diderot, upon reading *La Vie de
Richard Savage,* translated by Le Tourneur in 1771, procured Savage's *An Author to be Lett* and, as a result of these readings, incorpo-
rated changes into an existing version or *Le Neveu de Rameau.* According to Fabre, 1782 was the last year during which Diderot may
have altered or touched up his manuscript. The conclusion of his
review ("Cet ouvrage eût été délicieux . . . si l'auteur se fût proposé de faire la satire de son héros, mais malheureusement il est de
bonne foi") in fact defines what Diderot achieved: a masterful modern satire, derived from classical models and modified by the tragicomic lives of two wretched parasites—the English bastard with
poetic and aristocratic pretensions and the goodhearted eccentric
raté, Rameau's nephew, whom Diderot knew "de longue date" but
whom he may have understood more deeply through Johnson's *Life*
and Savage's *An Author to be Lett.*

With this in mind, Fabre's questions become answerable:
"Comment Diderot a-t-il dépassé l'anecdote et le pittoresque purs
sans tomber dans l'abstraction? Comment d'un excentrique à demi-
fou a-t-il fait un être si puissamment significatif et presque my-
thique? Comment a-t-il réussi la transfiguration de Rameau" (p.
liii)? The last question is crucial because Fabre denies Diderot the
power to create characters that seem alive: "Réduit à lui-même,
Diderot n'est pas capable de créer que de vagues fantoches. . . . Il
n'est pas de la lignée de Rabelais forgeant Panurge, ni de Jarry Ubu-
Roi. Mieux vaut alors avouer cette impuissance et désigner ses interlocuteurs par les lettres de l'alphabet" (p. xlv). Fabre views the
meeting of Diderot and Jean-François Rameau as a gift of life, an
encounter with a sponger Diderot found too extraordinary to be
reduced to a theorem or Condillac's statue. "Le personnage," writes
Fabre, "était en quête d'un poète, non d'un philosophe, et il a
contraint Diderot à le devenir" (p. xlv). But Diderot was not a poet,
either in the traditional or the modern sense; Spitzer even claims

that "he was deaf to the legato of the divine melody."[56] The one individual who could have opened Diderot's eyes to the tragedy of the alienated man was of course Jean-Jacques, who by 1760 had become his *bête grise, sinon noire,* and perhaps, next to Savage-Hackney, a second model for his *neveu.* It may well have been one of life's little ironies that the poetic transfigurative spark to which Fabre refers, may have been kindled by Johnson and fanned by offensive memories of Rousseau, who, according to Johnson, deserved to be exiled to America. Thus, the poetic gift for which Fabre fails to account in a manner satisfactory to him, the gift unacknowledged and never fully exploited by Diderot, came most likely from the English benefactor, fortunately in good faith towards his hero.

Speculating on the *neveu*'s literary ancestors, Fabre, who grants Curtius his critical due, links the *neveu* to an illustrious line of rascals and parasites:

> Diderot l'a vu forcément à travers sa culture et, comme cette culture, quoi qu'on en ait dit, était une culture essentiellement classique, maint souvenir est remonté de Lucien, de Plaute, de Térence, d'Horace, de Juvénal ou de Pétrone, de Rabelais ou de Boileau, pour donner une sorte de relief épique aux faits et gestes de Rameau. . . . Le relief de Rameau vient, en partie, de la conscience qu'il prend de lui-même ou que Diderot lui fait prendre, de cette illustre et famélique ascendance. . . . Le Simon de Lucien démontrait déjà à son interlocuteur que l'art du parasite l'emporte de beaucoup sur celui de l'orateur ou du philosophe. Rameau et Diderot, qui ont fait leurs classes, s'en souviennent et à merveille. Inutile donc d'invoquer Swift, ce Lucien des temps modernes, là où Lucien, ce Swift de l'hellénisme, avait déjà dit l'essentiel. Ou de déranger le docteur Sterne pour la cocasserie réaliste, les histoires à propos de bottes, et le récit discontinu, si l'on en trouve autant dans le *Roman Comique* de Scarron. Le *Neveu de Rameau* ne doit rien qu'indirectement à ces deux Anglais, que Diderot n'admirait tant que parce qu'il retrouvait en eux un air de famille; son originalité est d'autant plus savoureuse qu'elle s'insère dans une tradition décidément classique. (pp. lvi–lviii)

One wonders what Fabre's view of Diderot's indebtedness to English literature would have been, had the critic been acquainted with Johnson's *Life of Savage* as well as with Diderot's puzzling

book review, not to mention Savage's *An Author to be Lett*. Would
he have revised his conclusions concerning Diderot's originality
"d'autant plus savoureuse qu'elle s'insére dans une tradition clas-
sique"? Inasmuch as the classical models of biography were surely
as familiar to Johnson as to Diderot, it is Johnson's transcendence
of these models that constitutes his achievement. We should add
that, according to his reckoning, it took him only thirty-six hours
to write this biography. Exemplary of the enthusiasm with which
the book was received is that of Sir Joshua Reynolds. Boswell relates that the painter, having discovered the *Life of Savage* some-
where in Devonshire and "knowing nothing of its author . . . began to read it while he was standing with his arm leaning against a
chimney piece. . . . It seized his attention so strongly, that, not
being able to lay down the book til he had finished it, when he
attempted to move, he found his arm totally benumbed" (L,
1:165)—a reaction comparable to that of Goethe who, upon first
reading *Le Neveu de Rameau,* compared it to a bomb exploding in
the midst of French literature.[57] Indeed, one is tempted to claim
that Johnson does for Savage what Boswell will do for Johnson and
what Rousseau will do for himself: renew traditional formulations
of archetypes (Johnson of the parasite, Boswell of the conversationalist, and Rousseau of the self-made man)—in short, "existen-
tialize" literary types into specific mortal men.

Such metamorphoses which result in an individualization of a
type into a unique man—for example, the *parasite* Savage becomes
Richard Savage, the parasite—can only occur by virtue of a powerful sense of identification. Paul Fussell states the matter very well:
"As Johnson proceeds to recount Savage's career, it becomes clear
that his writing the whole *Life of Savage* . . . is in part the result of
his perceiving himself in Savage and his own literary career. We
sense that we are in the presence of that kind of 'autobiography
disguised as biography' of which André Maurois speaks."[58] No
one, I think, has better expressed the delicacy of the tribute that
Johnson paid to his profligate and insolent friend than Sir Walter
Raleigh, whose assessment deserves to be quoted in full:

> Only a man of the broadest and sanest sympathies could have
> performed this task, which Johnson does not seem to find
> difficult. Towards Savage he is all tenderness and generosity,

yet he does not for an instant relax his allegiance to the virtues which formed no part of his friend's character. He tells the whole truth; yet his affection for Savage remains what he felt it to be, the most important truth of all. His morality is so entirely free from pedantry, his sense of the difficulty of virtue and the tragic force of circumstance is so keen, and his love of singularity of character is so great, that even while he points the moral of a wasted life he never comes near to the vanity of condemnation. It is abundantly clear from the facts, which he records with all the impartiality of a naturalist, that Savage, besides being hopelessly self-indulgent and dissolute, was violently egotistic, overbearing, and treacherous to his friends. Johnson's verdict on these faults is given in the closing sentences of his *Life:* "The insolence and resentment of which he is accused were not easily to be avoided by a great mind, irritated by perpetual hardships, and constrained hourly to return the spurns of contempt and repress the insolence of prosperity; and vanity surely may be readily pardoned in him, to whom life afforded no other comforts than barren praises and consciousness of deserving them."[59]

To be sure, Diderot also perceives himself in his portrait of Lui, but never in the tragic mode. The mood seems gay, brittle, intellectual—but is it? Fabre writes:

> Aversion, dégoût, mépris, pitié, tels sont les sentiments qu'il Diderot éprouve, ou croit éprouver en sa présence, . . . mais, en fait, il s'agit de désarroi, d'admiration, d'envie, de remords et comme de honte de soi-même. De sympathie, surtout, et d'une espèce quasi organique. Car Rameau . . . compagnon de jeunesse et de bohème, est resté ce que Diderot a été, ce qu'il a failli devenir. . . . Encore Rameau a-t-il conquis, par son renoncement même, le droit d'avouer et de vivre son échec. Le philosophe, au contraire, est condamné, dans son angoisse, aux faux-semblants et aux demi-mensonges. . . . La rancune du philosophe contre le loup Jean-Jacques, hirsute et maigre, mais libre, s'explique en partie par là: il sent en sa conduite, celle d'un être qui essaye de vivre sa morale, comme un reproche ou un remords. (pp. lxvi–lxvii)

Fabre concludes his analysis by showing us a Diderot threatened by pharisaic bourgeois values: "Du moins, Diderot sent-il monter de Rameau comme un regret ou un appel. A un esprit aussi robuste

que le sien, il est plus facile de mettre en question l'univers que
soi-même. Le fait que *Moi* est enfin, non pas seul, mais d'abord,
mis en cause, donne sa résonnance tragique au *Neveu de Rameau*"
(lxix). In short, Diderot feels sorry for himself; Johnson, for Savage.
But, save for these fleeting shadows—"ce n'est rien, ce sont des
momens qui passent" (p. 16)—Diderot's satire of himself remains
good-humored. "Dans le *Neveu de Rameau*," notes Fabre, "la satire
ne parait jamais aussi impertinente ni savoureuse que lorsqu'elle se
tourne contre Diderot. Le plaisir est alors d'une espèce plus subtile
et plus rare; il naît de la découverte railleuse de soi-même, au delà
de la bonne conscience et des attitudes de parade: mais il reste
toujours un plaisir" (xliii).

Fabre's reference to Jean-Jacques, *loup hirsute et maigre, mais
libre,* brings to mind Donald O'Gorman's imaginative book *Diderot
the Satirist,* in which he suggests that *Le Neveu de Rameau* may
embody a caricature of Rousseau:

> Is it really possible, critics have asked themselves, that
> resentment towards a third-rate author like Charles Palissot
> should have inspired a satire of such extraordinary richness and
> power? What is more, can we honestly believe that for twenty
> years of his life Diderot came back constantly to retouch the
> portrait of an insignificant musician like Jean-François
> Rameau? These anomalies have led scholars to fathom the soul
> of Diderot the satirist in the effort to uncover other secret
> sources of his motivation. Thus far, no fully satisfactory
> explanation has been found.

After having shown that *le neveu* embodies traits of Charles Palissot
and Charles Duclos, O'Gorman proceeds to convince his readers
that "Jean-Jacques Rousseau is one of the several contemporaries of
Diderot concealed beneath *Lui*'s leering mask" and that such an
identification should cause no surprise.[60] O'Gorman's two initial
questions strike me as very reasonable, and his main argument,
artfully orchestrated, convinces me tentatively yet does not seduce
me. On reading O'Gorman's book, a nonspecialist might well ask
what Rousseau and *Le Neveu de Rameau* can possibly have in common. But, on reading Diderot's vitriolic diatribe against his former
friend in his *Essai sur les règnes de Claude et de Néron,* where he

proposes to write on Rousseau's monument "Ce Jean-Jacques que vous voyez fut un pervers," the reader will realize how differently Diderot and his *amis philosophes* perceived Rousseau from the way we perceive him today.[61] If the reader recalls the affinities that I discern in the parallel lives of Rousseau and Johnson and if he feels, as I do, the presence of Savage-Hackney behind the ever-changing masks and grimaces of Diderot's *neveu*—in short, if he subjects *le sujet* Rameau to a series of existential metamorphoses—then he may well applaud O'Gorman's flair. Like a psychic sleuth, he will sense behind the facade of *Le Neveu de Rameau* powerful human presences, antagonists infinitely more disquieting than Lui is to Moi. Among these we must count not only Rousseau's spirit haunting intermittently Diderot's second satire but also that of Samuel Johnson, alias Savage, as well as the spirit of Savage, alias Hackney.

However, I disagree with Professor O'Gorman when he admires the veracity of Diderot's portrait of Jean-François Rameau, for, as I have tried to show, the *neveu* is a construct, a psychological collage—a fact which might explain why so many find this satire hard to understand. It is not the references that confuse the readers, but the composite character of the *neveu:* "A glance at the documents assembled by M. Fabre in the Appendix of his edition of *Le Neveu de Rameau* leaves the reader in amazement at the skill with which the author succeeded in capturing the essential traits of the younger Rameau as he is described by his closest friends." In all fairness to O'Gorman, one has to note that he qualifies the faithfulness of Diderot's portrait:

> But the brilliance of this artistic triumph must not be allowed to blind us to the fact that our knowledge of the historical individual is meagre in comparison with the wealth of detail concerning *Lui* to be found in Diderot's satire. Therefore, however closely Rameau's nephew resembles the portrait, it remains quite possible that the portrait is more unlike than it is like Rameau's nephew, especially in its moral dimension. We can be certain that at least some of the sentiments and ideas lent to *Lui* were either imagined by the author in the interest of universality or borrowed from other contemporaries for purposes of satire, but no one has yet determined to what

extent Diderot saw fit to depart from the intellectual and moral idiosyncracies displayed by the living model.

O'Gorman concludes the section, entitled "Details of a Literary Portrait," as follows:

> For those who find the Diderot-Lui theory [*le neveu* supposedly engendered by affinities between Jean-François Rameau and Diderot] implausible, there remains another possibility: that Diderot chose to depict Jean-François Rameau for the simple reason that the latter was a living parody of another "original," Jean-Jacques Rousseau. This hypothesis assumes that there are some traits which, at least in Diderot's view, the two men had in common, but that the portrayal of Rameau is subservient to the caricature of Jean-Jacques. We have already seen evidence to show that *Lui,* who espouses all of Rousseau's theories on music, has also been endowed with two outstanding characteristics—inconsistency and cynicism—that could have been modelled upon similar traits manifested by Jean-Jacques.[62]

Such, in essence, is O'Gorman's view of the matter, and he may well be right. However, from my viewpoint, the inconsistency and cynicism which, according to him, Diderot senses in Rousseau and transfers to his *neveu* also manifest themselves in Johnson's *Life of Savage* and, perhaps even more so, in Savage's *An Author to be Lett.* Keeping in mind Diderot's puzzling book review of *La Vie de Richard Savage* and the striking resemblances between Diderot's *neveu* and Johnson's Savage, as well as thematic resemblances between the *neveu* and Iscariot Hackney that result perhaps from the Pope-Palissot-Diderot connection, we shall safely conclude with Goethe that "Diderot ist Diderot"[63] and that Jean-François Rameau is his uncle's nephew. We may also conclude, less assuredly, that Diderot's *neveu* is not only a parent to an English cousin Savage, the bastard, as well as to Savage's "nephew" Iscariot Hackney, but that the *neveu* is also the godchild of two godfathers who disapproved of each other—one from Lichfield, the other from Geneva—godfathers who would have been horrified had they known what an irritating misfit they had managed to sponsor, unbeknownst to each other and to themselves.

Given the importance of Johnson's *Life of Savage,* it is surprising that few scholars have integrated this extraordinary biography into literary history. In fact, only Benjamin Boyce has traced filiations between it and Defoe's account of the beautiful Roxana, whose maternal reactions at times bear comparison with those of the Countess of Macclesfield. Boyce shows convincingly that Johnson's evocation of Savage's mother includes traits derived from eighteenth-century criminal biographies as well as from Defoe's fiction. He concludes: "So he creates her in a new image, worse than any of the previous ones and more shocking than the pictures of Roxana or Moll or even the old bawds in Richardson's novels. Cymbeline's queen and Lady Macbeth, though cruel, have not her lust. Perhaps the elder Annesleys as seen in the *Memoirs* are the nearest to her, but they are men. Mrs. Brett {Lady Macclesfield} is Johnson's own terrible vision of the debauched lady of fashion."[64] Another Johnsonian, Paul K. Alkon, makes *The Life of Savage* his point of departure for a study of the different readings accorded to a "key passage in which Johnson brilliantly analyzes the mental mechanisms of rationalization, denial, and projection by which Savage managed to avoid blaming his misfortunes on himself." Furthermore, he shows that Charles Whitehead's novel *Richard Savage: A Romance of Real Life* (1841), whose plot Alkon likens to a tragic *Tom Jones,* reveals the influence of *Oliver Twist* and that "it is likely that Whitehead's Richard Savage had some influence on Dicken's portrayal of the Estella-Pip relationship as well as on other aspects of *Great Expectations.*" Alkon concludes: "If so, then Johnson's *Life of Savage* must also be credited with an impact on the evolution of novelistic, as well as biographical techniques."[65]

But there are other veins to be exploited: for example, the theme of the parasite, first treated in Greek comedy by Epicharmos—a theme related to that of the flatterer or *kolas.* These stock characters reappear in Roman comedy and satire and most likely are related to Attic comedy. Not to be forgotten are the panderers and parasites of English and American literature. Next to Falstaff stands Mosca in Ben Jonson's *Volpone* and, much nearer to us, Kate Croy and Charlotte Stant who scheme in *The Wings of the Dove* and *The Golden Bowl.* Closer to us is the host-parasite relationship of Leventhal and Kirby Allbee in Saul Bellow's *The Victim,* where

Allbee the sponger turns into a specter invading the consciousness of his host Leventhal and thus precipitates a dreadful intimacy which ultimately fuses both men into symbiotic patterns compounded of hate and compassion. Lord Tyrconnel has been possessed by a Savage versed in Dostoyevskian gray magic. As for Robert Frost's "The Death of the Hired Man," could one not interpret Silas's homecoming as an elegy on a New England parasite? It is not a matter of chance that one of the epigraphs to this essay derives from Proust, whose incomparable fresco includes *pique-assiettes* like the comte de Crécy, Saniette, and Charlus's beloved and reprehensible Charlie Morel, alias Bobette. And it is not surprising that Proust comments on Marcel's need to surround himself with hangers-on after Albertine's death:

> Peut-être alors la fatigue et la tristesse que je ressentais vinrent-elles moins d'avoir aimé inutilement ce que déjà j'oubliais, que de commencer à me plaire avec de nouveaux vivants, de purs gens du monde, de simples amis des Guermantes, si peu intéressants par eux-mêmes. Je me consolais peut-être plus aisément de constater que celle que j'avais aimée n'était plus au bout d'un certain temps qu'un pâle souvenir, que de retrouver en moi cette vaine activité qui nous fait perdre le temps à tapisser notre vie d'une végétation humaine vivace mais parasite, qui deviendra le néant aussi quand elle sera morte, qui déjà est étrangère à tout ce que nous avons connu et à laquelle pourtant cherche à plaire notre sénilité bavarde, mélancolique et coquette.[66]

Whereas it is not easy to situate Johnson's *Life of Savage* within the framework of Anglo-American literature, it is even more difficult to "fit" *Le Neveu de Rameau* into the Gallic scheme of things, impossible to define and yet ever so real. The *neveu* does not seem to resemble anyone of importance in French fiction or in French life. To be sure, Tartuffe and Charlie Morel are immoral parasites (I assume that there are moral ones) equipped with good taste, but unfortunately they lack the *neveu's* courageous self-awareness. As for French men of letters with parasitic inclinations, one thinks immediately of La Fontaine and, in the eighteenth century, of young Jean-Jacques who may be said to have led a sponger's existence during his tender years under the wings of Mme de Warens.

Perhaps we ought to add that the last page he ever wrote is devoted to a lovely transfiguration of these parasitic years into a "bonheur pur et plein," lived in a "maison isolée au penchant d'un vallon,"[67] when, in fact, Maman was already in the strong arms of Wintzenried. His elegiac recollection is matched by Johnson's touching reference to Henry and Hester Thrale's country estate Streatham Place: "I long to come to that place which my dear friends allow me to call home."[68] Curiously enough, the theme of the parasite was never perfected in German literature, and this lack may well explain Goethe's enthusiastic reaction to Le Neveu de Rameau. Spanish literature, to be sure, teems with pícaros, but one is hard pressed to point to a Hispanic parasite of heroic proportions. What holds true for Spain holds true for Italy, even in the province of the Inferno, where spongers may have been subsumed in Dante's mind under the category of ignavi, spineless cowards whom he hates even more than sinners of every persuasion. As for Russian spongers, the first to be mentioned has to be Kozovkin, a major character in Turgenev's two-act comedy A Poor Gentleman, who eats "alien bread" at the table of a commoner, a St. Petersburg official, whose wife turns out to be Kozovkin's natural daughter. Oblomov (1859), by Gontcharov, does not fit the parasitic paradigm, since the enervated hero does not sponge but only lives off serf-labor and eventually off the emotions of his landlady and future wife. Next in line are parasites in Chekhov's short stories, as, for example, "A Father" (1887). However, the authentic successor to the neveu in the realm of fiction has to be Foma Fomitch, protagonist of Dostoyevsky's novel The Friend of the Family (1859). Avraham Yarmolinski summarizes it in terms germane to the Life of Savage and Le Neveu de Rameau:

> As in most of the early stories, the character dominating the action is a man who for years had eaten the bread of humiliation, his dignity outraged and trampled upon. Dostoyevsky takes a new tack here by placing him in a position where he is the master, revered, pampered, adulated, and watches his antics as the absurd creature gives free rein to his limitless conceit, lords it over everyone in his neighborhood, and smothers all in unctuous rhetoric. The

author achieves its effect through overstatement, hyperbole, excess, until one sees his Foma Fomich, larger than life, the embodiment of a monstrous vanity that is merely his overcompensation for insults previously endured.[69]

The tables have been turned. Rameau's fantasies—his *Wunsch-träume*—have been fulfilled: "C'est alors que je me rappellerois tout ce qu'ils m'ont fait souffrir; et je leur rendrois bien les avanies qu'ils m'ont faites. J'aime a commander, et je commanderai. J'aime qu'on me loue et l'on me louera. . . . Cela sera delicieux" (p. 38).

It is beyond the scope of these speculations to trace upon the illusory grid of the history of ideas the growth of ideas and feelings that have made possible changes in the significance of such time-honored sociological paradigms as "host-parasite" or "master-slave." In this evolution, Rousseau's *Discours sur l'origine de l'iné-galité* (1755), Sade's *La Philosophie dans le boudoir* (1795), and Hegel's *Phenomenology of Mind* (1807) represent high-points against a historical background convulsed by the French and the Industrial revolutions, as well as by progress in the "hard" sciences. I shall permit myself a reference to Hegel's treatise, not because it is common knowledge that *Rameaus Neffe* plays a dramatic role in the section entitled "Spirit in Self-Estrangement—The Discipline of Culture and Civilization" but only because the analogies between *Le Neveu de Rameau* and the *Life of Savage* could be amplified, if the *Life* could be evaluated tentatively according to the grandiose system of the Sage of Tübingen. And lest it seem sacrilegious to subject the *Life of Savage* to a German Idealist analysis, it should be remembered that many Johnsonians have applied psychoanalytic concepts to Johnson and Savage and that Hegel is, after all, much closer to Johnson than is Freud. Only twenty-three years separate Johnson's death in 1784 from the publication of the *Phenomenology of Mind* in 1807. Even if the reader is not familiar with this work's dynamic structure and special terminology, the relevance of the short passage to which the footnote refers should be obvious.[70] Indeed, Johnson's political philosophy relates quite well to the Hegelian concept of "the noble consciousness." However, his defer-ential submission to Anglican orthodoxy limits the usefulness of this concept as a means of understanding Johnson in the light of Hegelian philosophy—a submission which becomes quite mean-ingful through the concept of "the contrite consciousness" ("the alienated soul which is the consciousness of self as a divided nature, a doubled and merely contradictory being").[71] But Richard Savage, as recalled by his friend, fits not only the paradigm of "the noble consciousness"—one imagines that he would have liked to—but also that of "the vile consciousness." Again, the reader should turn to the illuminating analysis by Trilling, who shows how "the movement from 'nobility' to 'baseness' is not a devolution but a development. So far from deploring 'baseness,' Hegel celebrates it. The 'honesty' of Diderot-Moi, which evokes Hegel's impatient scorn, consists in his wholeness of self, in the directness and con-sistency of his relation to things, and in his submission to a tradi-tional morality. Diderot-Moi does not exemplify the urge of the Spirit to escape from the conditions which circumscribe it and to enter into an existence which will be determined by itself alone."[72] As for the *neveu,* who clearly embodies "the vile consciousness," it should be noted that Hegel's interpretation of Diderot's anti-hero stresses, above all, hate and resentment, whereas Diderot's *neveu* exhibits a lightness of touch sorely missing in Hegel's characteriza-tion. Without this grace and playfulness, Diderot is no longer himself anymore than is his *neveu.*[73] Having undergone a teutonic metamorphosis, the latter reappears in Saint Petersburg, according to the dictates of his karma, as a denizen of the undergound, intro-ducing himself as "ill, full of spleen, and repellent."[74] Rancor, malice and, above all, *ressentiment* are his weaknesses—*ressentiment* being also characteristic of the *neveu* as well as of the "artificial bastard."

   This very notion of *ressentiment,* extremely useful in the detec-tion of psychological elements common to the two works under discussion, represents a focal point in Max Scheler's thought. He views it as "a self-poisoning of the mind which has quite definite causes and consequences. . . . It is a lasting mental attitude, caused by the systematic repression of certain emotions and affects which, as such, are normal components of human nature. . . . The emotions and affects primarily concerned are revenge, hatred, mal-

ice, envy, the impulse to detract, and spite."[75] Johnson's perspicacity in analyzing the anatomy of resentment not only matches
Diderot's insight into the dynamics of power and hate but also
foreshadows Scheler's phenomenological analyses grounded in
Nietzschean utterances:

> Examples need not be sought at any great Distance to prove
> that Superiority of Fortune has a natural Tendency to kindle
> Pride, and that Pride seldom fails to exert itself in Contempt
> and Insult; and if this is often the Effect of hereditary Wealth,
> and of Honours enjoyed only by the Merit of others, it is some
> Extenuation of any indecent Triumphs to which this unhappy
> Man may have been betrayed, that his Prosperity was
> heightened by the Force of Novelty, and made more
> intoxicating by a Sense of Misery in which he had so long
> languished, and perhaps of the Insults which he had formerly
> born, and which he might now think himself entitled to
> revenge. (p. 66)

This longing for revenge is, however, quickly repressed whenever
he lacks the strength to fulfill it. In the words of Johnson, "he
submitted with a good Grace to what he could not avoid, and
. . . discovered no Resentment where he had no Power" (p. 112).

   As one reflects on Savage's severance from all comfort and care,
one wonders whether there ever was a redemptive prostitute in his
life, a Lisa upon whom he could vent his rage and *ressentiment* in
loveless love. From what we know of his marginal and jarred existence among the poor and rich of London, it is likely that he met
such a woman; a century later, Baudelaire, evoking Paris at the
break of dawn, expressed feelings that may have been familiar to
such as her and Savage:

> Comme un visage en pleurs que les brises essuient,
> L'air est plein du frisson des choses qui s'enfuient,
> Et l'homme est las d'écrire et la femme d'aimer.

   Are men like Savage to be written off as an unfortunate loss to
society? What are we to make of troublesome and quarrelsome
parasites? Are forced labor and punishment satisfactory procedures
for delinquent poets and arrogant transients? Whatever an ethical
answer to these questions might be (there are no realistic ones),

Samuel Johnson and Diderot would have understood, even subscribed to, the thought of the author of *Beyond Good and Evil* who
speculates: "it is not unthinkable that such a society might attain
such a *consciousness of power* that it could allow itself the noblest
luxury possible to it—letting those who harm it go unpunished.
'What are my parasites to me?' it might say. 'May they live and pros-
per: I am strong enough for that!' "[76] Is this contempt for punishment not matched by Johnson's unwillingness to condemn the mis-
fits of his age among whom we must surely count his friend
Richard Savage? Does the Nietzschean view concerning societal
attempts "to sanctify *revenge* under the name of justice"[77] not cast a
new light on Johnson's almost proverbial unwillingness to upbraid
"those wretched females . . . fallen in the lowest state of vice,
poverty, and disease" (L, 4:321)? Does it not illuminate also the
secret significance of his celebrated answer to a lady who asked why
he so constantly gave money to beggars and was told with great
feeling: "Madam, to enable them to beg on"?[78] Given the pious
guilt that darkened Johnson's life, one marvels that he succeeded in
sparing Savage from its corrosive and subtle effects— his childish
and proud friend who was so vulnerable when he trusted the present and intermittently spiteful or serene when it deceived him. By
way of conclusion to these pages in which "nothing is concluded,"
we may ask ourselves whether *le neveu* did not play symbolically in
the life of Denis Diderot a role similar to the one enacted existen-
tially by Richard Savage in the life of Samuel Johnson—the role of
a man seemingly unscathed by guilt and untroubled by what he
owes to others, an insouciant and self-justifying parasite who fasci-
nates and repels us because tawdry tempters like him embody the
innate longing to abandon ourselves once more to her who carried
us and cared for us until, set free, we had to fight, dance, or beg for
daily bread.

Notes

Introduction

1. Pascal, *Pensées,* ed. Léon Brunschwicg (Paris, 1936), 1:53.
2. Georges May, *L'autobiographie* (Paris, 1979), 12.
3. Edition Pléiade. Concerning the development of Rousseau's "virtual" selves, consult the stimulating book by Huntington Williams, *Rousseau and Romantic Biography* (Oxford, 1983).
4. Plutarque, *Vies,* ed. Budé (Paris, 1975), 30.
5. Cf. Rousseau, *Confessions,* 1:9: "Plutarque, surtout devint ma lecture favorite."
6. *Rasselas* and *Candide* are unique. There are no comparable apologues or *contes philosophiques* in English and French literature.
7. Jan Brandt Corstius, *Introduction to the Comparative Study of Literature* (New York, 1968), 159.
8. Sheldon Sacks, *Fiction and the Shape of Belief* (Berkeley, 1967), 239. The same critic also observes: "*Rasselas* is a disjointed novel, but an excellent apologue."
9. Quoted by Jean-Albert Sorel, *Histoire de France et d'Angleterre* (Paris, 1950), 144.
10. Frederick C. Green, *Minuet* (London, 1935), 12.
11. Alice Green Fredman, *Diderot and Sterne* (New York, 1955), 14.
12. Ibid., 7.
13. Green, *Minuet,* 289. The only way Rousseau's success in Germany can be explained is to postulate that his thinking is "German." Luminaries such as Kant, Goethe, Schiller, Fichte, Hölderlin, and Hegel, to mention a few, all testify to his influence on their thought.
14. Frederick C. Green, *Eighteenth-Century France* (London, 1929), 29–69.
15. Edward Bulwer-Lytton, *England and the English,* introd. by Meacham (Chicago, 1970), xvi.
16. André-Michel Rousseau, *L'Angleterre et Voltaire,* 3 vols., in *Studies on Voltaire and the Eighteenth Century,* vol. 146, p. 285.
17. Diderot, *Entretien entre d'Alembert et Diderot,* Ed. Pléiade (1951), 876.
18. Henri Roddier, *J.-J. Rousseau en Angleterre au XVIII* siècle (Paris,

1950). Consult also Jacques Voisine, *J.-J. Rousseau en Angleterre à l'epoque romantique* (Paris, 1956).

19. Concerning cosmopolitism during the Age of Enlightenment, consult the excellent study by René Pomeau, *L'Europe des Lumières* (Paris, 1966).

1.   Johnson and Rousseau

Quotations from Rousseau refer to the Edition Pléiade, 4 vols., with the exception of *L'Essai sur l'origine des langues,* ed. Belin (1817), reprinted by *La Bibliothèque du Graphe* in *Cahiers pour l'Analyse,* supplement to no. 8 (Paris, 1967). References to the Edition Pléiade and to the *Essai* are integrated into the text.

1. Denis Diderot, *Le Neveu de Rameau,* ed. Jean Fabre (Paris, 1950), 4.

2. Donald Greene, ed., *Samuel Johnson: A Collection of Critical Essays* (New York, 1965), 1.

3. See Donald Greene, "Do We Need a Biography of Johnson's Boswell's Years?" *Modern Language Studies* 9, no. 3 (1979): 128–36.

4. Frank Brady, "The Strategies of Biography and Some Eighteenth-Century Examples," in *Literary Theory and Structure: Essays in Honor of William K. Wimsatt,* ed. Brady, Palmer, and Price (New Haven, 1973), 247.

5. Donald Greene, *The Age of Exuberance* (New York, 1970), 4.

6. Only six scholars have devoted their efforts to elucidating the relationship between Johnson and Rousseau and, without exception, their analyses are fragmentary or part of a larger scheme. As early as 1907 Robert Kleuker compares the doctrines of the two thinkers. Sigyn Christiani reviews all Kleuker's arguments in her summary of Johnson's opinions on Rousseau and centers her attention on Johnson as a transitional figure between Neoclassicism and Romanticism, as a man who did not dare to draw the consequences of what he understood: "Zu Ende gedacht, müssen seine Anschauungen ihn ins romantische Lager führen—aber Samuel Johnson weicht vor letzten Entscheidungen zurück und bleibt so doch im wesentlichen noch ein Pseudoklassizist und ein echter Engländer zugleich" (*Samuel Johnson als Kritiker im Lichte von Pseudo-Klassizismus und Romantik,* in *Beiträge zur Englischen Philologie,* ed. Max Förster, vol. 18 [Leipzig, 1931], 31). Richard B. Sewall and Albert Schinz elaborate and refine views expounded by Kleuker, who deserves much credit for his pathbreaking treatment long before any Johnsonians and Rousseau scholars became aware of the curious affiliations between their respective heroes. In 1950 and 1956, the late Henri Roddier and Jacques Voisine

published major studies on Rousseau's influence in England. Roddier's book is entitled *J.-J. Rousseau en Angleterre au XVIIIe Siècle* (Paris, 1950); Voisine's, *J.-J. Rousseau en Angleterre à l'epoque romantique* (Paris, 1956). Both works are *ouvrages de fond,* and I shall refer to them whenever necessary. As for Kleuker, I shall only quote his conclusion: Johnson agrees with Rousseau's fundamental arguments; he rejects *die Überkultur* as unnecessary for happiness and, like Jean-Jacques, believes that peace reigned during the childhood of mankind, that men are born free, and that the desire for property has gradually destroyed a serene and quiet way of life. Furthermore, Johnson, according to Kleuker, shares Rousseau's views on the development of social and political organizations and proclaims, like Rousseau, that the people are the rulers of the state, whose powers are restricted to the executive. And yet, according to Kleuker, Johnson opposes violently all of Rousseau's proposals as dangerous to the welfare of the state: "In short, Johnson hates in Rousseau not the philosopher, but the discontented fault-finder (*Nörgler*) in all that exists . . . the worst enemy of public peace and happiness" (*Dr. Samuel Johnsons Verhältnis zur französischen Literatur* [Strassburg, 1907], 154 [my transl.]). Richard Sewall not only amplifies ideas suggested by Kleuker but also shows that Burke and Johnson had Rousseau in mind when they wrote *A Vindication of Natural Society* (1756) and *Rasselas* (1759): "The probability that Dr. Johnson intended certain passages in *Rasselas* as a satire upon Rousseau's ideas on the state of nature can . . . be established only by circumstantial evidence and internal parallels" ("Rousseau's Second Discourse in England from 1755 to 1762," *Philological Quarterly* 17 (1938): 105). Specifically, Sewall highlights the episodes evoking the shepherds and the hermit, "whose fancy riots in scenes of folly" (chap. 21), as well as the episode contained in chap. 22 entitled "The Happiness of a Life Led According to Nature," wherein we meet the smug philosopher who informs us that "the way to be happy is to live according to nature, in obedience to that universal and unalterable law with which every heart is originally impressed; which is not written on it by precept, but engraven by destiny, not instilled by education, but infused at our nativity." Sewall's demonstration seemed correct to me until I came upon an article by Donald Greene ("Johnson, Stoicism, and the Good Life" in *The Unknown Samuel Johnson,* ed. Burke and Kay [Madison, 1983], 17–38), which establishes quite convincingly that the philosopher in *Rasselas* is meant to represent a Stoic philosopher rather than a caricature of Rousseau. The fourth critic to follow Kleuker's lead is Albert Schinz, well known to all Rousseau scholars. His lively but brief confrontation not only opposes Rousseau and Johnson as *philosophes,* restating Kleuker's findings, but also compares them as *men,* moral purists in an age of elegance and hypocrisy: "Et d'abord, nous pouvons passer sans guère nous y arrêter sur le trait qui fait si bien de Johnson un véritable frère siamois de Rousseau, à savoir cette combinaison de l'ours avec l'homme aux grandes délicatesses de coeur— tous deux adoptent consciemment le rôle d'Alceste dans la société du XVIIIᵉ siècle méprisant les Philinte indulgents jusqu'à l'hypocrisie" ("Les Dangers du cliché littéraire: Le Dr. Johnson et Jean-Jacques Rousseau," *Modern Language Notes* 57[1942]: 575). In a second article, "Dr. Johnson, Rousseau, and Reform" (1949), Richard Sewall clarifies further the opposition between the two thinkers by comparing them on "grounds which each would have considered fair" ("Dr. Johnson, Rousseau, and Reform," in *The Age of Johnson: Essays Presented to Chauncey B. Tinker* [New Haven, 1949], 307). According to Sewall, "Johnson and Rousseau were getting at the same thing: the problem of what to do about the ailing society in which they found themselves. Each man assumed constantly throughout his career the role of moralist or spiritual physician to his age, and to compare them on this basis is both legitimate and suggestive. Johnson's abusiveness can be seen for what it is, and Rousseau appears in his proper light" (p. 307). Much of Sewall's article constitutes a review of Rousseau's achievements, perhaps of more interest to Johnsonians than to *rousseauistes*. Regardless of some similarities in mood as suggested by Schinz, Sewall concludes that these resemblances "show merely that neither lacked humanity or a sense of justice. Fundamentally, Johnson believed Rousseau's schemes to be tainted at their source, mistaken in principle, and fraught with possibilities for disaster" (p. 314). Perhaps the most interesting part of Sewall's comparison is his conclusion concerning Rousseau's spiritual influence in England, later amplified by Roddier and Voisine in their detailed studies: "But that Rousseau read the times more clearly, there can be little doubt. . . . England was developing a conscience, for which Rousseau provided both encouragement and method. In Scotland during the third quarter of the century a more concerted movement showed that a new and non-Johnsonian view of man and society could be assimilated into the British Tradition with fruitful results. Adam Smith, Adam Ferguson, Hume, Kames, Monboddo (leaders in what has recently been called 'The Scottish Inquiry'), all felt his influence in one way or another" (p. 315). Another critic to relate Johnson to Rousseau is Jean Hagstrum: "It may surprise those who associate Rousseau only with Romantic release to discover in *Emile*—and almost everywhere, for that matter—a respect for reality and disciplined common sense worthy of Samuel Johnson, who nevertheless feared and loathed the French writer as a major and moral menace" (*Sex and Sensibility,* [Chicago, 1980], 221–22).

I have referred to the studies of Professors Roddier and Voisine. Both works, too often ignored or passed over by Anglo-American critics, fix the general outlines as well as the details of the complex relationship

between Rousseau and England. Professor Voisine's treatment of my subject matter teems with *aperçus* as learned as they are humane. Indeed, his
Rousseau en Angleterre combines the virtues of French scholarship with the
delights of English biography; studded with interesting and often curious
facts, it reviews much of the literary history of the second part of the
eighteenth century and the beginning of the nineteenth. Moreover, Professor Voisine's facts respect the facts of life; that is to say, his precision
never damages what should be left inviolate: the ambiguities of a writer's
destiny and the incommensurable truths of a work of art.

7. In the introduction to her edition of *Thraliana,* Katharine Bal-
derstone writes concerning Mrs. Piozzi's *Anecdotes:* "It was the first account of any value to appear, and it has remained the most intimate
picture of him, surpassing in that respect even the far greater and far more
exhaustive record of Boswell" (p. xviii).

8. Frank Brady and Frederick A. Pottle, eds., *Boswell on the Grand
Tour: Italy, Corsica and France, 1765–1766* (New York, 1953), 260–61.

9. Another lady to lump together Rousseau and Johnson is Fanny
Burney. G. B. Hill comments in his edition of Boswell's *Life of Johnson*:
"Miss Burney, in her Preface to *Evelina,* a novel which was her introduction to Johnson's strong affection, mentioning Rousseau and Johnson,
adds in a footnote: 'However superior the capacities in which these great
writers deserve to be considered, they must pardon me that, for the dignity of my subject, I here rank the authors of *Rasselas* and *Eloïse* as Novelists' " (2.1.12).

10. Lévi-Strauss, *Tristes Tropiques* (Paris, 1955), 421–22.

11. Paul de Man, *Blindness and Insight* (New York, 1971), 111–12.

12. See Mark Temmer, *Art and Influence of Jean-Jacques Rousseau*
(Chapel Hill, 1973), chap. 5: "Rousseau and Thoreau."

13. Ibid., chap. 3: *"La Nouvelle Heloïse* and *Wilhelm Meisters Lehrjahre."*

14. Sir Walter Raleigh, *Six Essays on Johnson* (Oxford, 1910), 21.

15. T. S. Eliot, "Johnson's 'London' and 'The Vanity of Human
Wishes,' " *English Critical Essays: Twentieth Century,* ed. D. Jones (London,
1933), 303–4.

16. For a general discussion of Samuel Johnson's poetry, see Donald
Greene, *Samuel Johnson,* chap. 2.

17. Jean de la Fontaine, *Oeuvres diverses,* ed. Clarac, Ed. Pléiade,
(Paris, 1958), 8.

18. See Bertrand H. Bronson, *Johnson Agonistes and Other Essays*
(Berkeley, 1965), 151. Professor Bronson writes: "In the end, I suspect—
and over and above what has been said earlier of Johnson's untheatrical
imagination,—the basic trouble lies in the style. The persons, to be sure,
are stiff and insufficiently vitalized. They are so, however, not primarily

because of what they do or say, but because of the way in which they say it."

19. See Temmer, *Art and Influence of Jean-Jacques Rousseau*, 105–6.

20. Bronson, *Johnson Agonistes*, 157: "Like any other author, Johnson exists for us in his works. But he exists for us also like a character in one of our older novels, and on the same level of objectivity and familiarity."

21. If ever two men have failed to fulfill Vergil's exhortation, they have to be Johnson and Rousseau:

> incipe, parve puer, risu cognoscere matrem—
>
> . . . .
>
> incipe, parve puer: qui non risere parenti
> nec deus hunc mensa, dea nec dignata cubili est.

George Oppen's translation of the end of the *Fourth Eclogue* reads as follows: "*Parve puer* . . . 'Begin, / O small boy / To be born; / On whom his parents have not smiled / No god thinks worthy of his table, / No goddess of her bed' " ("From Virgil," in *Collected Poems* [New York, 1975], 84–85).

22. Bronson, *Johnson Agonistes*, 115: "Perhaps surprisingly, at the very time when Johnson was engaged on the composition of *Irene,* another dramatist across the Channel was working on the same theme. Composed at Strasbourg, the *Mahomet Second* of Jean Sauvé de la Noue was first acted in Paris on the 23rd of February, 1739. It was so successful as to hold the stage for more than a generation."

23. Voisine, *Rousseau en Angleterre*, 42–44.

24. Bernardin de Saint-Pierre, *Oeuvres* (Paris, 1826), 12:37–38.

25. Every Johnsonian knows about his hero's cat Hodge to whom, when old, he fed oysters. Curiously enough, Rousseau, feline by nature, loved his dog Sultan, who accompanied his master to England. Hume encountered trouble when he attempted to persaude his moody guest to leave Sultan *chez lui* so that they might attend a performance at the theater where everyone, including George III, was waiting to have a look at the pseudo-Armenian. Concerning this episode, consult Roddier, *Rousseau en Angleterre*, 270. Rousseau's first dog was called Achate, perhaps a pun.

26. Bernardin de Saint-Pierre relates that the only faithful picture of Rousseau he had ever seen was an engraving done, he believes, in England. Rousseau is depicted "en bonnet et en habit d'Arménien" (*Oeuvres,* 12:38). This engraving has to be a copy of Ramsay's beautiful portrait now in Edinburgh. Concerning this and other portraits of Rousseau, consult Voisine, chap. 3, 39–40. Voisine relates that Rousseau disliked this painting and accused Ramsay of having depicted him with "la figure d'un cyclope affreux."

27. I refer the reader to an essay by Peter M. Newton, entitled "Samuel Johnson's Breakdown and Recovery in Middle-Age: A Life Span Developmental Approach to Mental Illness and its Cure," *International Review of Psycho-Analysis* 11 (1984): 93–118.

28. The discussion of Rousseau's contradictory experience of life is taken from my book *Time in Rousseau and Kant* (Geneva, 1958), 58–60.

29. Samuel T. Coleridge, *Philosophical Lectures,* ed. Kathleen Coburn (London, 1949), 308.

30. J. W. Cross, ed., *George Eliot's Life as related in Her Letters and Journals,* 3 vols., (Edinburgh, 1885), 1:198.

31. See G. W. F. Hegel, *The Phenomenology of Mind,* trans. J. B. Baillie, 2d ed., 251.

32. See Bronson, *Johnson Agonistes,* 42–43: "It is of the essence of Johnson's nature that his very acceptance should be strenuous, hard won and with difficulty held. 'To strive with difficulties,' he once wrote, 'and to conquer them, is the highest human felicity; the next is, to strive, and to deserve to conquer: but whose life has past without a contest, who can boast neither success nor merit, can survey himself only as a useless filler of existence; and if he is content with his own character, must owe his satisfaction to insensibility.'" Johnson's article of faith negates the very ideal of the *promeneur solitaire* who delights so often in the *dolce far niente.*

33. Brady and Pottle, eds., *Boswell on the Grand Tour, 1765–1766,* 300. See also R. A. Leigh, "Rousseau's English Pension," in *Studies in Eighteenth-Century French Literature Presented to Robert Niklaus* (Exeter, 1975), 109–22.

34. Bernardin de Saint-Pierre, *Essais sur J. J. Rousseau,* in *Oeuvres,* 12:78–79.

35. See Paul de Man, *Allegories of Reading* (New Haven, 1979), 138. Commenting on "Rousseau's ambivalence with regard to such key notions as property, civil authority and even technology," de Man states: "The ambivalence of Rousseau's attitude towards property is one example: on the one hand, he makes it sound as if property were theft; on the other hand, law is at times glorified, in almost extravagant terms, as defense of property."

36. Geoffrey Tillotson, *Augustan Studies* (London, 1961), 238.

37. Samuel Johnson, *A Dictionary of the English Language* (London, 1828), 1116.

38. Jean Starobinski, *La Transparence et l'obstacle* (Paris, 1958), 154.

39. Torquato Tasso, *Aminta,* ed. G. Baiardi (Urbino, 1976), 2.2.891.

40. See Charles Hughes, *Mrs. Piozzi's Thraliana* (London, 1913), 21.

41. Rousseau, *Lettre à d'Alembert* (Geneva, 1948), 106.

42. Bernardin de Saint-Pierre, *Oeuvres,* 12:44–45.

43. Personal communication.

44. Paul K. Alkon, *Samuel Johnson and Moral Dsicipline* (Chicago, 1967), 42–43.

45. It seems worthwhile to compare Rousseau's admonition to adults concerning their treatment of children to a statement recorded by Mrs. Piozzi: "There is in Life says Mr Johnson so very little Felicity to be possessed with Innocence, that we ought surely to catch diligently all that can be had without the hazard of Virtue: something like this same Principle was always discoverable in Mr. Johnson's thoughts on Education: he hated the cruel prudence by which Childhood is made miserable that Manhood may become insensible to Misery by frequent Repetition, yet no one more delighted in that general Discipline by which Children were restrained from tormenting their own grown up friends, nor more despised the Imbecility of Parents who are contented to profess their want of Power to govern: how says he is an Army governed" (T, 181).

46. James Gray, *Johnson's Sermons* (London, 1972), 230: "The sermons are not, of course, prose poems. Nor are they rhapsodic visions cast in a homiletic mould. They are, as this study has attempted to demonstrate, the unique productions of a great mind, steeped in the sermon literature of the past and in the Bible and in the Book of Common Prayer, nurtured in the Anglican tradition, and at the same time aware of the other tides and cross-curents of beliefs and interpretation that had swept the English-speaking world."

47. Concerning the relationship between *La Profession de foi* and English religious thought, consult Roddier, *Rousseau en Angleterre*, 178–210.

48. Stendhal, *Oeuvres Complètes*, (Paris, 1956) 18:249.

49. *The Letters of Samuel Johnson*, ed. R. W. Chapman (Oxford, 1952), letter 850, 3:35.

50. Bernardin de Saint-Pierre, *Oeuvres complètes*, 12:57.

51. Brady and Pottle, eds., *Boswell on the Grand Tour, 1765–1766*, 18. If her letters tell the truth, Girolama Piccolomini, known as Moma, was a sensitive and loving woman who cared for Boswell long after he had become indifferent to her. To do these letters justice, they must be read in Italian. Jean Hagstrum's *Sex and Sensibility in the Eighteenth Century* amplifies wittily and learnedly Moma's pithy conclusion.

52. Indicative of Johnson's respect of women is his unusual support of women writers. He encouraged and backed them whenever possible, and his relationships with Elisabeth Carter, Fanny Burney, Hannah More, and Charlotte Lennox testify to a most "un-English" attitude. In this one respect, Johnson could have been French, because in France women writers have always enjoyed much esteem—for example, Marie de France (perhaps an illegitimate daughter of Henri II), Louise Labé, Marguerite de Navarre, Mme de Lafayette, Mme de Sévigné, to mention some of the

important authors before the eighteenth century. Consult a forthcoming article by Gae Holladay entitled "Johnson as Patron" in *Greene Centennial Studies,* to be published by the University of Virginia Press. Rousseau, however, speaks unkindly about *les femmes auteurs* (1:554–55).

53. Chapman, ed., *Letters of Johnson,* letter 157, 1:157.

54. Quoted by W. H. Craig, *Doctor Johnson and the Fair Sex* (London, 1895), 28. Craig's book makes for delightful reading.

55. Brady and Pottle, eds., *Boswell on the Grand Tour, 1765–1766,* 300.

56. Chapman, ed., *Letters of Johnson,* letter 307.1, 1:324.

57. Concerning "le sentiment de la nature chez Rousseau," Professor Voisine writes: "On a trop écrit sur ce thème dangereusement facile, sans toujours se souvenir de l'aveu de l'auteur des *Confessions* 'Si je veux décrire un beau paysage, il faut que je sois dans les murs.' . . . Rousseau n'est tout de même pas encore de la génération des poètes ou des peintres du XIXᵉ siècle qui transporteront leur carnet ou leur chevalet en pleins champs. Lorsqu'il cherche la solitude de la forêt de Saint-Germain, c'est pour écrire le *Discours sur l'Inégalité;* les belles pages sur le lac de Bienne ont été écrites rue Platrière, d'après des souvenirs vieux de dix ans. Le souvenir compte plus ici que l'impression originale" (p. 141).

58. Chapman, ed., *Letters of Johnson,* letter 417, 2:62.

59. Bernardin de Saint-Pierre, *Oeuvres,* 12:39.

60. Bate (*From Classic to Romantic,* [Cambridge, 1946], 2) makes this pronouncement the beginning of an analysis of neoclassical ideals.

61. Voisine, *Rousseau en Angleterre,* 212: "Rousseau est un des premiers poètes—qu'il soit conscient ou non de cette fonction poétique, peu importe—à écrire en prose."

62. See ibid., chap. 14 ("Wordsworth entre Rousseau et Godwin"), 203–22.

63. Joseph Texte, *Jean-Jacques Rousseau et les origines du cosmopolitisme littéraire* (Paris, 1895), x–xi.

64. See Roddier, *Rousseau en Angleterre,* 76–77.

65. Chauncey B. Tinker, *Dr. Johnson and Fanny Burney* (New York, 1911), xxxi, xxxviii.

66. Richard Schwartz, *Boswell's Johnson: A Preface to the Life* (Madison, 1978), 101–2.

67. Concerning Rousseau's interest in Plutarch, consult vol. 1 *(Les Confessions),* in *Oeuvres complètes,* Ed. Pléiade, 1237–38. Articles by André Oltramare in *Mélanges Bernard Bouvier* (Genève, 1920), 185–96, and by Jean Morel in *Revue d'histoire moderne* (April/May 1926): 81–102, center on issues pertaining to the "moral" influence of the Greek historian. Neither article deals with issues regarding style or narrative technique.

68. Surprisingly, Marshall Waingrow's introduction to the Yale edi-

tion of *The Correspondence and other Papers of James Boswell Relating to the Making of the Life of Johnson* (New York, 1969) does not broach the matter, despite an almost flagrant similarity between Rousseau's and Boswell's introductory statements.

69. Concerning contemporary reception of Boswell's *Life*, consult J. L. Clifford's introduction to *Twentieth Century Interpretations of Boswell's Life of Johnson: A Collection of Critical Essays*, ed. Clifford (Englewood Cliffs, N.J., 1970): "On the appearance of the *Life*, almost six years later, there was the same kind of shock as in the case of the *Tour to the Hebrides* over the frankness of the personal revelations it contained" (p. 22). It is extraordinary that Clifford never mentions Rousseau, the more so since he writes: "The earliest indication we have that Boswell was thinking of the form his work would take comes in an entry in his journal for October 12, 1780: 'I told Erskine I was to write Dr. Johnson's Life in Scenes. He approved.' But it was not until after Johnson's death in December 1784 that Boswell began seriously to consider the actual writing of the biography. Even then he was slow in starting" (p. 4). The first part of Rousseau's *Confessions* was published in 1782.

70. Quoted by Richard Altick, "Johnson and Boswell," in *Twentieth Century Interpretations*, ed. Clifford, 107.

71. My term; see Temmer, *Art and Influence of Jean-Jacques Rousseau*, 1–15.

72. See Paul Alkon, "Boswell's Control of Aesthetic Distance, in *Twentieth Century Interpretations*, ed. Clifford, 51–65.

73. See Richard Altick, "Johnson and Boswell," 108: "With the assistance of the people present at the Mitre or the Thrales', Johnson from 1763 to 1784 literally talked himself into his own biography." Concerning the difference between Rousseau's *Confessions* and Boswell's *Journal*, Frederick Pottle writes: "To the modern age with its insatiable interest in psychology, the confessional element of Boswell's journal may well be its most rewarding feature. His kind of confession is almost unique. He is writing, as he himself frequently said, a *history* of his own mind. Not an apologia but a history: the difference is enormous. The recurring theme of Rousseau's *Confessions* is, 'See how weak and vile I was, but yet how much better I was and am than other people' " (*Boswell's London Journal, 1762–1763*, ed. Pottle [New York, 1950], 13). With due respect to Professor Pottle, his interpretation strikes one as a bit biased, for Rousseau's undertaking is very complex and Boswell must have been among the first to appreciate Rousseau's attempt to offer mankind "l'histoire de [son] âme" (1:278). Concerning Boswell and Rousseau, consult a pungent article by R. A. Leigh, entitled "Boswell and Rousseau," in *The Modern Language Review* 47(July 1952): 289–317. Professor Leigh concludes: "Boswell's interest in Rousseau was something more than a passing craze, something

less than a permanent attachment. Compared with Rousseau, of course, Boswell was, intellectually, a minnow. He was a wandering ivy, eternally in quest of a handy or suitable oak. Temperamentally, in spite of his uniqueness, he was in many ways the common man writ large—distorted, as it were, by some psychological equivalent of those geographical projections which exaggerate proportions, shapes and areas in certain regions of the globe. For this reason alone, the story of his relations with Rousseau is not without interest. In this 'projection' of the ordinary eighteenth-century Briton's attitude towards Rousseau, one may perhaps recognize a common pattern" (p. 317). From an intellectual viewpoint, Professor Leigh's assertions may not be unfounded; but Boswell's immortality is based on his artistic achievement.

Still, apropos Boswell and Rousseau, I should like to voice a suspicion which, to the best of my knowledge, has not plagued anyone except Donald Greene: doubts as to the veracity of Boswell's record of his conversations with Rousseau, whose answers ring with Boswellian overtones. Consider, for example, Rousseau's supposed reply to his interviewer's remarks about the Christian religion: "BOSWELL. 'Yet, to tell the truth, I can find no certain system. Morals appear to me an uncertain thing. For instance, I should like to have thirty women. Could I not satisfy that desire? ROUSSEAU. 'No! BOSWELL. 'Why?' ROUSSEAU. Ha! Ha! If Mademoiselle were not here, I would give you a most ample reason why'" (*Boswell on the Grand Tour: Germany and Switzerland, 1764*, ed. F. A. Pottle [New York, 1953], 253). In view of the fact that this exchange took place while Rousseau was suffering from severe urinary retention, I doubt that his sense of humor was so wry. Evaluated in the light of Boswell's grand conquest of Mademoiselle (*i.e.,* Thérèse), the conversation assumes a prophetic tone. In any case, I feel certain that his interview with Rousseau is less authentic than the one with Voltaire, who after all spoke and wrote English, whereas Rousseau could not. Commenting on Boswellian banter with Voltaire, Donald Greene offers a cautionary note well worth remembering: "indeed those who form their opinion of Johnson's ideas from Boswell's edited reports of conversations at which Boswell happened to be present, instead, as they should, from Johnson's writings, should keep in mind Johnson's caution: 'While the various opportunities of conversations invite us to try every mode of argument, and every art of recommending our sentiments, we are frequently betrayed to the use of such as are not strictly defensible. . . . We learn to satisfy ourselves with such rationcination as silences others; and seldom recall to a close examination that discourse which has gratified our vanity with victory and applause' (*Works,* ii. 416; *Adventurer,* no. 85)" ("Voltaire and Johnson," in *Enlightenment Studies in Honor of Lester Crocker,* ed. A. J. and Virgil Topazio [Oxford, 1979], 116 (n. 15).

74. W. C. Dowling suggests a similar impression in deconstructionist terms: "As much as Johnson's writings or his letters or his speech, the *Prayers and Meditations* are only a system of language or discourse, and behind them there exists no Johnson more or less real than any other—behind them there exists, quite simply, nothing at all. Yet the absence they define is not the same as that defined by Johnson's writings or his letters or his speech, and the question that ultimately demands an answer is how an illusion of presence, of a Johnson more real than any other, ended by drawing us to a nonexistent center, a world of private discourse to which nothing and no one corresponds" (*Language and Logos in Boswell's Life of Johnson* [Princeton, 1981], 95).

75. Proust, *La Prisonnière* (Nouvelle Revue Française, 1924), 6:255.

2. *Candide* and *Rasselas* Revisited

All quotations from *Rasselas* and *Candide* are taken from *The History of Rasselas—Prince of Abissinia*, ed. R. W. Chapman, (Oxford, 1927) and *Candide*, ed. André Morize (Paris, 1959). Parenthetical page references are to these editions.

1. Charles Whittuck, *The "Good" Man of the XVIII Century* (London, 1901), chap. 5; Martha Pike Conant, *The Oriental Tale in the Eighteenth Century* (New York, 1908; reprint, 1966); Joseph Wood Krutch, *Samuel Johnson* (New York, 1944); J. L. Clifford, "Some remarks on *Candide* and *Rasselas*," in *Bicentenary Essays on Rasselas*, ed. Magdi Wahba (Cairo, 1959), 7–13; Elmer Suderman, "*Candide, Rasselas* and Optimism," in *Iowa English Yearbook*, vol. 2 (1966): 37–43. For details concerning the publication of *Rasselas* and the publication of a translation of *Candide* in London, consult the above-mentioned article by J. L. Clifford. A recent book by F. M. Keener reflects contemporary trends towards abstraction: "In *Candide*, the various synecdochic associations constructed by the characters and the narrator have a splendid parodic symmetry. For the most part, the trope of irony persists rhetorically and dominates the epistemological and linguistic synecdoches, as in Cunégonde's unconsciously ironic recourse to custom, the narrator's deliberately ironic specification of doors and windows, and mainly in comic transformations of Optimism" (*The Chain of Becoming* [New York, 1983], 203). Perhaps . . . but why be theoretical in evaluating two masterpieces so exquisitely personal?

2. André-Michel Rousseau, *L'Angleterre et Voltaire*, 147:867. By the same token, the index of Ahmad Gunny's *Voltaire and English Literature* (in *Studies on Voltaire and the Eighteenth Century*, vol. 177) does not contain a reference to *Rasselas*.

3. Elie Fréron, *Année littéraire* (Paris, 1760), 3:145–67.

4. Legouis and Cazamian, *Histoire de la littérature anglaise* (Paris, 1924), 157–58.

5. Hippolyte Taine, *Histoire de la littérature anglaise* (Paris, 1866), 4:157–58.

6. Boswell never accepted the full implication of this analysis: "I told him, that his *Rasselas* had often made me unhappy; for it represented the misery of human life so well, and so convincingly to a thinking mind, that if at any time the impression wore off, and I felt myself easy, I began to suspect some delusion" (L, 2:317).

7. Alkon, *Samuel Johnson and Moral Discipline*, x.

8. W. K. Wimsatt relates *Rasselas* to works by Samuel Beckett: "Johnson's *Rasselas* has much in common with modern versions of the absurd—with a *Godot* or a *Watt*. One main difference, which may disguise the parallel for us, is that the modern versions of the descent take place at a level which is, to start with, subterranean, the very sub-cellar or zero level of modern man's three-century decline from the pinnacles of theology and metaphysics. Johnson's descental exercise, with its saving theological clause in the Catacombs, takes place at a level still near the top of the metaphysical structure" ("In praise of *Rasselas:* Four Notes (Converging)," in *Imagined World: Essays on Some English Novels and Novelists in Honour of John Butt,* ed. Maynard Mack and Ian Gregor [London, 1968], 130). See also Patrick Henry, *Voltaire and Camus: The Limits of Reason and the Awareness of Absurdity,* in *Studies on Voltaire and the Eighteenth Century,* vol. 138 (1975).

9. See René Pomeau, ed., *Candide* (Paris, 1959), 5 (n. 5): "C'est seulement en 1739 qu'il [Voltaire] prit connaissance de ce traité, cf. D 1936 (13 mars 1739): 'Entre nous, la métaphysique n'est qu'un jeu d'esprit: c'est le pays des romans; toute la *Théodicée* de Leibnitz ne vaut pas une expérience de Nollet.'" It is doubtful wherher Voltaire had ever read this treatise with care. Concerning Voltaire and Leibniz, consult Richard A. Brooks, *Voltaire and Leibnitz* (Geneva, 1964).

10. A. O. Lovejoy, *The Great Chain of Being* (Boston, 1942), 212.

11. See Alexander Pope, *An Essay on Man,* ed. Maynard Mack (New Haven, 1947), xlvii. Examining the *Essay* in the light of Renaissance thought and literature, Maynard Mack writes: "Here the ideas that we have dealt with so far on the philosophical plane can be studied in formulations elaborated and particularized by the literary imagination of centuries, and arranged in a pattern or formed *Weltanschauung* that seeks to take hold of the relations of God and man not through theorem but through symbol." Mack's statement defines a major characteristic of baroque art.

12. To be sure, Johnson's comments on the *Essay* in his *Life of Pope* suggest disapproval of optimism which he carefully distinguishes from

the artistic merits of the work: "Philosophy and poetry have not often the same readers, and the essay abounded in spendid amplifications, and sparkling sentences, which were read and admired with no great attention to their ultimate purpose: its flowers caught the eye which did not see what the gay foliage concealed" (Johnson, *Lives of the English Poets,* ed. G. B. Hill [Oxford, 1905], 3:164).

13. See Donald Greene, *Samuel Johnson* (New York, 1970), 133: "Nothing is known about the actual genesis of *Rasselas.*" Cf. Jean Sareil, *Essai sur Candide* (Droz, 1967), 13: "Candide est un chef-d'oeuvre qui n'a pas d'histoire." This is the first sentence of Sareil's excellent study.

14. G. B. Hill, ed. *History of Rasselas* (Oxford, 1898), 23. Regarding *Rasselas* and *Candide,* Hill amplifies Fréron's and Boswell's viewpoints: "There was not a touch of bitterness in his nature. From Swift's savage humour and from Voltaire's biting irony he was equally free. Life is unhappy, but it may be made less unhappy by wisdom, by moderation, and by the resolute discharge of duty. Innocent pleasures must be enjoyed whenever they are offered, and 'the short gleams of gaiety which life allows us' must not be needlessly clouded. But after all, 'there is but one solid basis of happiness; and that is, the reasonable hope of a happy futurity'" (p. 26).

15. See Donald M. Lockhart, "'The Fourth Son of the Mighty Emperor': The Ethiopian Background of Johnson's *Rasselas,*" *PMLA* 78 (1963), 516–28. Also pertinent is an article by J. W. Gardner, "Blameless Ethiopians and Others," in *Greece and Rome,* 2d ser. (October 1977): 185–93.

16. André Morize, *Candide,* critical edition (Paris, 1931), xiii–xiv.

17. Ibid., xiv.

18. Morize's edition appeared in 1913; *The Great Chain of Being,* in 1936.

19. See Sareil, *Essai sur Candide,* 35: "Seulement ce n'est pas parce qu'il [Voltaire] combat l'optimisme qu'il doit être taxé de pessimisme. Qu'il ait forcé la note pour les besoins de la démonstration est indéniable. *Candide* n'a pas pour but de nous rélever l'idée que Voltaire se fait de l'univers; c'est une satire, ce n'est pas une confession."

20. Richard Schwartz, *Samuel Johnson and the Problem of Evil* (Madison, 1975), 79.

21. Leibniz, *Essais de Théodicée sur la bonté de Dieu, la liberté de l'homme et l'origine du mal* (Amsterdam, 1730), 74–75.

22. Johnson, Review of Jenyns's *A Free Inquiry into the Origin of Evil* (London, 1757), in *The Literary Magazine* 2 (1757): 173.

23. Lia Formigari, *Dictionary of the History of Ideas,* vol. 1 (New York, 1947), 329.

24. Note 2, by Hill, gives Voltaire's reaction concerning this famous

dispute: " 'Le célèbre philosophe Leibnitz . . . attaqua ces expressions du philosophe anglais dans une lettre qu'il écrivit, en 1715, à la feue reine d'Angleterre, épouse de George second; cette princesse, digne d'être en commerce avec Leibnitz et Newton, engagea une dispute réglée par lettres entre les deux parties. Mais Newton, ennemi de toute dispute, et avare de son temps, laissa le docteur Clarke, son disciple en physique, et pour le moins son égal en métaphysique, entrer pour lui dans la lice. La dispute roula sur presque toutes les idées métaphysiques de Newton: et c'est peut-être le plus beau monument que nous ayons des combats littéraires.' Voltaire's *Oeuvres*, 1879, xxii. 408."

25. Voltaire, "Chaînes des êtres," *Dictionnaire philosophique*, ed. Benda and Naves (Paris, 1961), 101–2.

26. See *Life*, 1:425: "Bayle's Dictionary is a very useful work for those to consult who love the biographical part of literature, which is what I love most." See also: "In one of his little memorandum-books I find the following hints for his intended Review or Literary Journal: '*The Annals of Literature, foreign as well as domestick.* Imitate Le Clerk—Bayle—Barbeyrac' " (1:285). Johnson owned the second, enlarged edition of Bayle's *Dictionnaire*, 3 vols. (Rotterdam, 1702).

27. Pierre Bayle, *Dictionnaire historique et critique*, 5th ed., ed. Des Maiseaux, 4 vols. (Amsterdam, 1740), 4:644–45. Concerning Bayle's scepticism, consult the excellent article by Richard H. Popkin, "Pierre Bayle's Place in 17th Century Scepticism," in *Pierre Bayle Le Philosophe de Rotterdam*, ed. Paul Dibon (Paris, 1959), 1–19.

28. Jean-Pierre Crousaz, *Examen du Pyrrhonisme ancien et modern* (A la Haye, 1733), preface.

29. See Johnson, *A Commentary on Mr. Pope's Principles of Morality or Essay on Man* (London, 1739). The story of Crousaz's attack against the *Essay* has been told by Emile Audra, L. F. Powell, Maynard Mack, Jacqueline de la Harpe, and George Sherburn. Robert Shackleton summarizes very well the often amusing complications that resulted from Silhouette's prose translation in 1736, and du Resnel's verse translation during the following year, and comments on the roles in the controversy played by Warburton, Louis Racine, Rousseau, and of course Voltaire. See Robert Shackleton, "Pope's *Essay on Man* and the French Enlightenment," in *Studies in the Eighteenth Century*, ed. R. F. Brissendon (Toronto, 1973), 2:1–15.

30. Bayle, *Dictionnaire historique et critique*, 4:305–6.

31. Lovejoy, *Great Chain of Being*, 209.

32. Soame Jenyns, *A Free Inquiry into the Nature and Origin of Evil* (London, 1757; New York, 1976), 33–34, 37.

33. Pope, *An Essay on Man*, ed. Maynard Mack (New Haven, 1947), epistle 1, ll. 99–100, and epistle 3, ll. 44–45.

34. Johnson, *Lives of the English Poets,* 3:144. Cf. Pope on Voltaire: "Do not smile when I add, that I esteem him for that honest-principled Spirit of true Religion which shines thro' the whole; and from whence (unknown as I am to M. de Voltaire) I conclude him at once a Free thinker and a Lover of quiet; no Bigot, but yet no Heretick" (Pope's letter to Bolingbroke, April 9, 1724, *The Correspondence of Alexander Pope,* ed. George Sherburn [Oxford, 1956], 2:229). Regarding Johnson's fondness for anecdotes, Donald Greene writes: "A fair number of the more striking anecdotes in the *Lives of the Poets,* it has been established, were apocrypha that Johnson's 'strong imagination caught greedily at,' which 'a second inquiry' would have corrected—and not merely the two anecdotes of Voltaire in the *Life of Pope* which Voltairean students have sometimes attributed to Johnsonian malice instead of to Johnsonian (and Voltairean) love of a good story" ("Voltaire and Johnson," 118). Long after Pope's death, Voltaire wrote in 1772: "Ceux qui ont crié que tout est bien sont des charlatans. Shaftesbury, qui mit ce conte à la mode, était un homme très malheureux. J'ai vu Bolingbroke rongé de chagrins et de rage, et Pope, qu'il engagea à mettre en vers cette mauvaise plaisanterie, était un des hommes les plus à plaindre que j'aie jamais connus, contrefait dans son corps, inégal dans son humeur, toujours malade, toujours à charge à lui-même, harcelé par cent ennemis jusqu'à son dernier moment. Qu'on me donne du moins des heureux qui me disent, tout est bien" (*Oeuvres,* 29:164, quoted by G. B. Hill in *Lives of the English Poets,* 3:144).

35. Voltaire, *Préface du poème sur le désastre de Lisbonne,* in *Oeuvres complètes* (Paris, 1977), 9:468.

36. Pomeau, *L'Europe des Lumières,* 17.

37. Rousseau, *Lettre à Voltaire,* in *Oeuvres complètes* (Paris, 1969), 4:1067. For a history of the manuscript and editions of "la lettre à Voltaire," see Ralph A Leigh, "Rousseau's Letter to Voltaire on Optimism," in *Studies on Voltaire and the Eighteenth Century,* vol. 30 (1964). Also consult the *Notice bibliographique* by Bernard Gagnebin in *Oeuvres complètes,* Ed. Pléiade, 4:1880–84, 1060, and "A Letter about Pope's *Essay on Man,*" in *Rousseau: Religious Writings,* ed. R. Grimsley (Oxford, 1970).

38. Also consult Greene's article, "Johnson, Stoicism, and the Good Life," in *The Unknown Samuel Johnson.*

39. Robert G. Walker, *Eighteenth-Century Arguments for Immortality and Johnson's Rasselas* (Victoria, 1977), 36.

40. Rousseau, *Lettre à Voltaire,* 1072.

41. Quoted by Joseph W. Krutch, *Samuel Johnson,* 7.

42. Krutch, 178–79.

43. Jenyns, *A Free Inquiry,* 60.

44. See Sareil, *Essai sur Candide,* 20: "En un sens, *Candide* n'est qu'une succession de catastrophes."

45. Alkon, *Samuel Johnson and Moral Discipline,* 20.

46. William Beckford, *The History of the Caliph Vathek* (London, 1888), 2.

47. William F. Bottiglia, *Voltaire's Candide,* 2d ed., *Studies on Voltaire and the Eighteenth Century,* 7A(1964), 77–81.

48. French literary heroines, characterized by a great deal of strength, are always stronger than the men they love or cherish. For example, Chrétien de Troyes's Laudine tames and manipulates Yvain, Phèdre towers over Hippolyte, and Julie de Wolmar dominates Saint-Preux (*La Nouvelle Héloïse*). Other strong heroines are Mme de Mortsauf (*Le Lys dans la vallée*) and Marcel's grandmother, to mention a few.

49. Auerbach criticizes bitterly Voltaire's conception of reality: "Voltaire arranges reality so that he can use it for his purposes. There is no denying the presence, in many of his works, of colorful, vivid, everyday reality. But it is incomplete, consciously simplified, and hence—despite the serious didactic purpose—nonchalant and superficial." Unquestionably, Auerbach's experiences during the Second World War caused him to take a dim view of Voltaire's parodies (*Mimesis,* trans. by W. R. Trask [Princeton, 1953], 411).

50. Concerning the story of la Vieille, Sareil writes: "Le passage est remarquable, non seulement par la clarté avec laquelle la contradiction entre la pensée et les actes est exposée, mais surtout par la façon étonnante dont Voltaire s'est servi de notations humoristiques pour alléger le texte, lui ôter toute force dramatique, sans rien faire perdre de son sérieux à la pensée" (*Essai sur Candide,* 47).

51. Proust, *Du côté de chez Swann* (Paris, 1954), 1:116.

52. See Pomeau, ed., *Candide* (1959), 53: "Marionnettes, silhouettes, croquis: ces mots s'imposent à qui traite du personnage voltairien. Dénué d'imagination psychologique, l'auteur de *Zaïre* fait dans le conte de pauvreté vertu. Le genre n'admet que de légers dessins. Mais les coups de crayon doivent être bien placés. Or c'est à quoi Voltaire excelle."

53. My point of view does not contradict Pomeau's assertion (*Candide* [1959 ed.], 21): "Sans le spectacle de la guerre de Sept Ans, Voltaire n'eût pas écrit *Candide* tel que nous le lisons." Rasselas and his companions do not experience any natural or man-made catastrophes.

54. See André Delattre, *Voltaire: L'impétueux* (Paris, 1957), 11: "Il y a chez Voltaire, le besoin de bouffoner quand il parle de choses sérieuses; même quand il s'agit de lui-même"; Henri Bergson, *Le Rire,* Ed. Pléiade (Paris, 1959), 388.

55. Ira O. Wade, *Voltaire and Candide* (Princeton, 1959), 321–22.

56. Keener, *The Chain of Becoming,* 24; Jacques van den Heuvel, *Voltaire dans ses contes* (Paris, 1967), 290.

57. See Temmer, *Art and Influence of Jean-Jacques Rousseau,* chap. 3, 41–68.

58. John Locke, *An Essay on Human Understanding,* ed. Peter Nidditch (Oxford, 1975), 2:108.

59. Wilhelm Dilthey, *Das Leben Schleiermachers,* 2d ed. (1922), 1:317; Dilthey, *Das Erlebnis und die Dichtung,* 8th ed., (Leipzig, 1922), 393–94 [my translation]. The term *Bildungsroman* was not coined by Dilthey; it appeared first in two lectures by Karl von Morgenstern in 1819.

60. Goethe, *Wilhelm Meisters Lehrjahre* (Zürich, 1962), 525.

61. L. Dora Schmitz, trans., *Correspondence between Schiller and Goethe* (London, 1877), 1:190.

62. Goethe, *Werke* (Hamburger Ausgabe), ed. Trunz (Hamburg, 1965), 7:467.

63. Rousseau, *La Nouvelle Héloïse,* 2:336.

64. Sainte-Beuve, *Volupté* (Paris, 1927), 2:225.

65. See Pomeau, ed., *Candide,* 64: "Candide a vécu, et il a mûri, cette marche du temps étant soulignée par le vieillissement, simultané et plus évident, de Mlle Cunégonde." We are told that she is aging, but nothing more. Voltaire does not suggest the feeling of time.

66. Rousseau, *La Nouvelle Héloïse,* 2:35.

67. Goethe, *Werke,* 7:594.

68. Jacques Maritain, *Trois réformateurs: Luther, Descartes, Rousseau* (Paris, 1925), 78.

69. Goethe, *Werke,* 7:578.

70. Ibid., 7:565.

71. La Bruyère, *Les Caractères,* no. 10, "Des femmes" (Paris, 1962), 115.

72. Voltaire, *Lettres d'amour de Voltaire à sa nièce,* ed. Theodore Besterman (Paris, 1957), 193. Regarding a succinct summary of Voltaire's relationship with his niece, consult Hayden Mason, *Voltaire: A Biography* (Baltimore, 1981), 42–43. Also see Hugues Micha, *Voltaire d'après sa correspondance avec Madame Denis* (Paris, 1972). Concerning Voltaire's sentimental life, Micha declares: "Trois faits marquent sa vie intime: il fut orphelin de mère à l'âge de sept ans, ne fut jamais époux et n'eut d'autres enfants que ses livres. Madame du Châtelet disait de lui: 'Il aime aimer'" (p. 7).

73. Voltaire, *Lettres d'amour,* 106, 105.

74. Cf. Micha, *Correspondance avec Mme Denis,* 85: "Son histoire n'est-elle pas celle d'un Candide, enfin détrompé après ses errances et ses désillusions courtisanesques, cherchant refuge, aux portes de la France, dans le travail qui chasse l'ennui et le besoin, auprès d'une Gretchen d'une Cunégonde qui s'appelle Mme Denis?" Also pertinent is this observation by Roland Barthes: "Il y a toujours, dans le discours sur l'amour, une personne à qui l'on s'adresse, cette personne passât-elle à l'état de fantôme ou de créature à venir. Personne n'a envie de parler de l'amour, si ce n'est *pour* quelqu'un" (*Fragments d'un discours amoureux* [Paris, 1977], 88).

75. Quote from Wimsatt, "In praise of *Rasselas*," 119; Karl Schlechta, *Goethes Wilhelm Meister* (Frankfurt, 1953), 57.

76. See *Rambler*, no. 4, p. 19: "The works of fiction, with which the present generation seems more particularly delighted, are such as exhibit life in its true state, diversified only by accidents that daily happen in the world, and influenced by passions and qualities which are really to be found in conversing with mankind. This kind of writing may be termed not improperly the comedy of romance." Johnson means that, as in Aristotle's account of comedy in the *Poetics*, the "new" novel deals with individuals of a lower class than the nobles and kings of tragedy as well as romance. Hence the ordinary modern reader is able to "identify" with them. See also Boswell, *Life*, 1:49: "when a boy he was immoderately fond of reading romances of chivalry, and he retained his fondness for them through life; so that (adds his Lordship Bishop Percy) spending part of a summer at my parsonage-house in the country, he chose for his regular reading the old Spanish romance of FELIXMARTE OF HIRCANIA, in folio, which he read quite through. Yet I have heard him attribute to these extravagant fictions that unsettled turn of mind which prevented his ever fixing in any profession." Geoffrey Tillotson comments on *Rasselas:* "He was not setting out to write a novel, but a work in a much stricter form. A novel for him came lower down the scale of practical usefulness than a tale, for a novel found room in itself for what he considered to be accidentals. The set of his mind, so far as thinking went, was towards generality" (*Augustan Studies* [London, 1961], 238).

77. Pascal, *Pensées*, ed. Louis Lafuma (Paris, 1956), 149. "Suppose a man puts himself at a window to see the passers by. If I pass I cannot say that he stood there to see me, for he does not think of me in particular. Nor does any one who loves another on account of beauty really love that person, for the small-pox, which kills beauty without killing the person, will cause the loss of love. Nor does one who loves me for my judgment, my memory, love me, myself, for I may lose those qualities without losing my identity. Where then is this 'I' if it reside not in the body nor in the soul, and how love the body or the soul, except for the qualities which do not make '*me*,' since they are perishable? For it is not possible and it would be unjust to love the soul of a person in the abstract, and whatever qualities might be therein. So then we do not love a person, but only qualities. We should not then sneer at those who are honoured on account of rank and office, for we love no one save for borrowed qualities" (*The Thoughts of Blaise Pascal*, trans. C. Kegan Paul [London, 1885], 80).

78. Wimsatt, "In Praise of *Rasselas*," 123. Concerning the structure of *Rasselas*, Wimsatt declares: "*Rasselas* has the kind of structure which satisfies, more or less, its modest requirements as a quasi-dramatic narrative—not the causal progression, the beginning, middle, and end of the Aristotelian 'whole,' but a structure of accumulation, something like

that of a series of laboratory reports, or a series of chapters on animals sighted or taken, on a hunt across the veldt with gun or camera." Wimsatt proceeds to comment on the well-known essay by Gwin J. Kolb, "The Structure of *Rasselas*," *PMLA* 66 (1951). Kolb attempts "to argue the adequacy of the structure of *Rasselas* in relation to that end" (p. 699). Kolb finds little of interest in Pekuah's misfortunes: "her tale presents a sharp contrast to many oriental adventure stories, in which a noble lady's abduction often initiates or continues a series of marvelous happenings. The beginning is the only mildly exciting part of the whole adventure; the remainder consists, by and large, of Pekuah's efforts to prevent *ennui*. All potentially 'romantic' aspects of the affair are made flat and prosaic" (p. 711).

79. Wimsatt, "In Praise of *Rasselas*," 114–15. There is some confusion concerning the amount of the ransom. In Chapter 37 the Arab chief tells Pekuah that her freedom will cost two hundred ounces of gold. In Chapter 38, the Arab receives one hundred ounces of gold "for the fifty that were promised." In any case, it is Pekuah who hands him the gold. That act has to have some meaning.

80. See Kathleen M. Grange, "Dr. Samuel Johnson's Account of a Schizophrenic Illness in *Rasselas*," in *Medical History* 6 (1962): 162–68. Also see Richard B. Hovey, "Dr. Samuel Johnson, Psychiatrist," *MLQ* (December, 1954), 321–25.

81. Voltaire, *Précis du siècle Louis XV* (Paris, 1908), 305.

82. Stendhal, *La Chartreuse de Parme*, in *Oeuvres complètes*, ed. Georges Eudes (Paris, 1951), 12:138.

83. Stendhal, *Racine et Shakespeare*, in *Oeuvres complètes*, 16:97.

84. Taine, *Histoire de la littérature anglaise*, 164.

85. G. K. Chesterton, preface to *The History of Rasselas* (New York, 1926), x.

86. T. B. Macaulay, "Essay on Johnson," in *Macaulay's and Carlyle's Essays on Samuel Johnson*, ed. W. Strunk, Jr. (New York, 1895), 60–62. See W. K. Wimsatt, *The Prose Style of Samuel Johnson* (New Haven, 1941), 50.

87. Wimsatt, quoted by B. H. Bronson, in his preface to *Rasselas, Poems and Selected Prose* (New York, 1971), xvii; Wimsatt, "In Praise of *Rasselas*," 71. It should be understood that this orotund style, characteristic of *Rasselas*, should not be held typical of Johnson's prose; he commands other styles.

88. Lanson, *L'art de la prose*, 13th ed. (Paris, 1908).

89. See Donald Greene, "Boswell's *Life* as 'Literary Biography,'" in *Boswell's "Life of Johnson": New Questions, New Answers*, ed. John A. Vance (Athens, Ga.: 1985), 167–68. Greene discusses specific instances that exemplify Boswell's insistence on preserving the Johnsonian essence of Johnson's speech—the "'translation' into 'his own style' [which] was

seized on by Macaulay as the text for a vehement denunciation of 'John-sonese'" (p. 167).

90. Voltaire to Octavie Belot, May 16, 1760, *Correspondence*, ed. Theodore Besterman, vol. 42, letter 8174. Mme Belot was the first translator of *Rasselas* into French (*Histoire de Rasselas, prince d'Abissinie* [Amsterdam, 1760]). The expression "philosophie aimable" has little meaning and represents nothing more than a polite remark.

91. "In his Preface to *Shakespeare,* Johnson treated Voltaire very contemptuously, observing, upon some of his remarks, 'These are the petty cavils of petty wits.' Voltaire, in revenge, made an attack upon Johnson, in one of his numerous literary sallies, which I remember to have read" (L, 1:498–99). Hill furnishes the quotation in which Voltaire writes: "Je ne veux point soupçonner le sieur Johnson d'être un mauvais plaisant, et d'aimer trop le vin; mais je trouve un peu extraordinaire qu'il compte la bouffonnerie et l'ivrognerie parmi les beautés du théâtre tragique" (*Dictionnaire philosophique, Oeuvres complètes,* 23:566, quoted by Hill in Boswell's *Life,* 1:499). See also *Life,* 1:434–35.

92. Marvin Mudrick, *The Man in the Machine* (New York, 1977), 92.

93. Concerning the concept of "mother tongue," Edward Stankiewicz writes: "The concept of the integrity and uniqueness of individual languages is surrounded by an aura of connotations that are largely derived from the views on the mother-tongue, the language which is 'sucked in with the mother's milk,' which is in constant growth and advance . . . which is full of unexplored possibilities, and which cannot be locked into a closed set of rules. Like the mother tongue, each language has its unique qualities which include not only its particular grammatical structure or richness of idioms, but also some hidden impalpable properties" ("The 'Genius' of Language in Sixteenth Century Linguistics," *Logos Semantikos Studia Linguistica in Honorem Eugenio Coseriu* (Berlin, 1981), 181.

94. See F. W. Hilles, *"Rasselas,* an 'Uninstructive Tale,'" in *Johnson, Boswell, and their Circle: Essays Presented to Fitzroy Powell* (Oxford, 1965), 111–13: "We do not read *Rasselas* for the story, we read it for a view of life that is presented majestically in long, sweeping phrases. . . . Diction, rhythms, character and plot are all of a piece." See also George Saintsbury, *A History of English Prose Rhythm* (Bloomington, 1965), 269: "Not merely does Johnson probably aim at, and certainly secure, much more rhythmical character than had been seen for nearly a century; but he secures it, to a large extent, by recurrence to the manipulation of the individual foot, as well as of the clause or block."

95. Montesquieu, *Lettres Persanes,* ed. Antoine Adam (Geneva, 1954), letter 24, p. 64. Concerning Voltaire's interest in puppets, see Bottiglia, *Voltaire's Candide,* 83–95. Bottiglia relates that in 1746 at Sceaux, Voltaire assumed the role of Polichinelle.

96. Wade, *Voltaire and Candide,* 250.

97. C. R. Tracy, "Democritus, Arise!," *Yale Review* (Winter 1950): 306; Alvin Whiteley, "The Comedy of *Rasselas*," in *English Literary History* 23 (1956): 49; W. J. Bate, "Johnson and Satire Manqué," in *Eighteenth Century Studies in Honor of Donald F. Hyde* (New York, 1970), 150.

98. It should also be noted that this principle of deflection finds its most genial application in Heine's *Bäder von Lucca*, which could be interpreted as a fusion of Johnson's and Voltaire's wittiest virtues.

99. Bergson, *Le Rire*, 389.

100. Jean Starobinski, "Sur le style philosophique de *Candide*," in *Comparative Literature* 18, no. 3 (1976): 195.

101. See Pierre Aubery, "Voltaire et les Juifs: Ironie et démystification," in *Studies on Voltaire and the Eighteenth Century*, 24:67–69.

102. André Delattre, *Voltaire: L'impétueux*, 10.

103. Theodor Reik, *Jewish Wit* (New York, 1962), 26.

104. Nicholas Joost, "Whispers of Fancy; or, The Meaning of *Rasselas*" in *Modern Age* 1 (Fall 1957): 166.

105. Sigmund Freud, *Jokes and Their Relation to the Unconscious*, trans. James Strachey, in *The Standard Edition of the Complete Works of Sigmund Freud* (London, 1971), 8:236.

106. André Delattre, *Voltaire: l'impétueux*, 37: "Voltaire a besoin de se venger de quelque chose. De quoi? Quel psychanalyste découvrira le fait qui a causé un choc dans sa jeune sensibilité?"; Delattre, p. 9.

107. W. B. C. Watkin's *Perilous Balance: The Tragic Genius of Swift, Johnson and Sterne* (Princeton, 1939), emphasizes Johnson's struggle against insanity. Concerning Johnson's relationship to his mother, which was far from ideal, see George Irwin, *Samuel Johnson: A Personality in Conflict* (Aukland, 1971), 2: "Though, like the uncle in *Idler*, No 62, Sam Johnson's mother was impossible to please and hence impossible to love, her son seldom missed an opportunity of proclaiming his love for her."

108. Like Johnson, Voltaire disliked his father. He believed that he was the son of Rochebrune, a *chansonnier*. For a subtle psychoanalytic interpretation of Voltaire, see José-Michel Moureaux, *l'Oedipe de Voltaire: Introduction à une psycholecture* (Paris, 1973). Consult also T. Besterman, *Voltaire* (Oxford, 1969), chap. 1, as well as René Pomeau, "Candide entre Marx et Freud," in *Studies on Voltaire*, 89:1305–23.

109. Chapter 22 appeared for the first time, *in toto*, in the Geneva edition of 1761 (edition number 15, according to Morize's list). See Morize, ed., *Candide*, 149: "Toute la fin du chapitre ne sera qu'une satire âpre de la vie de Paris; le thème est traditionnel, les points sur lesquels porte l'attaque sont toujours les mêmes; des *Caractères* de La Bruyère jusqu'à la fin du XVIIIe siècle, en passant par les *Lettres Persanes*, on pourrait en suivre les innombrables répliques."

110. Greene, "Voltaire and Johnson," 119.

111. Concerning this bouquet, consult Morize, pp. 211–12 (n. 1): "D'ailleurs la précision des noms de fleurs rappelle le Voltaire jardinier des Délices et de Ferney, 'l'amateur de tulipes' qui se réjouit de voir ses 'plates-bandes de tulipes au mois de février' (XXXIX, 170) [Moland] et les observe en mars, quand elles 'commencent à s'épanouir' (id. 200, 1757).—'Il y a un mois, écrit-il, que je jouis du plaisir de voir s'épanouir sous mes fenêtres . . . des *jacinthes*, des *renoncules*, des *tulipes*.' . . . Et plus loin: 'Quelle est la fleur qui prétendra, après celles que je viens de vous décrire, à l'honneur de fixer nos regards et de mériter nos justes hommages? Ah! C'est *l'oreille d'ours!*' " Is it a simple coincidence that Saint-Preux mocks "ces petits fleuristes qui se pâment à l'aspect d'une renoncule, et se prosternent devant des tulipes?" (*La Nouvelle Héloïse*, vol. 4, letter 11).

112. Joseph Baretti, *Discours sur Shakespeare et sur Monsieur de Voltaire* (Paris, 1777), 17. Concerning Baretti's translation of *Rasselas*, see Raffaella Carbonara, *Giuseppe Baretti e la sua traduzione del Rasselas di Johnson* (Torino, 1970). In her conclusion, Carbonara quotes "le acute osservazioni mosse da Noel Blakiston" who writes in *Dr. Johnson and Italy*, p. 80: "Baretti perfectly understood the English language. He gets the sense well enough. Yet some at least of [the translations] hardly attain an equivalence with the force and majesty of the English, and for an interesting reason. . . . Baretti, in my opinion to his loss, simply cannot keep up with Johnson's abstract words. . . . And with Johnson the abstract words are anything but vapid. They are as heavy as stone. He sets them about, like megaliths, where he wants them and whence nothing can budge them." For another opinion concerning Voltaire's knowledge of English, see *Life*, 1:435 (n. 1), where Hill quotes Pennant: "Pennant, who visited Voltaire in 1765, says that, 'in his attempt to speak English he satisfied us that he was perfect master of our oaths and curses.' Pennant's *Literary Life*, p. 6."

113. Krutch, *Samuel Johnson*, 175. Regarding the relationship between *Rasselas* and *Candide*, I should like to quote the viewpoint of my colleague William Frost: "The fact that *Rasselas* and *Candide* appeared within a year of each other has led, in my view, to an unfortunate tendency to compare and contrast them, to the exclusion of more appropriate candidates, in the case of each work, for such comparatistic exercises. In my view, the English work most worth juxtaposing to *Candide* for its richness and inventiveness of rapid, sometimes violent, symbolic narrative, and for its satiric thrust, is *Gulliver's Travels;* while as for *Rasselas*, in respect to ethical persuasiveness and meditative interchanges, its finest French analogue, in my opinion, is certainly *Rameau's Nephew*, which, like *Rasselas* and unlike *Candide*, also raises a searching question about the choice of life" (personal communication).

114. Quote from Johnson, *Dictionary of the English Language* (London,

1828), ii. See Pomeau, ed., *Candide* (1959), 55: "Dans ce conte, la réalité même est créée par le style."

115. Krutch, *Samuel Johnson*, 182.

116. Quotes in Wade, *Voltaire and Candide*, 312, 313. See Hilaire Belloc: "No good man is the better for having read *Candide*, but every man is the better for having read *Rasselas*" (*An Anthology of his Prose and Verse* [London, 1951], 267.

117. Rousseau, *Lettre à Voltaire*, 4:1074–75. In the ninth book of *Les Confessions*, Rousseau expresses the belief that *Candide* is Voltaire's answer to his *Lettre sur la Providence;* see *Oeuvres complètes*, 1:429–30.

3. Speculations on *Life of Savage* and *Le Neveu de Rameau*

Quotations from *The Life of Savage* and *Le Neveu de Rameau* are taken, respectively, from the critical edition by Clarence Tracy (Oxford, 1971) and the critical edition by Jean Fabre (Geneva, 1950). Page numbers, in parentheses, refer to these editions. Likewise, quotations from Savage's *An Author to be Lett* (London, 1729; Augustan Reprint Society, Los Angeles, 1960) are followed by a page number in parentheses.

1. Jean Fabre, Preface to *Entretien sur le Neveu de Rameau*, ed. Duchet et Launay (Paris, 1967), vii. Concerning the background and dates of composition, Fabre writes: "le *Neveu de Rameau* brasse, sous forme d'allusion un ensemble de faits historiques qui s'égrènent sur une vingtaine d'années: approximativement de 1760 à 1780. Mieux encore, l'examen de ces faits permet de dégager certains repères qui jalonnent cette durée apparemment aberrante: 1762, 1767, 1772 à 1774, 1778 et audelà, jusqu'au terme final que marque le manuscrit autographe et qu'il convient peut-être reporter à 1782." English readers, unfamiliar with Diderot, may well be interested in the extraordinary history of the manuscript. *Le Neveu de Rameau* was first published in Germany in 1805. This edition was a translation by Goethe, based on a manuscript which had been sent to him by Schiller to whom it had come from Russia. Goethe's translation was translated into French by Brière in 1821, the same year in which a French translation (by De Saur and Saint-Geniès) had been passed off as the original French text. In 1891, Georges Monval discovered the autographed manuscript on the quays of the Seine. It is now in the J. Pierpont Morgan Library in New York.

2. The only reference to Johnson's interest in a work edited by Diderot occurs in *Dr. Johnson and Fanny Burney, Being the Johnsonian Passages from the Works of Mme d'Arblay*, ed. Chauncey Tinker (New York, 1911), 3, 4: "My sister then played another duet with my father; but Dr. Johnson was so deep in the *Encyclopédie* that, as he is very deaf, I question if he

even knew what was going forward." It should be noted that Johnson owned a set of the *Encyclopédie*. See Donald Greene, *Samuel Johnson's Library, Annotated Guide,* English Literary Monographs, (University of Victoria, 1975), 55. Goethe confirms Diderot's reputation as a conversationalist: "Whatever one may have thought of him as a writer, his friends and enemies agreed that no one's conversation had ever surpassed his [Diderot's] in liveliness, strength, wit, variety, and grace" (*Goethes Werke, Deutsche National Literatur,* ed. Dünker, *Anmerkungen* [Stuttgart], 185 [my transl.]).

3. Arthur Wilson, *Diderot* (New York, 1972), 53.

4. Loyalty Cru, *Diderot and English Thought* (New York, 1913), 99.

5. Faguet, *Dix-Huitième Siècle* (Paris, 1890), 322–23.

6. Cru, *Diderot and English Thought,* 112.

7. Ibid., 444.

8. Diderot, *Oeuvres complètes* ed. Assézat and Tourneux (Paris, 1875), 9:451. The translation by Le Tourneur does not offer any more clues concerning a possible relationship between *The Life of Savage* and *Le Neveu de Rameau* than does the original English version. In fact, the French translation contradicts an old adage in that it is faithful *and* beautiful. It pulsates with the energy characteristic of Johnson's style and constitutes a remarkable achievement, since the tonic accent in French is not so strong as it is in English. I thought the translation flawless until I came upon an article by Paul Alkon who notes: "In the otherwise accurate French translation of Johnson's *Life of Savage,* for example, the phrase 'Compassion was indeed the distinguishing Quality of Savage' (Tracy, p. 41) becomes 'La compassion fut une des qualités distinctives de Savage' (p. 80). Compassion is here reduced to *one* of Savage's distinguishing virtues. In the life of Savage provided by Shiels for Cibber's *Lives of the Poets,* the phrase becomes: "Compassion seems indeed to have been among the few good qualities possessed by Savage" (*Journal of Modern Philology* 72, no. 2 [November 1974]: 143–44).

9. See Milton F. Seiden, "Jean-François Rameau and Diderot's Neveu," in *Diderot Studies* 1:143–91. See also Jean Fabre's preface and appendix.

10. Clarence Tracy, *The Artificial Bastard* (Cambridge, 1953), 18.

11. Johnson, *Preface to Shakespeare,* in *Johnson on Shakespeare,* vol. 7, ed. Sherbo, *Yale Edition,* (New Haven, 1971), 77.

12. Oliver Goldsmith, *The Citizen of the World,* in *Collected Works,* ed. Arthur Friedman (Oxford, 1966), 2:452–53. Concerning Savage's tragedy, see Frank Ellis, "Johnson and Savage: Two Failed Tragedies and a Failed Tragic Hero," in *The Author in his Work,* ed. Louis Martz and Aubrey Williams (New Haven, 1978), 337–46.

13. Edmund Bergler, M.D. considers Savage a masochistic parasite:

"That type of parasite belongs to a specific subgroup of orally regressed neurotics who secondarily rationalize their refusal to work in different ways. If they happen to be, or pretend to be, writers and artists, they claim that the world owes their genius automatically all means of subsistence. . . . Not all orally regressed neurotics are parasites, and not all parasites claim to be, or actually are, artistically gifted. The parasitic subgroup is encountered outright, without pretenses and rationalizations. The untranslatable word in the Jewish jargon, accepted in many languages, "Schnorrer," is relevant ("Samuel Johnson's 'The life of the poet Richard Savage'—A Paradigm for a Type," *American Imago* 4 [December 1947]: 53–54). Bergler's views are not without merit; however, they discount the creative and even delightful aspect of Savage's personality, as well as some of the deeper truths that emerge from Johnson's lucid, though compassionate biography.

14. John A. Dussinger, "Style and Intention in Johnson's *Life of Savage*," *ELH* 37 (December 1970): 571–72.

15. Diderot, *Entretien entre d'Alembert et Diderot—Suite de l'Entretien*, in *Oeuvres*, ed. A. Billy (Paris, 1965), 936.

16. Swift, *A Tale of a Tub*, ed. A. C. Guthkelch and D. Nichol Smith, 2d ed. (Oxford, 1958), 174. See also Apostolos Kouidis, *"Le Neveu de Rameau" and "The Praise of Folly"—Literary Cognates* (Salzburg, 1981).

17. Jacques Proust, *L'Objet et le texte* (Geneva, 1980), 182.

18. Georges May, *Quatre visages de Denis Diderot* (Paris, 1951), 173.

19. Herbert Dieckmann, *Cinq leçons sur Diderot* (Geneva, 1959), 93, 122.

20. Johnson's comments on Falstaff are extremely revealing with regard to his *Life of Savage*. Furthermore, these comments also dovetail with Diderot's review of *La Vie de Richard Savage* as well as with certain aspects of *Le Neveu de Rameau*: "But Falstaff unimitated, unimitable Falstaff, how shall I describe thee? Thou compound of sense and vice; of sense which may be admired but not esteemed, of vice which may be despised, but hardly detested. Falstaff is a character loaded with faults and with those faults which naturally produce contempt. He is a thief, and a glutton, a coward, and a boaster, always ready to cheat the weak, and prey upon the poor; to terrify the timorous and insult the defenceless. At once obsequious and malignant, he satirizes in their absence those whom he lives by flattering. He is familiar with the prince only as an agent of vice, but of this familiarity he is so proud as not only to be supercilious and haughty with common men, but to think his interest of importance to the Duke of Lancaster. Yet the man thus corrupt, thus despicable, makes himself necessary to the Prince that despises him, by the most pleasing of all qualities, perpetual gaiety, by an unfailing power of exciting laughter, which is the more freely indulged, as his wit is not of the splendid or

ambitious kind, but consists in easy escapes and sallies of levity, which make sport but raise no envy. It must be observed that he is stained with no sanguinary or enormous crimes, so that his licentiousness is not so offensive but that it may be borne for his mirth" (*Johnson on Shakespeare, Yale Edition,* 7:523).

21. Lionel Trilling, *Sincerity and Authenticity* (Cambridge, 1971), 34.

22. Proust, *The Past Recaptured,* trans. Andreas Mayor (New York, 1971), 141.

23. Trilling, *Sincerity and Authenticity,* 32.

24. Frank Brady, "The Strategies of Biography," 251.

25. Diderot, *Les Deux Amis de Bourbonne,* in *Oeuvres,* 728.

26. Tracy, *The Artificial Bastard,* 54.

27. See Frank Brady, *The Strategies of Biography,* 254: "In his independence, resentment, insolence, and self-delusion, there are some touches of Satan: ' . . . that fixt mind / And high disdain, from scene of injur'd merit . . . / And study of revenge, immortal hate, / And courage never to submit or yield.' *Paradise Lost,* I, 97–98, 107–08. But only touches."

28. Diderot, *Jacques le Fataliste,* in *Oeuvres,* 572.

29. Elisabeth de Fontenay, *Diderot ou le matérialisme enchanté* (Paris, 1981), 212; Roger Kempf, *Diderot et le roman* (Paris, 1964), 97; James Doolittle, *Rameau's Nephew* (Geneva, 1960), 57; Walter Rex, "Two Scenes from *Le Neveu de Rameau,*" *Diderot Studies* 20 (1981): 246.

30. Rousseau, *Les Confessions,* 1:391.

31. Jean-François Rameau, *La Raméide* (Paris, 1766), 18.

32. Diderot, *Ceci n'est pas un conte,* ed. Billy, 429.

33. Trilling, *Sincerity and Authenticity,* 52.

34. Dieckmann, *Cinq leçons sur Diderot,* 37.

35. Ellis, "Johnson and Savage," 342.

36. Robert Folkenflik states the issue very well: "Savage's genuine heroism is not based for Johnson on his putative nobility but on his intellectual gifts, and in writing this biography Johnson gives us an early example of a figure who was to become significant in the later eighteenth and nineteenth centuries, the poet as a hero" (*Samuel Johnson, Biographer,* [Ithaca, 1978], 201–2). Folkenflik's book, pleasantly unpretentious, makes for good reading.

37. May, *Quatre visages de Diderot,* 181.

38. This play was staged by Jean-Louis Barrault at the Théâtre d'Orsay in 1979.

39. Tracy, *The Artificial Bastard,* 48.

40. Ibid., 60, 62.

41. Donald Greene comments concerning this quasi-proverbial remark: "Alas, this so often quoted statement seems to be an invention by Boswell. All that his diary records for that day (when Samuel Johnson was

in the midst of a four-month stay in Staffordshire and Derbyshire), is that when Boswell was trying to get Samuel Johnson's approval (as he often did) for his moving from Edinburgh to London (Samuel Johnson always advised him against it), he said, 'You find no man wishes to leave it' (meaning, I suppose, no man wishes to give up a *pied à terre* in it). (*Boswell in Extremes, Yale Edition of Boswell's Papers* [1970], 171)." (Personal communication).

42. Prévost, *Manon Lescaut* (Paris, 1965), 40.

43. See C. E. Engel, *Figures et aventures du XVIIIe siécle* (Paris, 1939), 40–41.

44. Prévost, *Mémoires et aventures d'un homme de qualité* (Amsterdam, 1783), 2:269.

45. Georges May, "L'Angoisse de l'échec et la genèse du *Neveu de Rameau*," *Diderot Studies* 3(1961): 291.

46. Jean-François Rameau, *La Raméide* (Paris, 1766), 16.

47. See Tracy, *The Artifical Bastard*, 82. Richard Savage, *The Poetical Works*, ed. Clarence Tracy (Cambridge, 1962), 89.

48. Basil Willey writes: "Satire is by nature nonconstructive, since to construct effectively—to educate, for example, to reform, or to evangelize—one must study actual situations and actual persons in their historical setting and this kind of study destroys the satiric approach" (*The Eighteenth Century Background* [London, 1940], 106–7). Also pertinent to the issue under discussion is a comment by Howard D. Weinbrot: "I can only speculate on why formal verse satire declined later in the eighteenth-century, but one reason, I shall suggest, is that the traditions Pope unifies begin to split again" (*Alexander Pope and the Traditions of Formal Verse Satire* [Princeton, 1982], xviii). Given his subject matter, Professor Weinbrot refers neither to Savage's *An Author to be Lett*, nor to Diderot's *Neveu de Rameau*.

49. E. R. Curtius, *European Literature and the Middle Ages* (New York, 1953), 581–82.

50. Diderot, *Satire I*, in *Oeuvres*, ed. Billy, 1187, 1192.

51. Rousseau, *Les Confessions*, 278.

52. Charles Dédéyan makes a similar statement: "Quel dommage que ce ne soit pas Diderot, auteur du *Neveu de Rameau* qui se soit fait le biographe de Savage" (*L'Angleterre dans la pensée de Diderot* [Paris, 1958], 127). It is doubtful that Dédéyan read Johnson's *Life of Savage*. Had he done so, he would most likely have noticed the resemblance between the *neveu* and Savage-Hackney.

53. Prévost, *Le Pour et contre* (Paris, 1735), 7:270, 271, 274. Concerning the question of illegitimacy, consult an interesting article by Otis Fellows, "The Facets of Illegitimacy in the French Enlightenment," *Diderot Studies* 20 (1981): 77–97. Professor Fellows makes no mention of Prévost's views.

54. George R. Havens, *The Abbé Prévost and English Literature* (reprint: Haskell House, New York, 1965), 130.

55. Palissot, *Oeuvres*, 4 vols. (Paris, 1788), 2:369–70.

56. Leo Spitzer, *Linguistics and Literary History* (New York, 1962), 168.

57. See Roland Mortier, *Diderot in Deutschland* (Stuttgart, 1967), 224.

58. Paul Fussell, *Samuel Johnson and the Life of Writing* (New York, 1971), 260.

59. Raleigh, *Six Essays on Johnson*, 19.

60. Donald O'Gorman, *Diderot the Satirist* (Toronto, 1971), 136.

61. Diderot, *Oeuvres complètes*, ed. Azzézat and Tourneux, 3:91–92. See Jean Fabre, "Deux frères ennemis: Diderot et Jean-Jacques Rousseau," *Diderot Studies* (1961): 155–215.

62. O'Gorman, *Diderot the Satirist*, 153–54.

63. Mortier, *Diderot in Deutschland*, 306.

64. Benjamin Boyce, "Johnson's *Life of Savage* and Its Literary Background," *Studies in Philology* 53 (October 1956): 596.

65. Paul K. Alkon, "The Intention and Reception of Johnson's *Life of Savage*," *Journal of Modern Philology* 72 (1974): 141, 149.

66. Proust, *Albertine Disparue* (Gallimard, 1925), 7:65–66.

67. Rousseau, *Les Rêveries du promeneur solitaire*, Ed. Pléiade, 1: 1099.

68. Quoted by F. E. Halliday, *Doctor Johnson and His World* (New York, 1968), 701.

69. Avraham Yarmolinski, *Dostoyevsky* (New York, 1957), 144–45.

70. Hegel, *Phenomenology of Mind*, 525.

71. Hegel, 251.

72. Trilling, 36, 39.

73. Yoichi Sumi, *Le Neveu de Rameau: Caprice et logique du jeu* (Tokyo, 1975), 377: "D'un bout à l'autre du texte, qu'on le lise horizontalement ou verticalement, le jeu apparaît comme une constante qui fait toute la substance—thématique ou structurale—du *Neveu de Rameau*."

74. Dostoyevsky, *Letters from the Underworld*, trans. Hogarth (London, n.d.), 5.

75. Max Scheler, *Ressentiment*, ed. Coser, trans. W. Holdheim (New York, 1961), 45–46.

76. Nietzsche, *Genealogy of Morals*, in *Basic Writings of Nietzsche*, trans. W. Kaufmann (New York, 1968), 508.

77. Ibid., 509–10.

78. Quoted by Raleigh, *Six Essays on Johnson*, 171.

Index